LIS HARRIS

HOLY DAYS

The World
of a Hasidic Family

SUMMIT BOOKS
NEW YORK

10   9   8   7   6   5   4   3   2

Most of this work originally appeared, in slightly different form, in The New Yorker.

Library of Congress Cataloging in Publication Data

Harris, Lis.
    Holy days.
    1. Jews—New York (N.Y.)—Social life and customs.   2. Hasidim—New York (N.Y.)—Social life and customs.   3. Brooklyn (New York, N.Y.)—Social life and customs.   4. New York (N.Y.)—Social life and customs.   5. Hasidism—History.   6. Habad—History.   I. Title.
    F128.9.J5H215   1985   305.8'924'073   85-14784
    ISBN: 0-671-46296-2

TO WILLIAM SHAWN

Contents

CHAPTER ONE

The Neighborhood and the Family

I N the small hours of a cold fall morning, when most of Brooklyn was asleep, some five thousand bearded, dark-hatted men, wearing nearly identical dark suits and coats, danced around a decrepit synagogue, arms clasped. The synagogue, a converted pre-war apartment house, stood on the corner of Kingston Avenue and Eastern Parkway, a major thoroughfare, and the curious slowed their cars down as they drove past this strange spectacle. Some drivers lowered their windows and caught a few snatches of the songs the men were singing. Few of them could make out any of the words, because they were Hebrew, though some of the songs were just wordless melodies.

The men were Lubavitcher Hasidim, and they were celebrating the Jewish holiday called the Rejoicing of the Torah (Simchat Torah), a day when the final portion of the year's reading of the Torah is completed, the scrolls of the Torah are carried around the synagogue seven times

and the Hasidic community expresses its appreciation for
being intimately connected with the Torah with spirited
singing, dancing, and merrymaking that frequently last all
night. A smaller but still substantial number of Hasidic
women hovered along the edge of the sidewalks, smiling
but not dancing. I had come to witness this annual event
in the Crown Heights section of Brooklyn with two
friends, a man and a woman. Apart from the motorists, we
were the only spectators present. The man, a gentile, was
enjoying himself. The graceful, scholarly-looking old men,
bright-eyed little boys with long sidelocks, plump, disheveled householders, and pale, bespectacled students were
as exotic to him as any Fiji Islanders, and he spoke admiringly of the virility of the dancing and the religious fervor
of the dancers. The woman, a secular Jew, was not enjoying herself. She thought that the joy she saw was inspired
by vodka, not religion, and she saw the separateness of the
men and women as symbolic of the group's backwardness.
My own feelings about them oscillated between neutral
and familial. A secular Jew, like the woman, I had nevertheless felt for years that the Hasidim were a mystery I
wanted to fathom.

In a box of old photographs that my family kept, I had
once, long ago, found a picture of a fierce-looking, bearded
old man, wearing the sort of fur hat and long black coat
that Hasidic men wear. When I asked my mother (a Man-
hattan-bred lawyer) who he was, she peered at the photograph briefly and disapprovingly and shrugged, "Nobody
in our family." Indeed, the man stood out like a sore
thumb among the waistcoated shopkeepers, artisans, small
businessmen, and tightly corseted women that populated
the box. But she may have been wrong. Our progenitors
came from Austria, Romania, and Russia, and in the nine-
teenth century, three quarters of the Jewish population
of Eastern Europe was Hasidic. It was more than likely,
therefore, that that man or somebody like him was not

only "in" our family but a central figure in the families of
the majority of American Jews—most of whom can trace
their lineage back to Eastern Europe. Believing that the
Hasidim represented some antique version of myself, I
have always felt vaguely bound to them and curious to
know who they actually were—a curiosity that neither my
education, my social milieu, nor my reading of Hasidic
stories did much to satisfy. The outing with my friends in
Crown Heights was one of many tentative forays I made
to the gates of the Hasidic world over a number of years
until one day several years ago I decided to see if I could
breach them and find out what was on the other side. I
hoped to find a Hasidic family that would allow me a
privileged look behind its door.

Hasidism is a revivalist-pietistic movement that began
in Poland in the first half of the eighteenth century. Its innovativeness lay in the way it redefined traditional Jewish
values by placing prayer, mysticism, dancing, singing,
storytelling, and sanctification of daily life on an equal
footing with Talmudic scholarship. (Talmud is the name
given to the oral law of the Jews and the commentaries on
it written by Palestinian and Babylonian scholars from the
third to the fifth centuries A.D.) It has always been a
leader-centered movement and its leaders, men noted as
much for their charisma as for their piety and scholarli-
ness, have traditionally passed their leadership on from
generation to generation in dynastic fashion. The various
Hasidic groups, called courts, that developed over the
years were named after places in Europe that were the
seats of these dynasties or sometimes the birthplace of
their founders. The Belzers came from Belz, the Bobovers
from Bobov (both Galician towns) and so on. There is
even a homegrown American group of fairly recent vin-
tage, called the Bostoners, whose leader holds court in the
Boston suburb of Brookline.

It has been estimated that there are some two hundred

and fifty thousand Hasidim in the world today, about one fifth the number that existed at the turn of the century. Some two hundred thousand live in the United States, and about half of the American Hasidim live in Brooklyn. The Lubavitchers, whose name comes from the Belorussian city that was the seat of their dynasty for many years, are believed to be the largest sect worldwide (no official census exists) and are one of forty that survived the Holocaust and the Russian pogroms—although many of these survived only skeletally. Before World War II there were about fifty Hasidic courts. The Satmarers, another group, who live in the Williamsburg section of Brooklyn, claim the largest New York following, forty-five thousand. Originally from Hungary, they survived the war in greater numbers because the war did not come to their country until 1944. Most of the other groups (among them, the Gerers, the Bobovers and the Belzers) live in the Boro Park section of Brooklyn and number about thirty-five thousand. A smaller number live in Westchester, Rockland County, and New Jersey. The groups are more alike than unalike, but differences and even deep enmities have developed among some of them.

Despite the large Hasidic presence in and around the city, finding a family who would allow me into their lives proved to be no simple task. Most Hasidim are suspicious of outsiders, distrustful of the printed word, and tired of being depicted as cute but anachronistic—like the pygmies, or, worse, cultists. After months of pleasant but fruitless exchanges with members of some of the smaller groups, an acquaintance with ties to the Hasidic world suggested that I try the Lubavitchers. The Lubavitchers, who are familiar to most New Yorkers because of the aggressive sidewalk proselytizing campaign they conduct at the side of large white campers, have traditionally been more open to outsiders than other Hasidim. A Lubavitcher spokesman gave me the names of two families to try. Neither was interested in being interviewed, but word of my quest rapidly spread along the Lubavitcher grapevine, and before long someone gave me the telephone number of Moshe and Sheina Konigsberg (the name as well as certain identity-revealing details about their lives have been made up), a couple who lived in Crown Heights. Several women I talked with before I called the Konigsbergs said that their husbands would find it impossible to speak with a strange woman; others sounded as if they suspected I might be an operative of the K.G.B. Mrs. Konigsberg, whose firmly accented r's and flat a's betrayed origins more westerly than Brooklyn, New York, said that she and her husband rarely liked the articles they read about Hasidim outside the Jewish press, but it might be useful to other Jews if they could in some way clarify the picture people had of Hasidic life. The Konigsbergs agreed (after a brief family conference) to talk with me as much as I liked and invited me to pay them a visit that week.

Crown Heights, where most of the city's fifteen thousand Lubavitcher Hasidim live, is a tidy, quiet oasis surrounded by streets that have succumbed to decay and abandonment. For the ultra-Orthodox, mostly Eastern European, Jews who live there, the kosher butcher shops and restaurants, the religious schools and bookstores, the ritual bathhouses and scrupulously observed religious life are taken as much for granted as they would have been in any nineteenth-century shtetl. But to outsiders, even (or, perhaps, especially) to Jews who live in the ordinary world, it is a world shrouded in mystery. According to the city, the borders of the neighborhood are Atlantic Avenue to the north, Clarkson Avenue to the south, Ralph, East New York, and Utica Avenues to the east, and Ocean and Flatbush Avenues to the west. But the Lubavitchers' Crown Heights actually encompasses a far smaller area whose borders are loosely defined by their synagogue, schools, kosher shops, and the last Hasidic family on a block. The majority of the neighborhood's residents are, in fact, black, but perhaps because of the old-fashionedness of their clothes, or their high visibility when they gather in front of their synagogue, it is the Hasidim who dominate the landscape. In the postwar years, the neighborhood was predominantly Jewish, but with the arrival of large numbers of blacks and Puerto Ricans in the late fifties and sixties, most of the Jewish population departed. Those who wanted to live in an exclusively Jewish neighborhood moved to Boro Park, the more upwardly mobile moved to the suburbs. The Lubavitchers stayed.

On my first daytime visit to the neighborhood, I felt as if I had wandered into a dream. Pale, bearded, black-hatted, dark-suited men, looking remarkably alike, hurried along the sidewalks with downcast eyes, pointedly avoiding eye contact with civilians. Those who chanced to look up stared stonily into space, like figures in a Magritte painting. Every woman under forty-five appeared to be pregnant. Nineteen- and twenty-year-olds who looked like my baby-sitters pushed their own carriages and strollers, and high-spirited children hopped like rabbits everywhere. That day the community was celebrating Purim (the festival that commemorates the biblical story of Queen Esther's deliverance of the Jews from a murderous plot of Persia's Grand Vizier, Haman, to destroy them) and many of the children wore masks and colorful costumes. Giggling, mustachioed Hamans and gaudily crowned Esthers chased one another up and down the streets, their small bodies and masked faces adding a slightly madcap element to the dreamlike aura of the scene.

The Konigsbergs live on President Street, a beautiful, tree-lined avenue abutted by large, old-fashioned, architecturally diverse two-story houses that would not look out of place in a New England town. In the nineteen forties President Street housed so many of Brooklyn's doctors that one section of it became known as Doctors' Row. Now its residents are chiefly well-heeled Lubavitcher Hasidim or blacks, but the street has changed little in the last forty years. The Konigsbergs live in a three-story redbrick house with Italianate masonry trim that was built in the solid, generous style of the early nineteen hundreds. The house boasted a small plot of land, planted with rhododendrons and privet, that looked neat but unloved.

The shade behind the Konigsbergs' front window was down. Walking along, I had noticed that many of the houses in the neighborhood had their blinds closed, their curtains drawn, their shutters latched.

Sheina Konigsberg greeted me warmly and there was a long moment of mutual sizing up. Whatever stereotype I might have had in my mind about Hasidic women, Sheina did not fit it. She is an attractive, fashionably dressed, generously proportioned woman in her late forties who looks as if she could once have been a high school cheerleader. As I contemplated her short, remarkably burnished-looking red curls and general air of wholesomeness, two limpid, trusting-looking blue eyes gazed at me from behind oversized tortoiseshell glasses with interest. Like many of Sheina's neighbors, I too was pregnant at the time, and I had the distinct impression that the pregnancy not only conferred a welcome air of harmlessness upon me but earned me some unspoken laissez-passer.

"Hello. Come in. You're a little early. Moshe's not due back from prison for a while," she said, enjoying the shock effect of her words before adding with a smile, "He goes to Allenwood Federal Prison Camp on some holidays to lead the Jewish prisoners in services. If he didn't, they might not have any."

The house Sheina led me into was bright, cheerful, immaculately clean, and suburban looking. The parlor floor had been turned into a spacious open room with hexagonal tiles on the floor, an orange-and-blue square geo-

metric print on the walls, and colorful paintings everywhere. A quilted velvet couch, two chairs, and a coffee
table had been placed at the side of the room near a fireplace, and there was a piano, bookshelves filled with
books bearing mostly Hebrew titles, and a potted palm.
Somehow, the furnishings, though obviously chosen with
care, seemed like afterthoughts. The room had a public
air about it, as if it were more a meeting hall than a living
room, more a place where people might throng or pass
through than somewhere to migrate to with a book and
an apple. At the end of the floor was a bright yellow
modern kitchen—a room so orderly looking that I would
not have been surprised to find the cans on the shelves in
alphabetical order. Near the kitchen, at the far end of
the room, stood a heavy sideboard, a twelve-foot dining
table, and a dozen or so leather-backed chairs, all of which
were dominated by an unignorable full-length portrait of
Rabbi Menachem Mendel Schneerson, the Lubavitchers'
revered spiritual leader, universally referred to as "the
Rebbe." Rebbe is a variation on the word rabbi, which in
Hebrew means literally "my great one" but has come to
mean teacher or master. It is also the title given to leaders
of Hasidic courts. Rabbi Schneerson is the seventh Lubavitcher rebbe. The first, Rabbi Schneur Zalman of Liadi,
taught that the rebbe's central task was to "teach Hasidism according to the spirit of the times and the needs of
the people," a dictum that has been scrupulously adhered
to by all his successors.

Sheina led me over to the dining room table. In the center of the table was a huge pile of straw baskets, tanger-
ines, pineapples, cookies, hard candies, rum cordials, pints
of J & B Scotch, packets of nuts, chocolate pastilles, and
peanut-butter cups.

"Listen, we'll talk when we can, but you know it's Purim. I have to rush to make more *shalach manos* baskets."

"What are they?"

"Leah [the woman who gave me Sheina's name] said you were Jewish. Didn't your family celebrate Purim?" she asked, in a sympathetic tone that suggested that she already knew the answer to her question.

I explained that my family was not religious and that their attitude toward their Jewishness was more or less that of fans whose home team was the Jews. I did not add that my mother, no longer alive, had regarded Hasidim as fanatics and not a little repellent, nor that my octogenarian father, a pleasure-loving Yankeefied son of Russian Jews, whose family emigrated from St. Petersburg to Connecticut in the eighteen-seventies, had looked at me in wonder when I had told him I'd had a lifelong curiosity about Hasidic life and said, "But that's all old hat."

During the long period that I was to spend getting to know the Konigsbergs and their community, I never encountered a single Jew who didn't have a strong opinion about the Hasidim. Gentile friends who knew about my visits to the Hasidic world asked polite questions. The Jews I knew were usually in one of two camps: those who did not like them and were eager to share stories about alleged Hasidic hypocrisy—how they'd heard that they cheated in their business dealings, and so on—and those who shared a kind of wistful, idealized view of Hasidic life. The language of the detractors might have been drawn from the lexicon of classic anti-Semitism: "They're really dirty. Have you seen how they keep their homes?" "No one is pushier." "I hate their standoffishness." "Why do they think that they're better than everybody else?" "They're certainly unhealthy—you can tell that just by looking at them." Both camps were united in their (mistaken, as I was to learn) conviction that most Hasidic practices were somehow fundamentally different from those of ordinary Orthodox Jews.

Shalach manos, Sheina explained, as she filled a basket with fruit and candy, meant "sending out of portions," or

gifts of food and drink. It was customary for religious
Jews to distribute the baskets, usually transported by the
younger members of the family, to friends on Purim.
While methodically arranging the fruit and sweets in the
basket, Sheina went on to say that everyone in the community had gone to 770 Eastern Parkway—the place where
I had seen the men dancing—the main Lubavitcher synagogue (as well as the movement's official headquarters)
the night before for a reading of the scroll of Esther, in
which the story of Esther and Haman is related. That
morning she had gone to a neighbor's house to hear the
story read again. The word *Purim*, she said, was Hebrew
and meant lots. Haman drew lots to choose the date on
which he intended to kill all the Jews in the kingdom.

"Have you known about all this since you were a child?"
I asked.

"Some of it, but I never really understood the deeper
significance. I wasn't raised here, you know. I grew up
in Michigan—in Bloomfield Hills, a suburb of Detroit. My
dad is a businessman—he owns a large paint manufactur-
ing company—and I grew up like any well-to-do American
girl really. I went to movies and parties, I dated, and I
sort of drifted along like everyone else. My family called
themselves Orthodox but many commandments were not
strictly observed. I learned Hebrew when I was a girl and
we kept a kosher home and went to synagogue every Saturday but I know that neither of my two brothers nor my
sister and I ever profoundly connected with any of it.
Purim was never celebrated in a big way there, for in-
stance, although it says specifically in Esther that the holiday is supposed to be a day of feasting and merrymaking.
Here the day is like a carnival; we have a special Purim
feast and everything is completely unlike the rest of the
year. It's the only day of the year besides Simchat Torah
when it is considered appropriate to drink all day and the
whole community celebrates in one way or another. It's all

commemorative, of course, a celebration of an occasion when for once Jews were spared from the destructive whims of their ruler. The rituals keep people aware that the danger is always there. I never fully understood *any* of the reasons for Jewish rituals until I became a Lubavitcher.

"It was different for Moshe. He grew up among Hasidim and his family has always been Lubavitch; even so he's always studying—on his own and with his children. We were both married before, and both of us had five children [the average number in Hasidic families]. Moshe lost his wife in 1969 and I got divorced in 1974. It was the saddest time in my life, but this is the happiest because *baruch Hashem* [praise God] I've come to understand that, like all Jews, I'm here for a purpose."

"And that is?"

"To see the beauty and holiness in everyday things. To try to elevate ordinary life. The key is in the Torah [the Pentateuch] and the way to get there has been shown us in a practical way by the mitzvot. [The mitzvot are the six hundred and thirteen positive and negative commandments or precepts described in the Torah and referred to by Jewish sages in the first and second centuries A.D. In the fourth century A.D., a Palestinian rabbi divided them into positive and negative commandments but few attempts were made to enumerate them with any precision until the twelfth century, when Maimonides, in his typically lucid way, established that there were two hundred and forty-eight positive commandments and three hundred and sixty-five negative ones and wrote a treatise in which he described the scriptural origin of each of them. The list embraces virtually every facet of a religious Jew's day, indeed of his life, from resting on the Sabbath (positive commandment one hundred and fifty-four) to fasting on Yom Kippur (positive commandment number one hundred and sixty-four) to not increasing wealth from anything connected with idolatry (negative commandment

number twenty-five). Nothing is considered more central
to the lives of religious Jews than the fulfillment of the
commandments. Whatever impedes their fulfillment is considered to be in the realm of darkness; whatever contrib-
utes to carrying them out in the realm of light.] When the
Jews accepted God's challenge to follow his ways, he gave
us the mitzvot so that we'd know how to do it."

Sheina was interrupted by the boisterous entrance of
her husband and his two sons, Shmuel and Mendel, who
had accompanied him to Pennsylvania. One of the boys'
faces was flushed and his eyes looked somewhat over-
bright. They were both talking to their father at the same
time in loud, excited voices and, as they talked, their
hands never stopped moving. Some reveling, it seemed,
had already taken place. All three wore dark hats tipped
slightly back on their heads, dark rumpled suits, and
white shirts unbuttoned at the neck. Peeking out beneath
their jackets were the ends of their *talisim katan*, four-
cornered fringed undergarments Orthodox men wear like
a string around the finger to remind them to fulfill all their
religious duties. Like all Hasidim, they had beards, in keeping with the Biblical injunction, "Thou shalt not mar the
corner of thy beards" (Leviticus 19:27). Unlike many
other Hasidim, however, adult Lubavitchers do not wear
long *peyes*, or sidelocks, their sages having interpreted the
injunction against cutting beards as not including long
sidelocks. (Young Lubavitcher boys who do not yet have
beards are required to wear them.) They don't wear
shtreimls, the large fur hats favored by many Hasidim for
Sabbaths and other special occasions either, since the hats
belong to no purely Jewish tradition but were merely an
accessory East European Jews borrowed from their former oppressors, the Polish overlords. Other Hasidic groups
sometimes fault the Lubavitchers for not stressing the
niceties of traditional Hasidic dress or for not *davening*
(praying) with the same outward show of emotion that

many of them display. The Lubavitchers (I was to learn) shrug off this sort of criticism. They maintain that though they follow the customs of their ancestors the intensity of someone's religious feeling is a private affair that can't be calibrated by the amount of rocking back and forth he does while praying or by the fabric or style of his hat. One Israeli scholar who has written extensively about the Hasidim believes that variations in Hasidic dress came about as a result of compromises that had to be made when various tsars and kaisers issued decrees forbidding Jews to dress differently than the rest of the population. While Hasidim could not remove their hats (a sign of respect for God) under any circumstance, they could in good conscience adopt the hat styles of their fellow countrymen.

Moshe Konigsberg had dark, heavily hooded, lively eyes, softly rounded features, a balding pate, small delicate hands and a long white beard that made him look much older than his fifty-odd years. His eyebrows and what was left of his hair were still black. The brows sloped upward toward a deep furrow, giving his face a fixed quizzical expression, and he wore black-framed glasses which perched rather low on his nose and looked as if they might slide off at any moment. Like Sheina, to whom he gave a broad smile when he came into the room (Hasidic husbands and wives are forbidden to kiss, hug, or in any way embrace each other in public), he moved around a lot when he talked and exuded an air of quiet energy. When Sheina introduced us, Moshe stared at me with open curiosity, but his sons regarded me warily (the expressions of two British colonists surprised in their compound by a paint-bedaubed, spear-carrying tribesman would not have been too dissimilar) and their ebullience vanished behind clouds. Mendel, the younger boy, twenty years old, was a thin angular young man with olive skin, a thin mustache, and a rather oriental appearance. Shmuel, five years older, had a dark, bushy beard, a pot belly, and a preoccupied manner. Shmuel yawned and looked at Mendel. Mendel said that they were both tired, it had been a long drive back from Pennsylvania, but when Moshe and I headed toward the large round table in the family's sunny breakfast room next to the kitchen to have a chat they nearly tripped over each other following us and proceeded to station themselves on either side of their father like two yeomen. When I asked Moshe to tell me a little about his family history, both of them gazed at him unhappily.

"What's so interesting about his personal life? It's irrelevant. It's what we do as a community that matters," Shmuel said. His remark was addressed to his brother.

"Sha, it's all right, people want to know a little about these things too," his father said, giving him a reassuring look. Moshe talked fast and with a Yiddish accent (the first language of most Hasidic homes is Yiddish) that had slight Slavic overtones, and punctuated his words with little jabs of a cigarette, which he held in a black cigarette holder.

"My family has been Hasidic since the beginning of the movement in the eighteenth century, and nearly all of us have been Lubavitchers. Most of the stories I know about them begin with my great-grandfather Isaac, who was a ritual slaughterer and a disciple of the third Lubavitcher rebbe. My family came from a little town in the Ukraine, near Ekaterinoslav. At that time, which was about eighteen forty, the rebbe's followers all went to visit him in Lubavitch at least once a year, to take stock of their lives. It took several days for my great-grandfather to get there. Well, one year when he arrived at the rebbe's house he found the door to the rebbe's room closed and a little crowd of Hasidim huddled outside it.

"They were taking turns looking through the keyhole, so my great-grandfather looked, too. The rebbe was praying with such intensity that he was filled with awe. The rebbe's concentration and the deep feeling with which he

prayed stirred him so much that when he heard the rebbe
say, 'Ayn o d milvado' ["There is no one but God"] he
fainted. A few minutes later, when he'd been revived, the
rebbe called him into the room. 'Well,' he thought to himself, 'we're certainly going to talk about deep spiritual
matters today.' But, much to his surprise, the rebbe said
to him, 'Let's talk in practical terms about your life. You're
a good ritual slaughterer and you're respected by those
who know you. It's enough for you to be a pious man.
When you leave here you will prosper.' Naturally, my
great-grandfather asked him how he was to go about finding the path to this sudden prosperity. The rebbe told him
simply to seize the first opportunity that presented itself.
Sure enough, on the way home he met the landlord of the
village. The landlord had to buy some sugar in a distant
town but didn't want to make the journey himself. So he
asked my great-grandfather, who had a reputation for
trustworthiness, if he would get it for him. My great-
grandfather agreed, of course, and eventually did more
and more for the landowner and increased his responsi-
bilities until he became a wealthy man. By the way, my
great-grandmother died rather young and my great-grandfather's second wife, a widow, was Leon Trotsky's grandmother. My father was a young man when Trotsky was
around but he told me that they used to say that whenever
Trotsky came to town a bank would be robbed."

Since the arrival of Moshe and the boys, the doorbell
had rung about a dozen times. The visitors—small, cos-
tumed children, slightly older boys in sober dark suits, and
teenage girls dressed in starched, chaste dresses—would
scurry in, present Sheina with a generously filled basket,
wish everybody a *freilicher* (happy) Purim, chat for a few
minutes, then rush off to deliver baskets to other friends
and relatives. This was the stuff musical comedies were
made of and it all seemed so orchestrated that one could
easily visualize the giftbearers hallooing in the opening

scenes of the musical *Purim!* The room had begun to look
like a stateroom on the *QE 2* on sailing day. Cellophane-
wrapped baskets covered the coffee table, the dining
table, and the couch. The phone rang almost constantly,
and twice I overheard Sheina agree to put up out-of-
towners who needed a place to stay on the coming Sabbath. It was clear from her conversation that she had
never laid eyes on either of her prospective guests. Before
my visit, I had somehow imagined that the Konigsbergs'
house would be a dark cluttered place, full of crumbling
books and yellowed pamphlets. Instead, I seemed to have
stumbled into the Hasidic Hilton.

"My paternal grandfather was a working man, too—a
blacksmith—but he had knowledge and wisdom and he
was well-respected. In the little town where he lived there
was a rabbinical court, a *Beth Din,* and he was one of the
three men who sat on it. My mother's father was one of
the other men. After the revolution, when the Cossacks
were looking for vengeance they killed tens of thousands
of Jews. A marauding band came to my grandfather's
house and a Cossack pointed a gun at him. My mother
saved him. She just stepped in front of him and said,
'Kill me.' They were lucky. They'd been threatened by a
fellow who was impressed by gallantry. Others weren't so
lucky. In the Second World War my father's father was
killed by the Germans, along with all the other Jews of the
town. They just came one day and asked every Jew to
bring a shovel to the outskirts of town. Then they shot
them and buried them there. Just like that. My father,
thank God, had already married and left by then. He had
been sent as a young man to the Lubavitcher yeshiva in
Lubavitch to study. During the First World War he fought
with the tsarist partisans and became a German prisoner
of war. When he returned to the village, the pogrom
I was talking about had started so he joined the Jewish Defense Band of the Red Partisan Army. That's why

so many Jews became Bolsheviks at that time; not for
ideological reasons, but because it was the Bolsheviks that
saved them from the Cossacks. It was not long, of course,
before the Communists became the Jews' bitter enemies.
Later that year my mother and father moved to Petro-
grad. They thought that they'd find better opportunities
in the city. But it was hard to lead a full religious life.
There was no special place where Jews lived. They were
scattered all around, and fearful. Any communication with
the rebbe had to be couched in secret language and of
course the yeshivas had to be secret because religious education was forbidden."

I asked Moshe what he remembered of his own life in
Russia.

"I was born in 1928 and I have two sisters, one younger,
one older. In some ways we grew up like ordinary Russian
children. Most of the children in the neighborhood were
gentile and we played with them. My parents didn't like
it but that's the way it was. We went to circuses like other
children but we were not educated in Russian schools. We
had private tutors who could teach us Yiddish and Hebrew as well as other subjects. Of course we already spoke
Russian. My father told the authorities that we were too
bright for the local public schools. That's what all the
Hasidim did. We got away with it."

"What was your father's profession?"

"He was a stationer. For seven years after the revolution
people were allowed to have private businesses, so my
father opened up a stationery factory. When the government took it over in 1928, he just stayed on. But then working on the Sabbath became a problem so he started a
photography business which was kind of an adjunct to the
stationery factory. He opened up little photography stands
in the public parks and hired gentiles to work on Saturdays. We made a living but we were not really *living*. The
Bolsheviks completely disrupted the life of the Jewish

community. Everything we did had to be secret. We had
secret *mikvahs* [ritual baths], secret Torah-study groups,
secret circumcisions, secret businesses so Jews could work
at home and earn money and not have to work on Saturdays, and even secret places where we could pray in
peace. Many people got caught—especially the Hasidic
leaders who went around trying to hold people together
and organize the Jewish life of the community. Many of
them were sent to prison or to the labor camps. But I think
that it was the arrest of the sixth Lubavitcher rebbe in
1927—even though he was eventually released—that convinced people that Russia was not going to be a place
where we could *ever* lead a full religious life or count on
our safety. That was when my family decided to leave.
But of course deciding to leave was one thing, getting visas
another. The Russians, you know, don't like Jews *in* their
country but they don't like them to leave either. Paradox-
ical, yes? My mother started going to the visa office regularly in 1933. She went several times a week, but it wasn't
until 1937 that they finally gave them to her and we left
for Palestine."

"How did it feel to be in Palestine?"

"We felt like birds freed from a cage. For years, though
we were not Zionists, we would see pictures of Tel Aviv
and our hearts would pound. Three times a day in our
prayers we speak of longing to go to Zion, and there we
were. It felt . . . well, you just can't imagine how it felt
. . . wonderful. First, it was the Jewish homeland, and
secondly, it was a free country. My parents are gone now,
but they stayed in Israel until they died. They sent us to
Lubavitcher schools when we got there and then they sent
me to New York to continue my studies at the yeshiva here.
My older sister came here a few years later—she lives just
a few blocks away with her family, by the way—but my
younger sister and her family stayed in Israel. When I
thought about it, I guess I always expected that I would

be a teacher, but the Rebbe thought that I should be a
metal engraver, so I became a metal engraver. I married
my first wife, a Canadian woman, in 1952, and we lived
in Canada for a while. But we moved to New York in 1957,
and I've been here ever since. I used to work for somebody
else, but now I own my own business."

I asked Moshe what he considered to be the main differences between himself and an ordinary Orthodox Jew.

He pulled on his beard. "Well, there are more similari-
ties than differences, because Jewish law is Jewish law.
But we probably do things more wholeheartedly as a group,
we have a more mystical leaning, we never stop trying
to bend our natural characteristics toward more godly
ones, and maybe we pay more attention to the holiness of
things in the physical world. Isaac Luria [a sixteenth-
century kabbalist] said that everything had a soul, even
things in nature and inanimate things. We're taught to
show respect for these things. We're taught not to throw
bread, for example, or step on food. I remember walking
down the street with my father when I was a boy and
if he saw a piece of food lying on the street he'd pick
it up so no one would step on it. The previous rebbe
told a story about a walk he took with his father one day.
They were studying together and he was so deeply en-
grossed in whatever his father was saying that he absent-
mindedly tore a leaf off a tree. Well, he hadn't meant any
harm, of course, but his father chided him for doing it.
Why? Because there was a spark of godliness in the leaf
that deserved to run its own course."

"There are a lot of Orthodox people whose daily lives
look just like ours," Sheina called in from the dining room,
where she was still wrapping baskets and could overhear
us, "except that they don't live in communities quite like
ours or have a rebbe for a spiritual leader, so many of
them feel quite isolated; and of course there are the kinds
of Orthodox Jews like the ones I was telling you about

earlier, who like to consider themselves Orthodox but
really aren't." Peering into the breakfast room with a pineapple in each hand, she added, "But these labels—Orthodox, Conservative, Reform—have no real meaning to us.
As far as we're concerned, a Jew is a Jew; nobody's relationship to God can be conveyed by a label."

Shmuel nudged his father and looked at the clock, and
Moshe said that he had to go to evening prayers but suggested that I return the following Friday to spend the
Sabbath with the family. I accepted his invitation and
held out my hand reflexively to shake his—momentarily
forgetting that no extrafamilial physical contact between
the sexes, however casual, is permitted in the Hasidic
world—then quickly pulled it back when I realized my mistake. Moshe just gazed at the ceiling. The boys exchanged
knowing looks.

While the men were putting on their coats, Sheina, who
had gone back to filling baskets at the table, beckoned to
me. Looking up briefly as she nestled some Reese's Peanut
Butter Cups around a pineapple, she asked in a low voice
what my personal interest was in learning about Hasidic
life. It was to be the only time she ventured a question of
that nature and the only time anyone in the family ever
questioned me about my personal beliefs. I said that I was
merely intellectually curious but even as I said it, I realized that this probably wasn't entirely true. That Sheina
did not accept my answer as adequate was obvious from
the amused if forbearing look she shot at me. In fact, having known as many different kinds of Jews as I had gentiles in my life, I had never much troubled myself with
the whole "What is a Jew?" issue and considered it fairly
irrelevant. I accepted my own Jewishness as one of the
things that helped define me, like my dark hair, brown
eyes, and lefthandedness; but the foundation of my spiritual upbringing, such as it was, rested largely upon the
gentle New England civilities of my father's childhood

and the tolerant urban values of my mother's. I knew that many Jews still found plenty of nourishment in the synagogues and other institutions associated with the various Jewish denominations—Orthodox, Conservative and Reform—but nobody I knew well did, and the only personal glimpses I'd had of the religious life (droning congregants, unintelligible prayers and posturing rabbis) did not impel me to delve further into those waters. I had always taken it for granted that the diluted rituals and distracted congregations I had observed were merely faint echoes of a once vital tradition. Why else had so many generations of skeptical, spiritual people (most of whom today looked to everything else but religion—secular books, music, love, art, even sports—for spiritual uplift) remained loyal to it for thousands of years?

But if whatever was meaningful or attractive about Jewish communal religious life was absent from so many places now, where was it present? It was present in Jewish literature, of course, but at one remove, like the photograph of Freud a Polish emigré I know keeps to remind him of his grandfather who perished, along with the rest of his family and all mementos of them, during World War II. Apparently his grandfather resembled Freud, so he keeps the photograph because it is the closest he can get to his grandfather. But surely the Holocaust had not succeeded in eradicating all the strength and passion of religious communities except for that which had been needed to create and maintain a Jewish state? Newspaper articles alluded from time to time to the resurgence of interest in Orthodoxy and to various revisionist efforts to organize Jewish groups along more modern lines, but I suspected, I think, that I could recover the past in its most vital form in a Hasidic community. Jews, of course, had no monasteries or nunneries, since the central beliefs of Judaism are incompatible with notions of celibacy or prolonged separation from the hubbub of everyday life,

but if one were searching for a place where the practice
of religion was uppermost in the life of a Jewish community, the Hasidic court seemed to be the best place to
look. Perhaps, too, I saw in myself the same cultural alien-
ation, obsessiveness, and urge for transcendence that people attributed to the Hasidim and wondered, though I had
a horror of conformity (I am uneasy watching even the
happy marchers in parades, for example), if beyond my
own psychological makeup and secular values and preoccupations my attraction to them was not so much an
attraction of opposites as of one side of a coin wanting to
know what the other was like.

As he was leaving, Moshe turned to me and said, "Well,
good luck in your work."

"Thanks," I said. "By the way, are there any books about
Hasidism that you think might be helpful?"

"There are no books."

"No books! Why, what do you mean? You must know
that hundreds of books have been written about Hasidism."

"Books about Hasidic matters always misrepresent
things. They twist and change the truth in casual ways. I
trust Lubavitcher books, like the *Tanya* [a work written by
the movement's founder] and the collections of the rebbes'
discourses, because our Rebbe got the information in them
from the rebbe before him, and so on in an unbroken
chain. I trust scholars I know who I can talk to face-to-
face. But most books tell lies, even if it's unintentional. I
read secular books on Jewish subjects from time to time;
they're like the newspapers, if you know anything about
the subject they're writing about, you know that they
haven't got the facts straight. Most books distort things."

"But there has been a great deal of highly respected
scholarly work published about Hasidic matters," I said.

"Most of it written by outsiders. There are always errors.

Lots of errors. You want to know who we are? Read what we read. Read the Torah. Read Hasidic texts."

"Is there no outside scholar you trust?"

Moshe thought for a moment or two, shook his head, shrugged, and said, "No." Then he smiled and left, his sons following closely in his wake like escort galleons in a threatened fleet.

CHAPTER TWO

A Brief
Social and Religious History
of Hasidism

Innocent or not, let the Jew be fried.
PEDRO ARBUÉS (Spanish Inquisitor) c. 1480

Although Hasidism as a modern movement began in the eighteenth cenutry, its roots go back as far as Biblical times. The Hebrew word *hasid* means, literally, pious one, and has always denoted a kind of spiritual rigorousness. The word is mentioned in the Book of Psalms and in the Apocryphal books of Maccabees, One and Two. In the second century B.C., in Palestine, a group called the Hasideans joined in the revolt of Judas Maccabaeus against the Hellenized Syrian Antiochus Epiphanes, who attempted to Hellenize the Jews. These Hasideans, although known for their purity and saintliness, were not considered to be in any way different from their fellow Jews (as, later the Hasidim were); but they were admired by their coreligionists for their intense piety and stubborn faithfulness to their religion in the face of persecution.

A more recent antecedent of modern Hasidism was the Hasidic movement in Germany in the twelfth century.

This early movement, which never achieved the popularity of eighteenth-century Hasidism, flourished from about the middle of the twelfth to the middle of the thirteenth centuries and produced a widely read book, the *Book of the Pious,* an esoteric examination of the Pentateuch traditionally ascribed to Judah the Hasid of Worms. Although twelfth- and eighteenth-century Hasidism had little in common, both movements focused on mystical interpretation of the Law and helped unify large numbers of unlettered but pious Jews in eras marked by violence and upheaval.

Like so much Jewish history, the transmission of German Hasidism as well as other forms of German culture to Eastern Europe can be credited largely to a catastrophe, in this case the anti-Semitic campaigns of the Crusades, which forced thousands of Jews to migrate to Poland. It was the Muslims, of course, who were the avowed enemies of the Crusaders, but they were far away and costly to vanquish. The Jews, on the other hand, were never far away. Large numbers of Jews began to emigrate eastward during the very first Crusade, in 1096, when the Crusaders decimated the Jewish population of Mainz. It was said that the Crusaders killed more than a thousand Jews in a single day. Similar massacres took place in many Rhine communities along the Crusaders' route to the Holy Land. At our first meeting, Moshe had mentioned that he thought that some of his early ancestors were German, and might well have been among these eastward-bound immigrants.

Most of the history of Jewish life in that bleak period has been lost, but large chunks of it were unearthed by the Russian historian Simon Dubnow, the first serious independent scholar of Hasidism to place the movement in any kind of historical context, who was killed by the Nazis in Riga in 1941. Some of Dubnow's views about the Hasidim—especially his ideas about the role historical in-

evitability played in the movement's rise—are regarded as
outdated, but even the scholars who question Dubnow's
assumptions about Hasidism acknowledge a debt of gratitude to his research, to date unmatched in its comprehen-
siveness, on the early history of East European Jewry.
Dubnow would, I suppose, be a good example of the sort
of writer Moshe warned me against and one, I confess, of
many I was to repair to frequently nonetheless.

The great majority of the Hasidic texts Moshe approved
of were written for those whose knowledge of Hasidic
(not to mention Talmudic) luminaries and principles was
extensive. These texts rarely place the author's thoughts
in any sort of historical or temporal perspective and even
more rarely pause to define or explain the arcane philosophical terminology they employ. One reason they do
not, of course, is that most of them were written in the
form of homiletic snippets and refer to passing events or
esoteric phenomena that even scholars of Judaic matters
frequently find impenetrable; another is that since time
immemorial it has been the practice in Jewish religious
education to pore over every text line by line, subject it
to the closest scrutiny, and discuss it ad infinitum. The
seminal books of Hasidism were written by and for scholars for whom the notion of an inquiring reader sitting
alone in an armchair, far from the all-embracing womb of
a synagogue study hall was inconceivable. For such readers—and I was certainly one of them—outsiders like Dubnow and other more recent scholars provided a necessary
framework for the Hasidic masters' "never apologize, never
explain" excursions into the realm of pure thought.

In Dubnow's *History of the Jews in Russia and Poland,*
for example, he revealed that virtually the only constant
in the secular life of the Polish Jew in the Middle Ages was
danger. Various liberal kings tried to extend their protection to their Jewish subjects, but the Catholic clergy, which
wielded more practical power (they controlled the Polish

Diet) and was violently antagonistic to the Jews, nullified
most of the royal statutes and edicts designed to help them.
The clergy passed its own laws: forbidding Jews to keep
Christian servants, wet nurses, or nursery maids, forbidding Jews to live in the neighborhoods of Christians, forbidding Christians, at the risk of being excommunicated,
to invite Jews to a meal or to drink with them, or to buy
their meat (lest it be poisoned), requiring Jews to lock
themselves in their houses when church processions passed,
and requiring Jewish men and women to sew a ring of red
cloth on the left side of their upper garments. Any Jew
who was found to be living with a Christian woman was
subject to fine and imprisonment, and the woman was subject to a public whipping and permanent banishment from
the town. The Polish nobles, on the other hand, who were
frequently absentee landlords, welcomed the eastward-
migrating European Jews for their financial skills and their
proficiency as land and business managers. Eventually,
many Jews became the stewards of the absentee noblemen,
and in this role deflected much of the serfs' resentment of
the landlords to themselves.

As time went on, the Jews became ever more visible in
their adopted lands. By the sixteenth century, they had
become tailors, bakers, silversmiths, toll collectors, and
innkeepers; they had their own community town councils,
called *kahals*, and they had a flourishing educational system. In Poland, they became the tax collectors in the
towns and townlets that were privately owned by the
Polish nobles, and they became *arendars* (or lessees, originally of a farm, later of a tavern or any other source of
revenue for a landowner) who helped supervise the
dairies, mills and distilleries that brought the largest part
of their incomes to the noble landowners. It was, of
course, in the interest of the landlords to protect the Jews
from the clergy and from the anti-Semitic rabble, but
they did not. Notoriously weak and lazy, and living far

from their estates, they were ill equipped to protect anybody.

In the middle of the seventeenth century, the Ukraine,
where the Hasidic movement would flourish, witnessed
the worst series of pogroms Jews were to suffer until the
twentieth century. The peasants, most of whom belonged
to the Greek Orthodox Church, were oppressed by heavy
taxes and humiliated by the condescension and antagonism
shown them by the Roman Catholic clergy. Unprotected
by their Polish lords or the Polish church, they organized
themselves into warlike bands to fight off marauding Tatars
from the Russian steppes and the khanate of the Crimea.
Somewhat drunk with their success in defending themselves, they turned next against the Polish government,
and became a force to be reckoned with.

"The mutiny of the Cossacks and the Ukrainian peasants in 1648," writes Dubnow, inaugurated "in the history
of the Jews of Eastern Europe the era of pogroms, which
Southern Russia bequeathed to future generations . . .
In the spring of 1648 . . . one of the popular Cossack
leaders, Bogdan Khmelnitsky . . . unfurled the banner of
rebellion in the Ukraine and in the region beyond the
Dnieper Falls . . . peasants and town dwellers left their
homes, and, organizing themselves into bands, devas-
tated the estates . . . slaying their owners as well as the
stewards and Jewish arendars. . . . The rebels allowed
only those to survive who embraced the Greek Orthodox
faith."

A Russian historian of the time reported that "killing
was accompanied by barbarous tortures; the victims were
flayed alive, split asunder, clubbed to death, roasted on
coals, or scalded with boiling water. Even infants at the
breast were not spared. The most terrible cruelty, however, was shown toward the Jews. They were destined to
utter annihilation, and the slightest pity shown to them
was looked upon as treason. Scrolls of the Law were taken

out of the synagogues by the Cossacks, who danced on them while drinking whiskey. After this Jews were laid down upon them, and butchered without mercy. Thousands of Jewish infants were thrown into wells, or buried alive." It has been estimated that between 1648 and 1658 as many as three hundred thousand Jews perished.

In the latter part of the seventeenth century, religious trials, in which Jews were accused of outlandish, malevolent things (desecration of church sacraments and ritual murder of children, for example), were a common occurrence. A number of Polish kings again attempted to protect the Jews' business and property rights and to shield them from harassment. Most of these attempts were once again rendered meaningless, however, by the regulations of the Polish Diets, which were still controlled by the virulently anti-Semitic Catholic clergy.

Ever since 1492, when the Jews were expelled from Spain, ideas about exile and redemption had been a growing preoccupation of Judaic scholarship. Most rabbinic leaders—and probably most ordinary Jews—until the seventeenth century held that if God allowed the abuse of His chosen people and postponed the paradisaical era it was because they had failed to obey His laws stringently enough and were thus being collectively punished. To rectify this, rabbinic leaders enjoined their congregations to follow God's commandments more carefully and heed their ramifications as outlined by the sages of the Talmud. Opposing this view were the Jewish kabbalists, or mystics, who shared the belief that the Jews were not faithfully following the commandments—not, as the traditional rabbis believed, because they were not trying hard enough but because they did not fully grasp their significance.

For the kabbalists, this understanding was achieved by probing the hidden symbolism present in the sacred texts and daily life of every Jew. But no matter how far their eyes strained toward the heavens, Jewish mystics from

Biblical times to the present have traditionally had their
feet planted firmly on the ground, a phenomenon partially explained by the fact that Judaism is inextricably
bound to the practices of everyday life. For the most part,
they have also been members of communities. Since the
most manifest mystical experience of Judaism, the divine
revelation at Mount Sinai, was an experience shared by
six hundred thousand souls, Jewish mystics have always
assumed that even esoteric practices ought not to isolate
them from their communities (though community sometimes meant only one or two disciples). Not everyone was
deemed "prepared" for seeing what the great mystical
practitioners saw, of course, and all sorts of restrictions
relating to the age, sex (women were excluded), morals
and wisdom of initiates were imposed to prevent the hoi
polloi from gaining access to kabbalistic circles. The Bible
has always been the star that charted the Jewish mystics'
course through ritual, withdrawal from sensory vanities
and distractions toward intimacy with God, and whatever
their differences, all of them shared the belief that the
more they repressed their egos, the more they would be
like mirrors reflecting the bright image of God.

In the earliest phase of Jewish mysticism, the first century B.C. through the tenth century A.D., mystical teaching was largely oral and concerned with the creation of the
world, the first divine revelations, and finding pathways
to a deeper, usually visionary connection with God. The
pursuit of mystical knowledge was considered dangerous
for those not spiritually prepared for it. Through the ages,
Jews have been told about the fate of Ben Azai, Ben
Zoma, Ben Abuyah and Rabbi Akiva—all famous scholars
of the first century A.D. who delved where others feared
to tread in their pursuit of mystical treasure. Of the four,
only Rabbi Akiva emerged unscathed: Ben Azai "gazed
and died," Ben Zoma went mad, and Ben Abuyah became
an apostate. To protect the uninitiated from similar dan-

gers, mystical knowledge was usually passed down from master to disciple in oral form. When written mystical tracts surfaced, they were usually unintelligible to all but a handful of the Jewish population. Most were descriptions of the dazzling visions the adept might expect to behold and what he might experience at each step of his mystical inner journey. In this early stage of Jewish mysticism, chants, breathing exercises, and fasting were used as tools to ease the initiate away from the outer world, as they are in many Eastern religions.

The second phase of Jewish mysticism was ushered in with the appearance around 1175 in Provence of an anonymous (actually it was deliberately ascribed to a false author) work called the *Book of Brilliance,* whose main theme was the elusive divine order that exists in everyday life. The *Book of Brilliance,* which brought kabbalistic notions to the attention of many of the Jews of France and Spain, was a kind of esoteric guidebook for finding God's glory everywhere and recommended methods for achieving a higher state of consciousness that included focusing on a spiritual energy that was believed to flow through the body, a technique also used in many Eastern religions, including kundalini yoga.

Whatever resemblance Jewish mysticism had to other religions, however, it differed from most of them in the way it stressed commentary and interpretation. Scholars have noted that nearly all post-Biblical literature shares these two characteristics, and as the critic Harold Bloom has pointed out, this is especially curious for "a body of work professedly mystical and speculative . . . But this emphasis upon *interpretation* is finally what distinguishes Kabbalah from nearly every other variety of mysticism or theosophy, East or West."

At about the same time that the *Book of Brilliance* was circulating, the *Book of the Pious* appeared in Germany and was read by many of the Jews of Northern Europe.

Although German Hasidim were mainly concerned with esoteric examinations of the Pentateuch they were also curious about altered states of consciousness and explored such exotica as automatic or spontaneous writing as pathways to spiritual knowledge. Unlike his eighteenth-century namesake, the medieval Hasid was an ascetic, a man who was warned against enjoying even the innocent pleasures of keeping birds or spending time with children.

One of the few things everybody agrees about in the realm of Jewish scholarship is that there is amazingly little known about the lives of the great Jewish mystics. Gershom Scholem, who died several years ago and was the preeminent student of Jewish mysticism of our time, said of them that they "left us . . . mystical tracts and books from which it is difficult, if not impossible, to form an impression of their personalities." One of the major books of the Hasidic world, for example, is the *Sefer Ha-Zohar*, or *Book of Splendor*, which Scholem has described as a kind of "mystical novel," and even the authorship of that book has been disputed. The *Zohar*, as it is usually called, records the mystical conversations of the second-century Palestinian rabbi Shimon ben Yohai, the most illustrious teacher and leader of his generation, his son Eleazer, and various followers. Most Hasidim still believe that the book was written by Shimon ben Yohai, although Scholem established after years of research that it was almost certainly the creation of the Spanish kabbalist Moses de Leon, who died in 1305. In contrast to earlier kabbalistic works, which stressed asceticism and personal mystical experiences, the *Zohar* emphasizes, among other things, the interconnectedness of all things in creation, and, although it was by no means an easily accessible book, it was more plainly written than many earlier mystical works.

But no kabbalist had greater influence on the philosophy of East European Jewry than Isaac Luria (1534–

1572), the leader of the sixteenth-century Safad school of mysticism. Safad, a city near the northern shore of the Sea of Galilee in Palestine, was an important economic and spiritual center for Jews, particularly those who had been exiled from Spain, in the fifteenth and sixteenth centuries. Although Luria wrote no comprehensive description of his theories and died before he reached forty, his philosophical discourses and syntheses of earlier kabbalistic works (he is alleged to have spent eight years reading and absorbing the *Zohar*, for example, which he happened upon by chance) were recorded by a disciple, Chaim Vital, and eventually transformed into what Scholem called the "true *theologica mystica*" of Judaism. Luria's intricate and elusive system of thought, I think it is safe to say, would scarcely have become as popular as it did had it not offered at last a persuasive explanation for the exile and suffering of God's supposedly chosen people. Vital's interpretation of his master's teachings is couched in difficult, knotty language, and even Scholem's exegesis of them is a bit opaque, but the boldness of Luria's vision is clear. Luria suggested that the reason suffering and evil exist in the world is that not only Jewry but the "Divine Presence" itself is separated from its source. In order for the material world to exist, he said, God contracted part of His "Light," a space opened up (a process Luria called *tzimtzum*, or concentration and withdrawal) and divine "vessels" or "husks" were filled with God's "Light." Another result of the *tzimtzum* was the emergence of the ten *sefirot* (*sefirot* is the plural of the Hebrew word *sefirah*, meaning, *very* roughly, divine attributes or energy-essence, although no exact equivalent of the term exists in any other language) which according to the kabbalists represent all the human faculties and the physical and spiritual dimensions of existence. The earliest mystical work to mention this concept seems to have been the *Book of Brilliance*. The *sefirot* have been depicted diagrammatically in many ways, but most fre-

quently in the form of a Tree of Life which has its roots
in the heavenly spheres beyond the grasp of human comprehension. Sometimes they are referred to as God's "garments"; they have also been called "faces," "limbs," "col-
ors," and "names," but whatever name is used for them
they symbolize some outer manifestation of the always
hidden God to which they are closely bound. The meaning
and relevance of this esoteric concept, which is funda-
mental to all Hasidic belief, have inspired countless medi-
tations from scholars of every generation. Luria's kabbalistic disciples disagreed somewhat about what exactly
happened next but all agreed that it was a cosmic catastrophe—one that, to a contemporary reader, is oddly evocative of the Big Bang theory of modern physics. Unable to
withstand the energy of the divine "Light," the "vessels"
or "husks" shattered, and confusion reigned. Some of the
sparks returned to their source. The rest commingled with
the shattered husks and fell into every animal, vegetable
and mineral part of the world. It is the task of man, Luria
said, to separate "the holy sparks" from their husks or shells
so they can reascend to their source, or "roots," as he called
them. All generations have a role to play in this process
until the day when the final *tikkun*, or repair—redemption—
comes.

One can readily see how the persecuted Jews of Eastern Europe and the descendants of those who had been
exiled from Spain drew an analogy between their condition and the ideas expressed by Luria. As Herbert Weiner
put it, in his refreshingly lucid 9½ *Mystics*, "Since to
kabbalists all history is but the outer representation of
an inner spiritual process, expulsion from Spain . . . was
seen as the outer covering of the real catastrophe that is
still taking place in the inner world. The seeming absence
of God which the Jews of Spain experienced was anal-
ogous to the primal withdrawal of God. Israel is in exile
just as God is in exile. But there is a purpose to this scat-

tering of the Jews; they are to go everywhere to gather the sparks and prepare the world for its Great *Tikkun.* The condition of the Jew is, therefore, not the result of an accident and certainly not a challenge to the claims of his ancestral faith. On the contrary, his condition of exile is proof of the cosmic mission which devolves upon every individual Jew and upon the people of Israel as a whole. The world will not be restored or redeemed unless the Jew performs his task."

If Lurianic doctrine gave all the Jews of the diaspora an explanation for their dispersal, it also provided satisfying grounds for performing the six hundred and thirteen commandments. The prime reason for observant people to obey the commandments, of course, was and always will be because God commanded them to. But the theory of sparks and the *sefirot* and the Great *Tikkun* gave ordinary Jews a sense that carrying out the most mundane of God's commandments—whether it had to do with preparing for the Sabbath, or eating kosher food, or going to the ritual bath—fulfilled a deeper cosmic purpose. Three hundred years later—and one hundred years after the Hasidim were to bring these ideas to the doorstep of the masses of East European Jewry—a disciple of the third Lubavitcher rebbe was asked what advantage *hasidus* (the study of Hasidic thought) offered over traditional kabbalah and philosophy. He responded, "Kabbalah describes the *sefirot;* . . . philosophy explains how God is beyond description and definition, how one cannot really understand Him at all, for if one would know God he would be God; Hasidus, however, maintains 'Know Him and become like Him.' " Curiously, Luria believed that the process of restoration had nearly been completed and that the final redemption, which would be announced by the appearance of the Messiah, would come soon. His followers even went so far as to predict the year that the Messiah would come, 1648—a cruel irony for those who were aware of it,

since instead of divine salvation, 1648 brought the Jews
the Khmelnitsky pogroms.

Sixteen hundred forty-eight also marked the year that
Sabbatai Zevi, a wealthy Turkish Jew and one of the strang-
est avatars of mysticism in Jewish history, first suggested
in public that *he* was the Messiah. He was born in Smyrna
in 1626. Although he was a gifted student of Talmud and
a member of the rabbinical elite of Smyrna, his scholarly
gifts were called into question early in his life by his bizarre behavior. For long periods he avoided people and was
subject to deep depressions; at other times he was wildly
garrulous and euphoric. It was undoubtedly during one
of his euphoric periods that he declared himself the re-
deemer of mankind. At first, no one took him very seriously. Those who knew him regarded his pronouncement
as further evidence that he was a troubled man. His general behavior only confirmed this view: he was divorced
from his first two wives without having consummated
either marriage, and a third wife was rumored to be a
prostitute; he frequently boasted that he was experiencing
levitation; and he celebrated a ceremonial wedding service with the Torah as his bride beneath a traditional
Jewish wedding canopy. For antics of this kind, he was
eventually banished from Smyrna and Salonika by the local
rabbinates.

In 1665, the course of his life was changed, however,
when a rabbi of unquestionable probity named Nathan of
Gaza declared that he had had an ecstatic vision in which
he saw Sabbatai Zevi as the true Messiah. By 1666 (the
same year the English millennialists had predicted for the
apocalypse), Nathan predicted, the new Messiah would
come to restore the world, "riding on a lion with a seven-
headed dragon in its jaws." Nathan announced that he
was the prophet of the new Messiah, and his announce-
ment was followed by seven weeks of frenzied excitement
during which time Sabbatai Zevi frequently rode around

Gaza on horseback in regal robes. To underscore his seri-
ousness, he appointed some of his followers apostles.

Word of this startling turn of events spread rapidly by
letter and messenger throughout the Jewish world and a
kind of mass hysteria ensued in which not only the weary,
downtrodden masses of Eastern Europe but Jews of all
classes and countries of the diaspora joined a mass movement of repentance to prepare for the coming age of redemption. According to contemporary witnesses cited in
the Encyclopaedia Judaica, "People from the surrounding
countries flocked to him to receive individual penance or
wrote to him asking him to reveal to them the root of their
soul and tell them how to 'restore it.' Excessive fasts and
other ascetic exercises became the order of the day . . .
The first reports that reached Europe were, curiously
enough, not about Sabbatai Zevi, but about the appearance
of the lost ten tribes of Irsael, who were said to be marching under the command of a prophetic and saintly man of
God about whom all sorts of miraculous stories were told.
According to some versions they were conquering Mecca,
according to others assembling in the Sahara Desert, and
in a third version marching into Persia. Rumors of this
kind, coming from Morocco, reached Holland, England
and Germany . . . Detailed reports from many parts of
the Diaspora describe the excessive lengths to which the
penitents went. Fasts and repeated ritual baths, mortifica-
tions which were frequently of an extreme character, and
lavish alms-giving were practiced everywhere. Many people fasted for [a] whole week . . ." One observer noted
that "the ritual bath was so crowded that it was almost impossible to enter there."

The Encyclopedia also noted that "commerce came to
a standstill everywhere. Many sold their houses and property to provide themselves with money for the journey to
the Holy Land, while others made no such preparations,
being convinced that they would be transported on clouds.

More realistic wealthy believers made arrangements to transport the poor to Palestine. Reports from small towns and hamlets in Germany prove that the Messianic revival was not limited to the larger centers. From many places delegations left to visit Sabbatai Zevi, bearing parchments signed by the leaders of the community which acknowledged him as the Messiah and King of Israel . . ."

Not everyone was impressed by Sabbatai Zevi's claims, of course. Among the notable skeptics were the rabbis of Jerusalem, who threatened him with excommunication. To avoid this, he returned to his birthplace, Smyrna, where he was received by tumultuous crowds and where he continued to attract followers from all parts of Europe and North Africa. Then, early in 1666, the year that was to have ushered in the paradisaical era, he was placed under arrest by the Turkish sultan, who had tolerated him for a while, but finally decided the time had come to respond to the social and religious upheaval caused by this eccentric Jew. A short time later, the would-be Messiah was asked to choose between death and conversion to Islam, and, to the horror of hundreds of thousands of his followers, he chose to don a white turban, the sign of his conversion to Islam. According to all reports, he entered upon a luxurious life and had the honorary title of Sultan's Doorkeeper.

Sabbatai Zevi's apostasy had a devastating effect on Jews throughout the diaspora, particularly those of Eastern Europe. In the region of the Ukraine, which had probably suffered most in the various pogroms, those who had pinned their hopes for a better life on the self-proclaimed Messiah felt betrayed and abandoned. Adding to their confusion was the fact that certain of Sabbatai Zevi's followers continued to proclaim his legitimacy. They argued that his apostasy was only a mask, a forced conversion that was nullified by a "deeper" faith. It did not help matters either when another demagogic figure (and apostate to Catholicism), Jacob Frank, whose followers were rumored to indulge in incestuous sexual orgies, appeared on the scene to revive and reinterpret many of Sabbatai Zevi's ideas.

In the end, the result of all the furor was to make most Jewish community leaders deeply suspicious of any innovation, all new ideas. Ordinary Jews were told to obey the commandments and leave deeper matters, especially mystical ones, to the scholars who had the training and knowledge to pursue them. Thus, a schism developed between the bulk of the now largely ragtag, leaderless, poor and uneducated Jews and the few well-to-do rabbis and scholars who had the time to study.

The founder of modern Hasidism, Rabbi Israel ben Eliezer, who is generally credited with rousing East European Jews from their spiritual torpor, could not have been more different from the established spiritual leaders of his time if he had been born a hedgehog. Rabbi Israel was born in the Ukrainian province of Podolia in 1698. In Hasidic circles, he is usually referred to as the Besht—an acronym of Baal Shem Tov, or "Master of the Good Name." The Baalei Shem were itinerant healers and wonder workers who, because of their kabbalistic knowledge of the secret mystical names of God and their possession of various amulets, were believed to be able to cure people and exorcise demons. (Name magic is one of the oldest forms of mystical belief. As the folklorist Joshua Trachtenberg pointed out in *Jewish Magic and Superstition,* "To know the name of a higher supernatural being is to dominate the entire province over which that being presides. The more such names a magician has garnered, the greater the number of spirits that are subject to his call and command. This simple theory is at the bottom of the magic which operates through the mystical names and words that are believed to control the forces which in turn control our world. The spirits guarded their names as jealously as ever did a primitive tribe. 'Tell me, I pray thee, thy name,' Jacob demanded of the angel with whom he had wrestled, but the angel parried the question and his name remained his secret, lest Jacob invoke him in a magical incantation and he be obliged to obey."

The golem—literally, shapeless or lifeless matter—was a homunculus supposedly created by the invocation of various mystical names for God. Known about since Talmudic times but receiving wider attention in the twelfth century, the character and nature of the golems changed over the centuries. The earliest versions were visionary functionless creatures created to demonstrate the power of the Holy Name; later on, they acquired practical functions, clay bodies, and in some cases malevolent wills. Nowadays golems are considered a somewhat quaint part of the Judaic past. Even so, a comic book series entitled *Mendy and the Golem*, featuring a gigantic, infinitely powerful, helpful superhero made of clay, is one of the popular reading sources for the children of Crown Heights and the Orthodox community. The first issue of the series, published in the summer of 1981, explained to its readers that "a *golem* was like a statue made of clay. Many years ago, *golems* were used to protect the Jewish community in times of trouble.")

At least part of the Besht's holiness was allegedly hereditary, since according to Hasidic legend, his soul was an incarnation of a spark from the soul of Rabbi Shimon ben Yohai. The Besht was the polar opposite not only of the spiritual leaders of his era, but of most of the trailblazers of Jewish history. Most of the great spiritual Jewish leaders or Hasidic masters share a common biography: They are precocious in their studies, they are sober, serious little men who evince no great interest in the ordinary pursuits of childhood, and very early on they become the shining light of an intimate circle of enthralled elders. The Besht had none of these attributes. He was poor, given to wandering around in the woods when he was supposed to be studying, and in his early life even chose to hide his true nature behind a mask of doltishness. However, when in his mid-thirties he finally began to preach his message— that simple faith, inward passion and fervent prayer were as important as Talmudic scholarship—it was not long before he found a grateful and passionate following.

The Besht's teachings, which form the core of all Hasidic belief, emphasized the mystical presence of God in all things and had as a goal the infusion of all aspects of life—eating, praying, lovemaking, social intercourse—with holiness and joy. For decades, the rabbinical scholar, lost in the minutiae of the law, or the reclusive mystic, steeped in secret kabbalistic lore, had been out of touch with most ordinary Jews, and, for that matter, with educated Jews who yearned for an infusion of vitality in their devotion. Small wonder then that before the end of the eighteenth century more than half of the Jews of Europe would have closed ranks behind the Besht and his followers, who not only brought kabbalistic mysteries (especially the Lurianic kabbalah) to light in a digestible form but, equally importantly, regarded themselves as community leaders, as had scores of rabbis in earlier generations.

Like many of his predecessors, the Besht wrote down none of his ideas, but his disciples did. (One is struck time and again by this preference for anonymity among Jewish mystics. They seem virtually egoless—content to allow their collective wisdom to flow from one generation to the next unencumbered by the flotsam of personal glory.) No real biography of him exists. A semicohesive account of his life appears only in a book called *In Praise of the Besht*, a compilation of Hasidic tales written by his scribe's son-in-law that did not surface until 1814, fifty-four years after his death.

Two slightly different versions of the Besht's life emerge in the book: one written by the author, the other by the printer, who could not resist adding his own version of the facts in the form of a preface. The author focuses on the Besht's wonder-workings. The printer gives a rather more conventional, earthbound version of his life and emphasizes his hidden saintliness. He tells us that the Besht was born when his parents were quite old and that his father died soon afterward; that his community sent him to study with a local teacher but he was frequently absent and was said to prefer sitting alone in the woods to attending school; that, later on, he became a teacher's assistant and took the children to and from school; that he was reputed to have a beautiful voice; that he became a beadle at the local study house, where he secretly studied all night and slept all day so that people thought him doltish and laggardly; that his first wife died shortly after they were married; that his second wife's father knew him to be a holy man, but that his brother-in-law considered him to be a simpleton and urged his sister to divorce him; and that eventually he and his wife went to the country where he quarried clay, regularly secluded himself, and fasted.

In 1734, after seven years of this ascetic life, the Besht returned to his wife's village and soon afterward "put aside his mask," and began to teach. Little else of a nonlegendary nature is known about him. Hundreds of Hasidic tales have been passed along, however, about his life, all of them testifying to his clairvoyance, his compassion, his ability to perform miracles or exorcise dybbuks (restless souls of the dead), his ability to solve problems that had confounded the wisest scholars, and his mystical powers, which included being able to rise to the heavens. Many of the stories emphasize the Besht's concern that religion must be a living, vital thing. "Not," as it says in Deuteronomy, "in the Heavens . . . Neither is it beyond the sea . . . [but] very close to you."

The Besht traveled a good deal to distant towns and villages and word seems to have spread rapidly among the hamlets of Eastern Europe that according to his teachings no one needed ever again to feel left out in the spiritual cold. Even the poor shepherd who mumbled incoherently when his heart was full of love for God was heard. Moreover, his sincerity probably made more of an impression on the heavenly spheres than the dry supplications of the scholar who recited his prayers by rote. Although there were many itinerant *maggidim* (teachers who also functioned as preachers and storytellers) who circulated among the masses before the Besht came along, the preaching style of most local leaders was admonitory; on the rare occasions when community leaders condescended to step out of their study halls to address their communities it was usually to berate the faithful, in fire-and-brimstone tirades, for their alleged sins. The Besht stressed the everyday examples of faith and piety he encountered and tried to persuade community leaders to be more compassionate.

Before long, impressive numbers of Jews began to leave their villages' established congregations (and ritually ordained rabbis) to follow the Besht and his disciples, the *zaddikim* (righteous men). The reputation of the Besht and his followers as pious men who could use mystical techniques to heal, bless, comfort and enlighten every Jew eventually earned them the name "Hasidim." Unfortunately, it also aroused the deepest suspicions that they were ill-intentioned gadflies, if not heretics. But Scholem and others have pointed out that there was nothing heretical about them. In *Major Trends in Jewish Mysticism,* Scholem, citing the British scholar Evelyn Underhill, de-

clares: "The prevailing conception of the mystic as a
religious anarchist who owes no allegiance to his religion
finds little support in fact. History rather shows that the
great mystics were faithful adherents of the great religions." Many of the conservative enemies of the Hasidim
were also mystics; it was not the Hasidim's mysticism
that they objected to, but what they regarded as their
vulgarizing of it. It was certainly true that the Besht and
his followers never rejected a single tenet of Orthodoxy.
They did, of course, introduce certain innovations, among
them permitting the hours of prayer to vary, so that people could pray in less of a hurry and, it was hoped, with
more feeling; eliminating the cantor, long a fixture of
synagogue life, from the service so that any pious man
could lead it; and declaring that dancing and singing were
appropriate ways to express religious enthusiasm. Unlike
the followers of Sabbatai Zevi, whose spiritual energy was
directed outward, toward the person of their would-be
savior, the Besht's followers were urged to turn their focus
inward; the joyous dancing and singing, the vigorous,
rocking prayer style and the shouting of endearments to
the Deity in the course of a service that became the ear-
marks of Hasidic worship were only the overflow of excited religious feeling. Nonetheless, these peculiarities,
and the growing number of defectors to the movement,
did little to endear the Hasidim to the established rabbinic leaders, especially those whose memories of their
elders' tales about Sabbatai Zevi were still fresh.

It did not take long for the conservative sector of the
religious hierarchy (who came to be known as *mitnagdim*,
or opponents) to declare that the Besht and his followers
were dangerous heretics who were threatening the heart
of Orthodoxy with their denigration of Talmudic study
and vulgarization of worship. In 1755, the new "sect" (a
word which was understood to link the Hasidim to Sab-
batianism) was denounced and two years later the rab-

binates of the cities of Slutzk, Vilna, and Shklov placed a ban on the Besht and his teachings. This censure proved to be as effective in halting the growth of the Hasidic movement as a fisherman's net would have been in holding back a tidal wave.

CHAPTER THREE

Sabbath

> Six days shall you labor, and do all your
> work; but the seventh day is a Sabbath unto
> the Lord your God, on it you shall not do any
> manner of work . . . for the Lord blessed the
> Sabbath day and sanctified it.
>
> (EXODUS 20:9–11)

I T is one of the curious twists of history that the Hasidim,
once considered the enemies of Orthodoxy, today consider
themselves its bulwarks. Besieged from every direction by
what they perceive as a decadent, morally bankrupt world,
they shun its preoccupations, rebel against many of its social conventions, spend as much time as possible in their
neighborhood fortresses, and devote themselves to perpet-
uating the ideals of Jewish religious life. This is especially
evident on the eve of the Sabbath. To wander along Kingston Avenue, where the Lubavitchers do most of their mar-
keting, as I did one Friday afternoon some weeks after my
first visit to the Konigsbergs, is to enter a world whose
rhythms are dictated solely by religious custom and ritual.
Like most of her neighbors, Sheina had completed some
of her Sabbath preparations the night before, but she still
had some last-minute shopping to do, and invited me to
accompany her. She was in a good mood.

"I live from one Shabbos to the next," she said. "I look forward to it all week. We almost always have three or four guests. Sometimes they're neighborhood friends; at other times it's just family, but we're often asked by some official to provide a congenial Shabbos for someone who is traveling or for students who have no other place to go. In the last month we've had people show up from England, Iran, and South Africa; the door is never closed. It's totally unlike what I was used to growing up in Bloomfield Hills. Saturdays were a drag when I was a child. I didn't really understand what the Sabbath was about; no one ever talked about it. We observed it only in a half-hearted way, and neither my two brothers nor my sister and I ever really understood why we were doing any of it. In fact, I hardly understood anything about the deeper levels of Judaism until I became a *baalat teshuvah* [Hebrew for 'one who has returned']."

No one knows exactly how many *baalei teshuvah* there are, but in recent years a surprisingly large number of Jews have "returned" to Orthodox ways, and each year hundreds of them join the Lubavitcher world. Some have been sought out. Unlike other Hasidim, the Lubavitchers are unabashedly committed to bringing as many Jews as possible back into the fold. Some, like Sheina, found their own way.

"What was life like in Michigan?"

"It was like everywhere else: aimless. It would probably be hard to find a community whose values were more different from those of a Hasidic community than the one that I grew up in. I had a happy childhood, but we were completely isolated as Jews, and we certainly had no sense of being part of a larger Jewish world. Everybody was fairly well-to-do and self-absorbed. They really never gave two thoughts to their spiritual life."

In a corner fruit store, Sheina handed a short shopping list to a swarthy man in a yarmulke who filled a bag with fruits and vegetables as we talked. From time to time, the shopkeeper and Sheina discussed the comparative merits of various fruits. Sheina's voice was unusually even as she talked with him and the man seemed to be struggling with a powerful urge to fawn which, one surmised, he must have learned from experience would embarrass this customer. There were three other women in the store. All of them knew Sheina and came over to chat. Across the street, a "Glatt Kosher Dairy Cafeteria" (*glatt* means smooth; originally the word referred to the lining of an animal's lung, which was not considered kosher if wrinkled; it has come to mean assiduous) had signs in the window for cold borscht, mushroom barley soup and noodle pudding, and nearby a dark tiny store called "Benny's of Boro Park" offered ladies' clothing.

The general store down the block, where Sheina stopped next, was piled high with cartons. Customers sidled around the boxes and each other, flattening themselves to avoid physical contact, and generally acting like contortionists as they strained to reach boxes of Landau's Puffed Wheat, jars of Rokeach Gefilte Fish and cans of Season Sardines. Cartons of Shefa brand kosher milk filled the refrigerator cases. Little knots of Hasidim stood about talking, gesticulating, laughing, arguing, creating complex roadblocks. Shopping definitely played second fiddle here to conversation. Most of the conversations were in Yiddish, a few were in English. No one passed Sheina (whose command of Yiddish, she confided somewhat ruefully, was tenuous) without at least a nod, or, more often, "Ah, Sheina, how are you?" followed invariably by *"Baruch Hashem,* fine. And you?" There were many Yiddish accents and much of the English spoken reflected Yiddish syntax. Almost everybody used the word "by" for "at," for example, as in, "I was staying by Hannah last week." Except for the thin veneer of modernity represented by the refrigeration, the plastic food wrappings, and the fashionable wrappings of the women, the store seemed to have been freshly transported to Brooklyn from Sholem Aleichem's Kaserilevke.

All the canned goods and cartons were marked with a Ⓤ (for Union of Orthodox Jewish Congregations of America) or other little symbols signifying that the product had been approved as kosher by various rabbinical boards. No Hasid will buy any prepared food that does not bear this stamp of rabbinical approval, and one supervising rabbi may be deemed more trustworthy than another. We nearly made it to the fish store across the street without stopping to talk with anyone, but at the entrance a gray-bearded man stopped Sheina to ask her how the two Iranian girls he had sent over to her were doing. Sheina explained that more than nine hundred Iranian Jewish children had been sent to America by their worried parents, who feared for their lives because of the political unrest in that country. Almost all of them were taken in by Lubavitcher families, who were doing their best to cope with communications problems (few of the children spoke anything but Persian) and the characteristically indifferent religious background of their charges. Although the children were grateful for the Lubavitchers' help, most had shown little interest in pursuing a more religious life. The man who stopped her was in charge of the Iranian project. She told him that the girls were doing fine. "They keep to themselves a lot, but they try to enter into our customs as best they can." One of the chief characteristics of the Lubavitchers that distinguish them from other Hasidim is their Jewish social consciousness. Helping Jews of every stripe has traditionally been a Lubavitcher preoccupation.

In Raskin's Fish Store, the clerks, all in yarmulkes, joked a lot with their customers. The fish was piled in huge heaps and the atmosphere evocative of an oriental bazaar. Most of the women had made the traditional Sabbath food, gefilte fish, the night before, but for those who had

not had the time or the inclination, Raskin's sold its own
gefilte fish, frozen. I saw no one buying less than five
pounds of fish. In my neighborhood in Manhattan, at least
half the late Friday afternoon customers were young
working women buying the modest provisions for dinner
with their boyfriends—two artichokes, two fillets of something, two candles, and so forth. There were obviously no
intimate *soupers à deux* being planned here. The Books of
Leviticus (Chapter 11) and Deuteronomy (Chapter 14:3-
21) list the animals, fish, and fowl that are considered
kosher, or fit to be eaten by Jews. Only sea creatures that
have both fins and scales are considered kosher, so no
lobster, clam, oyster, crab, or shrimp is ever seen in a
kosher fish store. Other foods that are proscribed by Jewish law include meat from animals that do not both chew
their cud and have cloven hooves, twenty-four kinds of
birds (many of them birds of prey); insects, amphibian
creatures or any creature that crawls "upon the belly"; any
"winged swarming thing," rodent, or lizard; or any product
that might come from these creatures, such as milk, eggs,
or oil. Animals that are considered clean are cows, sheep,
goats, deer, chickens, turkeys, geese, ducks, and doves.
Other forbidden foods include pigs, camels, herons, storks,
hawks, ravens, pelicans, ostriches, eels, snails, rattlesnakes,
ants, and rock badgers.

Eating kosher food and meats that have been slaughtered in the ritually prescribed manner is one of the basic
disciplines of Jewish religious life. Reform Jews, who believe that the dietary laws are antiquated and serve no
practical function, point out that they are a major factor
in separating Jews from the rest of their fellowmen. The
Hasidim are opposed to joining the mainstream and, citing the scriptures, point out that God never intended that
they should: "I am the Lord your God who have set you
apart from the nations. You shall therefore separate between the clean beast and the unclean beast and the un-

clean fowl and the clean." If the Hasidim's habits and customs alienate outsiders, they are unconcerned. Unlike most
Jews, who tend either to shrug off, compartmentalize, or
firmly reject any idea of their exoticness, the Hasidim accept it as part of their role. In fact, it is a source of pride.
As one religious author put it, "What narrower minds look
upon as a picayune concern with trifling kitchen matters
is really an example of how Judaism elevates the mere
physical satisfactions of one's appetite into a spiritual act
by its emphasis on the everpresent God and our duty to
serve him at all times." So much ritual is associated with
eating in Orthodox homes that it sometimes seems that
the table is a form of altar. In fact, one unnamed Talmud
scholar mentioned in a curious tome that I came across,
called *To Be a Jew* by Rabbi Hayim H. Donin (one of
many such everything-you-wanted-to-know-about-Juda-
ism-but-were-afraid-to-ask volumes that have recently become popular in the booming spiritual-affirmation business), went so far as to suggest that the table has come to
replace the Temple altar: "When the Temple stood, sacrifices would secure atonement for an individual; now his
table does."

By midafternoon on Friday the streets of Crown Heights
are filled with women laden with shopping bags, hurrying
home to finish their preparations for the Sabbath. By late
afternoon the women have all disappeared and the landscape has become entirely masculine. As the shadows
lengthen under the maples and lindens of President Street,
dark-hatted men in somber clothes, alone or in groups of
two and three, are taking pains to reach home before sundown, when the Sabbath begins. Many of the men work
half days on Fridays, others leave work by midafternoon.
If an employer will not permit an early departure on Friday, a Hasid will not work for him. On Friday afternoon
the men go to the *mikvah*, or ritual bath, to purify themselves for the Sabbath. Many of them exchange their busi-

ness suits and ordinary fedoras for knee-length black silk
caftans and velvet yarmulkes. Crowds of men mill outside 770 Eastern Parkway. The look of boredom or patient
endurance one sees so often on their faces in the workaday
world has vanished. Their expressions are lively, and the
talk is animated. It is a pleasing scene—a *tableau vivant*
that cannot have looked much different two hundred years
ago. Few of these men have attended college. In the Hasidic world, secular education has traditionally been
viewed as a threat to religious life. In the past decades,
this view has changed in certain communities. There has
developed what the sociologist Egon Mayer, in his study of
the Boro Park religious community, referred to as a dual
status system. Upwardly mobile young men and women
have tried (helped by laws protecting them from religious
discrimination) to achieve distinction in secular careers
and still satisfy the demands of a religious life. In these
communities, being a good doctor or lawyer has come to
mean as much as being a good Jew. This change has never
occurred in Crown Heights. It is no surprise, therefore, that
there are few professional men in the crowd in front of
the synagogue. The conspicuous lack of interest in careers
that the anthropologist Jerome R. Mintz observed among
Hasidim in the nineteen-sixties and wrote about in *Legends of the Hasidim* (a study of Hasidic life based on
modern Hasidic tales) still prevails among the Lubavitchers of the nineteen-eighties. Some of them, like the
Konigsbergs, appear to make a good living despite this
handicap, but many do not. "A Hasid," said Mintz, "does
not have a 'career'; he is concerned simply with earning a
living in a way which will not interfere with his religious
duties. Most Hasidim . . . belong to the ranks of skilled
workers. They are employed in the diamond center as cutters, polishers, and dealers; they hold jobs as sewing machine operators, pattern cutters, watchmakers, linotype
operators, electricians, carpenters, and upholsterers . . . a

small but ever increasing number have established small packaging and wholesale businesses, often in response to the particular needs of the Hasidic community. Because of their disdain for what they consider inadequate precautions in fulfilling the ritual law, a number of Hasidim have succeeded in establishing enterprises concerned with matzoh, meat, milk, cheese, bread, noodles, salt, sugar, mayonnaise, and vitamins. Hasidic manufacturers and wholesalers can assure their customers that no condition will be permitted which might render their products impure. Still other concerns supply religious books and other articles. . . . A number of Hasidim have become ritual slaughterers or have opened highly successful butcher shops. Some have opened groceries, vegetable markets, fish stores, dry goods stores . . . These retail ventures are assured of a measure of success because of the customary endorsement of their Rebbe and the patronage of their own courts."

At the Konigsberg house, twenty-five minutes before sundown, Sheina, dressed in an elegant tan silk blouse and tweed skirt, was preparing to light the Sabbath candles. Her afternoon coiffure of short, feathery Titian curls had been completely transformed into a long, svelte pageboy in the few minutes it took her to change upstairs. I briefly entertained the idea that I might have been encountering my first kabbalistic wonder, then recollected that for reasons of modesty, married Hasidic women cut off most of their hair and wear wigs. She had merely changed wigs.

According to custom, Sabbath candles are lit twenty minutes before sundown. The meal had been cooked, the table elaborately set, the heavy, ornately wrought silver candelabrum polished, and the family and some guests were milling around the living room. The guests included a South African rabbi and his wife and two daughters; Moshe's second-oldest daughter, Chanah, who was preg-

nant; and her husband, Isaac, a small redheaded man with
intelligent, laughing eyes, who told me that they were
about to depart for Virginia to help organize the Jewish
community there; the two almond-eyed Persian girls, Gita
and Azita Medizhadi; and a young girl who had recently
decided to abandon her secular life and live in the dormitory the Lubavitchers run for young *baalot teshuvah*.
Several minutes after the guests were introduced to one
another, the women crowded around the candelabrum.
According to Jewish custom it is the obligation of married women to usher in the Sabbath by lighting the
candles. At least two candles are lit, symbolically repre-
senting the fourth commandment, to "remember" the Sabbath, and the twelfth verse in Deuteronomy, Chapter 5,
to "observe" it, but Sheina also lit additional candles for
her children and so did the rabbi's wife. Without saying
anything, Sheina handed me several candles and invited
me to repeat the blessing for lighting the candles after her,
which I did somewhat awkwardly. I had never done it
before. When I was young, I had seen my grandmother,
a plump, rosy Austrian beauty, light Sabbath candles once
or twice. But my mother, an adamantly modern soul who
thought that such rituals belonged in the same category as
curtseying and child labor, put the traditions of four thousand years behind her without a backward glance. Now,
watching the peaceful, absorbed faces of the women in
the glow of the candles, I felt a rush of nostalgia and
something like a sense of loss. It passed quickly, however,
when I realized that because of the prohibition against
using the phone on the Sabbath, I would be unable to call
my son to wish him goodnight.

The activities proscribed for the Sabbath either by the
Bible or by post-Biblical decree seem mind-boggling to
outsiders. They include cooking; baking; washing laundry;
chopping; knitting; crocheting; sewing; embroidering;
pasting; drawing; painting; writing; typing; fishing; hunt-

ing; cutting hair (or cutting anything else, with the exception of food); building or repairing anything; gardening; carrying or pushing anything farther than six feet in public; riding in cars, planes, trains, or buses; boating; buying or selling; horseback riding; playing a musical instrument; switching on any electrical apparatus, such as a TV set, phonograph or radio; handling any objects whose use is forbidden on the Sabbath, such as money, tools, or pencils; exercising or playing any sport; or traveling, even by foot, more than a short distance from the place where one is ensconced on the Sabbath. I asked Sheina how she felt about having her activities so restricted each week. Surveying the dinner table approvingly, as the men filed out the door to go to their evening service, she replied that she didn't think of it that way.

"I feel that I'm getting a break," she said, as she placed a heavy water pitcher on the table. "Once you get some of the more complicated things out of the way, like cooking the food in advance and setting a large urn of hot water on a metal cover over a low burner so that everybody can have coffee and tea to drink on Saturday, and covering some of the light switches so that no one will accidentally turn the important lights off, it feels more like a holiday. What if you were flown to a quiet tropical island every week? Wouldn't you be pleased if you were permitted, even obliged, to just put aside your everyday burdens and everyday chores? I don't really know what other people's lives are like, but I doubt that most families get the chance we do to just sit around and talk to one another every weekend. On weekends most Americans seem to play as hard as they work . . . The Sabbath is also a time when I can study Torah in an unhurried way, and we almost always have guests who have interesting things to say about life."

"You mean Jewish life, of course."

"Well, yes."

"Are your guests ever gentiles?"

"No. I'm aware that there are some fine gentile people; but their world is not our world. I may see an occasional play, or concert, or TV program—most of the people in the community don't have TV's, by the way, and don't go to the movies—but these are not the important activities in my life. Being a Jew and fulfilling the commandments *is* my life, and it's Moshe's. It takes up all our time. The rhythms of my life over the weeks and months follow those of the *Jewish* calendar. [The Jewish year is made up of twelve lunar months, with an extra month added every few years to make up for the annual eleven-and-a-quarter-day discrepancy between a lunar year and the solar one.] It's the same for everyone here, so it follows that the people that we see are going to be involved in the same kind of life."

"You don't feel that you're cutting yourselves off from any of the richness of life by shutting things out just because they're different?"

"No, I don't. I can't imagine a richer life than the one I'm leading. Anyway, we're not all that shut off from the world. Moshe and I travel."

"You do? Is that common here?"

"Well, it's quite common to go off to another city or country to help start or build a Lubavitcher center, but people here travel for pleasure, too. We went to London last summer."

"What did you do there?"

"We visited Lubavitcher families and the yeshivas in and near the city, but we also went to see the Victoria and Albert Museum and the Tower of London and Madame Tussaud's. Of course, when you do these things, you can sometimes get into trouble; we certainly did when we went to the Tower of London on a Friday," she said, smiling.

"What do you mean?"

"There was a tube strike while we were there, and even

though we left the Tower at four o'clock in the afternoon in order to be sure to make it to the friend's house
we were staying at in Golders Green by nine, when Shabbos began, we very nearly didn't make it. You could only
move around by bus—you couldn't find a taxi. We had to
change buses several times and the queues were endless.
At seven-thirty, we were still standing at the end of a
long queue at Oxford Circus and there were no buses
in sight. Moshe said, 'Let's walk.' We were both exhausted
by then and pretty frantic, and there didn't seem to be
any chance that we could make it, but off we headed toward Golders Green, which was about an hour away by
bus. I nearly started to cry. Then Moshe just bent over to
a fellow who had stopped his car at a light and told him
that he was a religious Jew and that we simply had to be
at our friend's house by sundown. He told him that he'd
give him whatever amount of money he wanted if he
would drive us there. The man looked at Moshe as if he
were crazy at first, but it turned out that he was a religious
Catholic. He was surprised that we couldn't get a special
dispensation because of the strike; *he* could have, he said,
but he agreed to take us, and we made it. He didn't even
want to take any money in the end, but we insisted because it didn't seem fair to have him go out of his way for
nothing."

"Why do you think that people really aren't supposed to
work on the Sabbath?" I asked. "Why does it honor God
more to desist from work than to work?"

Sheina bit her lip. "Ask Moshe when he comes back, he
knows more about things like that than I do."

About an hour and a half later, Moshe, Isaac, and the
rabbi from South Africa returned from the synagogue.
Sheina had mentioned earlier that her husband prayed
three times a day (as required by Jewish law) on week-
days at 770—which is how the Lubavitchers refer to their
synagogue—where there were always so many people

around that he was sure to find the quorum of ten men needed for public prayer. On Fridays and Saturdays, however, he prayed at a *shtiebl* (small synagogue) around the corner. Many Lubavitchers did the same thing, she explained, because they wanted to keep the little synagogues, which were built in the first half of the century and had lost most of their congregations in the fifties and sixties, going. Moshe, resplendent in a long black caftan and velvet yarmulke with gilt zigzagging, rubbed his hands together and regarded the room and his guests with obvious satisfaction. A few minutes later, his sons and a schoolfriend rushed breathlessly into the room. When Mendel spied me, he nudged his brother. Shmuel glanced my way briefly, but stared fixedly at his shoes when he greeted me. They had made it just in the nick of time, Sheina explained, since kiddush (the prayer of sanctification) had to be recited before six o'clock. It was five to six. They had been somewhat delayed coming in from Morristown, New Jersey, where they were all students at a Lubavitcher yeshiva, the Rabbinical College of America, and so had gone to evening prayers directly after they had arrived back in the neighborhood. The boys' friend was another visitor from South Africa. Everyone gathered around the table and the men sang the traditional "*Shalom Aleichem,*" a hymn that pays homage to the angels that accompanied them home from the synagogue. After the song I noticed Moshe looking rather intently at Sheina and reciting or singing something. She was smiling. Later that evening she explained that Moshe had been singing the thirty-first chapter of the Book of Proverbs, which contains the well-known phrase "A woman of valor, who can find; for her price is far above rubies." This paean to what seems to be the practical virtues of Jewish housewifery was in fact interpreted by the early kabbalists as a hymn to the *Shekhinah,* God's female aspect. I knew that Hasidic men sang this to their wives every Sabbath, but I had somehow expected that it would be a more public, declamatory ritual. The intimacy of the moment took me by surprise. One of the guests asked where Moshe's two other daughters were and was told that the eldest, Miriam, lived in Cape Town with her husband and children and that Bassy, the youngest, who was nineteen, was with her grandmother. Bassy, a slim, spirited girl who in the secular world would probably be taken for the captain of her field hockey team, had explained to me several hours earlier, as she hastily gathered a few belongings together and headed for the door, that she spent Shabbos with her widowed grandmother, who lived around the corner. "Sometimes she comes here for Shabbos but sometimes she likes to stay at home, so I help her prepare everything and I stay overnight to keep her company." When I said that most of the girls her age that I knew would not be eager to do that, she looked genuinely surprised.

"But I don't mind at all. It's no problem. You'll see when you meet Bubbe. She's great. Actually, I've spent every night with her since she had to have one of her fingers removed because of cancer last year. It's really no big deal."

Moshe filled a silver kiddush cup to the brim with sweet wine and, holding the cup in the palm of his hand, recited the kiddush, and then everyone trooped off to the kitchen in silence to wash hands for the meal. Like virtually every facet of Hasidic life, washing up before meals is accomplished in a ritually prescribed manner. One fills a chalice with water, pours the water first over the right hand, then over the left, then recites the benediction, "Blessed art Thou, Lord our God, King of the Universe, who has sanctified us with His commandments, and commanded us concerning the washing of the hands." One by one, the guests returned in silence to the table. Then Moshe removed a velvet coverlet from two home-baked challah breads (two to symbolically commemorate the extra portion of manna

that the Israelites were given on the first Sabbath eve of the
Exodus), poured everybody some wine, lifted the breads,
recited another blessing, then cut off a piece for everybody
at the table. Everyone dipped his chunk of bread in salt
(symbolic of the salt used in the ancient Temple during
ritual sacrifices) and the meal, trumpeted in by a great
outburst of talk, began in earnest.

A staggering amount of food appeared at the table, but
the guests seemed to like to talk even more than they liked
to eat, and much of the dinner was destined to sit un-
touched for long lapses, on people's plates. Sheina's dinner was so copious that it would not have been a calamity
if one or two courses had slipped away unnoticed, although I believe none did. The menu was inspired largely
by East Europe and the suburban Midwest, with East
Europe predominating. There was gefilte fish, a tossed
salad, chicken soup with matzoh balls, roast chicken,
braised beef, noodle pudding, a spinach-and-broccoli
mold, and a nondairy ice cream pie with a walnut crust
for dessert. Whiskey, wine, and cordial bottles were scattered across the length of a snowy, starched tablecloth. In
front of Moshe, who sat at the head of the table with the
other men seated around him, was a bottle of Chivas
Regal; the boys poured each other glasses of Israeli wine,
and the women sipped from a dazzling assortment of cordials—banana liqueur, Kahlua, Cherry Heering, and black-
berry brandy, some of which came from miniature bottles,
souvenirs, perhaps, of Purim. Over the matzoh-ball soup,
I asked Moshe why it was, apart from emulating the actions of the Creator, that ceasing to work on the Sabbath
honored God. His sons looked at me in astonishment,
scarcely believing that anyone would not know why Shabbos was Shabbos, but Moshe seemed pleased that I had
asked the question.

"What happens when we stop working and controlling
nature?" he asked, peering at me over the top of his

glasses. "When we don't operate machines, or pick flowers, or pluck fish from the sea, or change darkness to light, or turn wood into furniture? When we cease interfering with the world we are acknowledging that it is God's world."

The rabbi from South Africa, a robust, cheerful man with a thick, black, curly beard, added that the Sabbath was also a memorial to the exodus from Egypt.

"Once the Jews left Egypt they were no longer enslaved. But of course the ordinary workaday world always involves a kind of servitude, and for many people, especially poor people, work can be awfully grinding. But no one is the master of any Jew on the Sabbath. Every body and every soul is free on that day. Tyrannical countries have always tried to force Jews to work on Saturdays, to mock this gesture of independence. East European Jews fought anti-Sabbath edicts and statutes for centuries."

Moshe chose this moment to lead the men in a beautiful Aramaic hymn, familiar to everyone present, written by Isaac Luria, that depicted the Sabbath as a bride "adorned in ornaments, jewels, and robes. Her husband embraces her; through this gathering which brings her joy, the forces of evil will be utterly crushed." The Sabbath queen or bride is a popular metaphor in the literature of the mystics. Her husband, of course, is all Israel, that is, every Jew. Almost all religious Jews sing at the Sabbath meal. The songs they sing celebrate the joys of the Sabbath and were written chiefly during the Middle Ages. Lubavitcher Hasidim have their own melodies, or *nigunim*, most of which have been composed by their rebbes; they are sung on almost any occasion that offers itself. Among the Sabbath *nigunim* that were sung that weekend was one composed by the present Rebbe ("may we be united with the Supreme One in whom is the life of all things; may our strength be increased, and may our [prayer] ascend and become a [diadem] upon His head") and another composed by the first Lubavitcher rebbe ("Rejoice now at this

most propitious time, when there is no sadness. Draw near
to Me, behold My strength, for there are no harsh judge-
ments. They are cast out, they may not enter, these [forces
of evil which are likened to] insolent dogs").

Moshe had a fine, clear voice and sang with gusto,
sometimes closing his eyes to better concentrate on the
song. I remarked that he seemed to enjoy singing a lot. He
made a little self-deprecatory gesture and pulled on his
beard, but smiled. "I come from a musical family. My
grandfather played the violin for the soldiers when he was
in the Red Army. My Bassy is a good pianist, too, you
know." Songs were sung throughout the meal. The singing
grew more animated as the hour grew later. If the heavy
food anchored the guests ever more deeply into their
chairs, the songs acted as a kind of spiritual counterweight.
Unfamiliar as I was with the songs, I felt a strong urge to
join in, though I had not failed to notice that none of the
women had been singing. While the noodle pudding was
being passed, I asked the young girl next to me, who was
studying Lubavitcher ways, if it didn't bother her to be
left out of the singing.

"A little," she admitted, "but I sort of sing along to
myself."

"Do you know why women aren't supposed to sing?"

"Well," she said, plunging a big forkful of noodles into
her mouth and gazing placidly at me over a freckled nose,
"women's voices can be highly arousing to men, so our
sages thought it best that we didn't sing in front of them.
It doesn't work the other way around though, because
women have always been considered more spiritual, so a
man's singing is not going to upset them or anything."

Seeing what must have been an ill-disguised expression
of bemusement on my face as I gazed at the freckle-faced
girl, the boys' friend from South Africa, a gentle looking
pink-cheeked boy of about nineteen, said to me in a re-
proving tone, "Everybody thinks the modest ways of Hasi-

dic women are absurd and unnecessary, don't they? But they're wrong. Last week a group of us were speaking about Hasidic life at one of the universities, and a student said to us, 'You know, it's really ridiculous, the way your women cover their elbows and their knees, and the way you make married women wear wigs. I'm not turned on by elbows and knees, and I'm not going to ravish anybody's wife just because her hair is beautiful.' And most of the people there either laughed or smiled. 'Well,' I said, 'it's too bad if beautiful hair and legs and arms don't arouse you. They do me.' Uh, and that's true. It takes a lot to turn people on today, because there's so much public nudity and promiscuity. People have become coarsened. No wonder the simple sight of beautiful flesh doesn't mean much. But in our world, where there is no exposure to such things and where the sexes are separated so much of the time, things are different."

Perhaps, I thought, looking around the table at the attractively dressed, carefully made-up women present. But why hair, elbows, and knees? Why not eyes, hands, napes of necks, and trim ankles? And what about mouths? Muslim women's mouths were considered so tempting that they had to be veiled.

Gazing at the young boy approvingly, Moshe said, "Dovid came into our midst because of what people call our proselytizing campaign, although that's really the wrong word for what we do. The Rebbe started a program some years ago of sending young couples around to places where there were sizable Jewish communities, not only in our country but all around the world. He hoped that they would quicken awareness of what Judaism had to offer our people. We sent the Mitzvah Tanks [the Lubavitcher campers that carry students around asking passersby, 'Are you Jewish?'] out for the same reason. They usually come back amazed by the welcome they receive. The most unlikely people sometimes respond to what they have to say.

My daughter Miriam and her husband in Cape Town
never expected what they found: a lot of people who were
willing to take on the obligations of a more religious life.
Dovid is one of them."

Looking slightly embarrassed, Dovid explained that
until recently he had lived with his family on a large
South African cattle ranch and attended the University of
Cape Town. But his conversations with Moshe's daughter
and son-in-law at the university convinced him that a lot of
the things that he missed in his life—a sense of purpose and
commitment, a feeling of community—could be supplied
by Judaism and more particularly by the Lubavitchers'
way of life. He thought about it for several months and
then decided to leave the university, come to New York
and study at the Lubavitcher yeshiva. "It was the smartest
thing I ever did," he added.

"Did your parents give you a hard time?" asked the girl
with the freckles.

"Not really," said Dovid.

"Well, mine did. And they still do. They think that the
Lubavitchers are some kind of weird cult, like the Moonies.
They hated it when I started observing Shabbos and they
hated it when I told them I really wanted to study Judaism seriously and to lead a more religious life. Sometimes I think that they'd rather have me smoke pot than
pray." Everybody laughed.

"From the beginnings of the Hasidic movement outsiders have wanted to think of us as cult or a sect," said
Moshe. "That's why we were excommunicated in the eighteenth century. But we never were a sect. On the contrary,
from the beginning the Besht intended that all Jews
should be brought closer together because of his ideas. If
the various Hasidic dynasties that formed in different
towns after his death came to be regarded as separate en-
tities, that was never what was intended. The Lubavitchers

in particular, from our founder, Rabbi Schneur Zalman, to the present Rebbe, have always tried to reach all Jews. If we seem so different from other Jews it's more because of what has happened to them than anything that happened to us. We've stayed the same; it's they who've changed."

"You know there is a saying among Hasidim that the Messiah will come 'when the wellsprings of the Baal Shem Tov spread out,'" said Sheina, as she eased generous wedges of cocoa-colored pie onto plates and passed them down the table, "that is, when everything that he taught becomes the common practice of all Jews in the diaspora. That's why the Rebbe has sent the young people around in the campers and around the world. Jews don't really stick together because there is a breach among us. He wants to heal it."

At about ten o'clock the women began to clear the table. Moshe carried one or two things to the kitchen but Shmuel was still eating a second helping of dessert and the boys got into some knotty discussion of a point of Hebrew semantics just as the clearing up began. They did not resolve it until the table was cleared of everything but the still softly glowing candelabrum. Moshe entered into the discussion after a while and I noticed that though he spoke English when he talked with Sheina, he and the boys spoke to one another in Yiddish. Some of the guests lingered at the table, some drifted over to the couch and chairs at the fireplace. One of the guests, the woman from South Africa, asked Shmuel, who was seated in an armchair, his stomach protruding over his belt, how a certain friend of his was getting on. Shmuel said that he was married and that he and his wife had recently had their second child. He looked at his shoes as he answered.

"And what about you?" the guest asked pertly. In these circles, a twenty-five-year-old is considered a bit long of tooth for bachelorhood.

"What about me?" Shmuel answered, keeping his eyes glued southward. There was a defensive edge in his answer, but also a real note of misery.

"Oh, Shmuel will settle down when the right time comes," said her husband, looking at him evenly and drawing his wife away to look at some books across the room. Shmuel raised himself heavily from the chair with a little sigh, found a book, and retired to a quiet corner to study. Five minutes later, Mendel joined him and their heads remained bent together for the rest of the evening. During the winter months when it got dark earlier, Moshe met with a group of Lubavitcher neighbors every Friday night to study, he said, but in the months when it turned dark late he studied either with the boys or by himself at home on Shabbos. Conversation among the rest of the guests continued in an animated way until the early hours of the morning. At 2:15 I excused myself and retreated to Bassy's cheerful, frilly second-floor bedroom, which, unlike that of every other teenage girl of my acquaintance, was innocent of posters of rock godlets, photographs of boyfriends, clippings of Snoopy cartoons, or fey messages.

All that met the eye were several shelves filled with religious books and some neatly arranged cosmetics on top of a dresser. The sole wall decoration was a blue and white banner that (like the bumper sticker on the car I had seen in the driveway) proclaimed that "Jewish Mothers and Daughters Light Shabbos Candles." Heavily ballasted with matzoh balls and conversation, I sank into sleep almost immediately. As I pulled a soft blue and white comforter over my head, it occurred to me that not one word had been spoken about any nonreligious subject. Tomorrow, I thought, as I drifted off, there will undoubtedly be some conversation about secular matters. A few hours later, I was awakened by a street noise. I glanced at my watch. It was 4:15. A low hum of conversation drifted up from below.

On Saturday, the conversation turned frequently to Biblical events and their relation to the lives of those assembled at the house, to upcoming religious holidays, and to some of the Rebbe's recent talks. Subjects such as jobs, politics, movies, the environment, secular books, or the latest football scores never even entered the fringes of discussion. There was a bit of gossip, but it was mostly about who was getting married or was having a baby. Several times I overheard Moshe mention Yitzhak and Avraham. I thought he was talking about some neighbors. It turned out that he was talking about the Biblical Isaac and Abraham. Throughout the day, I was struck by the familiar even intimate way in which Moshe, Sheina, and the others spoke of Biblical people and places. Isaac and Abraham all but hovered near the stove, miraculous deeds had more credibility than newspaper stories, and none of the Biblical heroes had lost their luster. This personal mystical connection with the literalness of the Bible serves, of course, as a kind of Jewish relic or monument to the past, its only religious monument, in fact, since, unlike other religions, most of the material relics—such as the Temple and many of the sacred books—have been destroyed. Like the shtetl Jews that Mark Zborowski and Elizabeth Herzog wrote about in *Life Is With People,* an anthropological study of shtetl life, the Hasidic community today "traces its line of march directly back to Creation. The Exodus from Egypt, the giving of the Law on Mount Sinai, are seen as steps along the way, historical events no less real than the Spanish Inquisition or the Russian Revolution."

Like their shtetl forebears, the Hasidim believe that the oral and written law, which was codified chiefly in the centuries following the exile, amount to a Magna Carta or constitution of a kind of spiritual government in exile and only the adherence of the Jewish faithful, they believe, "has enabled a weak and homeless people to survive the great empires of Egypt and Babylon, Greece and Rome,

Byzantium and Islam, and has caused their sacred books to enter into the holy writ of half the world."

If the Konigsbergs live in a kind of perpetual Biblical present, in which the events of their everyday lives are constantly being linked to their spiritual past, their rebbes have traditionally been the guides who have interpreted the interconnectedness of the two. While I watched the *Havdalah* ceremony (*Havdalah* is the Hebrew word for separation) that signaled the end of the Sabbath, Saturday night—a plaited candle is lit, wine is drunk, a benediction is said, and a spice box is passed around to raise spirits that might be saddened by the passing of the Sabbath—I remembered some of the names of former Lubavitch and other Hasidic leaders that had been evoked during the day as if they were old friends. "Ah, the *frierdike* [previous] rebbe used to say . . ." or, "Did that happen to you? The same thing happened to the *Tzemach Tzedek* [the third Lubavitcher rebbe]." The history of these Hasidic ancestors, too, is inextricably bound to the lives of their descendants.

CHAPTER FOUR

The Rise,
Fall, and Reascendance
of Hasidism

I N the seventeen-forties and -fifties, as word of the Baal
Shem Tov's teachings spread and his followers became
more numerous, the entrenched leaders of many East European Jewish communities grew more nervous and hostile. Despite the fact that the Besht never stressed messianic issues or laid the slightest claim to any messianic
role, the whiff of heterodoxy that surrounded him was
enough to rouse the deepest suspicions of those whose
memory of the havoc wreaked by the false messiah was
still relatively fresh. The established hierarchy regarded
the Besht's un-Jewish sounding emphasis on joy with no
little consternation, and believed that his elevation of the
simple man to a place in the social and religious hierarchy
equal to the Talmud scholar (to them!) threatened the
Jewish community with chaos and anarchy. How were
local authorities going to admonish their unlettered flocks
to follow every nicety of the law when the Besht assured

them that it was their purity of heart and the spirit of their devotion that mattered, not their ability to memorize tractates?

The partition of Poland in the years 1772–95 would eventually give Hasidism as great a forward impetus as its spiritual leaders did. The three foreign governments who took over the country—Russia, Prussia, and Austria—disregarded altogether the old communal authorities that had kept Polish Jewry together for centuries. In the southern, less citified regions, Hasidism spread rapidly. But even before that era Hasidic prayer houses began to sprout up everywhere, and, in many quarters, praying had ceased being so solemn. "Our Father in Heaven hates sadness," said the Besht, "and rejoices when His children are joyful." To be sure, there was still plenty of solemnity in Hasidic praying, but now intensity of feeling and spontaneity were valued more. The song and dance that played such a central role in the Hasidic gatherings served not only as a sociologically unifying force but as a mystical rite of passage.

The Besht and his followers were not the first Jews to sing and dance their way closer to God. Isaac Luria and his circle often sang and danced outdoors when performing their rituals, and one of the members of that circle, Israel ben Moses Najara (1542–1619), who lived in Syria as well as Palestine, adapted many Arabic, Greek, Turkish, and Spanish melodies to fit Hebrew texts. Najara's songs were eventually carried to all parts of the Jewish world and became a part of everyday synagogue life. But the Besht and his followers gave singing and dancing a higher spiritual status than they had ever enjoyed before and convinced great numbers of Jews of music's unique power to transport them quickly from the mundane and oppressive realities of their lives to the realms of ecstasy and joy. Often, Hasidic masters wrote their own tunes, but they also borrowed their music, as Najara had, from contemporary sources such as ballads, folk tunes and even military marches. The founder of Hasidism taught that music heightened spiritual awareness and made it easier to appreciate the beauty of the world, and belief in the potent spiritual power of song and dance has remained undiminished among Hasidim for more than two hundred years.

The Hasidim also adopted a prayer book (and consequently an agenda for synagogue praying) based on the teachings of Luria that differed from the one generally in use in its order of prayers, in its omission or inclusion of various liturgical hymns, and in some small changes in textual phraseology; they made some slight changes in the methods of slaughtering cattle (they permitted the use of a honed steel knife instead of the traditional iron one); and they dressed in white on the Sabbath. Everywhere the Besht traveled tales were told of his miraculous healing powers and, perhaps even more important, of his psychologically comforting ideas.

It was not unusual to see the Besht and his followers assembled in the woods or meadows, or gathered companionably around a table. (The openness of these gatherings went far to allay the suspicion that the Hasidim were heretics; since their meetings were open to all for scrutiny, they obviously had nothing to hide.) There was no formal preaching, no discourse delivered from a pulpit, and he never instructed his pupils in a methodical expository way. Distrusting the written word, he preached through stories, anecdotes, aphorisms, and parables: the chief teaching method practiced by Hasidim today. Sheina's quotation about the Messiah coming when the "wellsprings of the Baal Shem Tov spread out" came, I learned afterward, from one of the few documents in the Besht's own hand that survived after his death: a letter he wrote to his brother-in-law in 1750, describing a mystical encounter his soul had with the Messiah in a journey it made to heaven.

Unlike so many of his mystical predecessors, and despite his own early history, the Besht was opposed to asceticism, and discouraged his followers from excessive fasting or similar acts. "The body," he said, "must be strong for the worship of the Lord."

It came as no small surprise to me to learn, as I quickly did in talking to the denizens of Crown Heights, that the chief twentieth-century popularizer of Hasidic thought and tales, Martin Buber, is considered by most Hasidim to have misconstrued both the message of the Besht and the essence of Hasidism. They feel that he placed too much emphasis on the legends and too little on kabbalistic doctrine. Scholem (whom the Hasidim also dislike because of what they regard as his anarchic intellect) agreed. In Buber's version of Hasidism its adherents find "joy in the world as it is, in life as it is, in every hour of life . . ." In reality, Scholem said, the method used for finding joy was "to extract, I may even say distill, the perpetual life of God out of life as it is . . . It is not the fleeting Here and Now that is to be enjoyed, but the everlasting unity and presence of Transcendence." Buber presented to the world a Hasidism which "does not acknowledge any teaching about *what* should be done but puts the whole emphasis on intensity . . . Therefore, references to the Torah and the commandments, which to the Hasidim meant everything, become extremely nebulous in Buber's presentation."

From the little that I had thus far glimpsed of Hasidic life, it seemed to me that Scholem had it right; the charm of the Hasidim's stories, the quaintness of their appearance, and, for those who understood it, their mystical theology were symbols to the world of their singularity and of their essence. They made it easy to think of Hasidism as a cult, which, as Moshe had pointed out, it never was. But the core of Moshe and Sheina's life was the Law: the Torah and the commandments; their mysticism, their vigilant studying, and even their Rebbe were merely mining tools. Were their story to appear in Buber's *Tales of the Hasidim*, Sheina's tweediness, Moshe's good humor,

Bassy's adolescent energy, and the boys' xenophobia would never be mentioned; we would learn only about "a good woman," "a pious man," "a dutiful daughter," and her "studious brothers." But in real life what was amazing about the Konigsbergs and those around them was the passion with which they strove to submerge themselves, with all their quirks and weaknesses, to better serve what Scholem calls "the everlasting unity" and to see in the world, with all its quirks and weaknesses, "the presence of transcendence." In a sense, my first impression of their life, on Purim, a day of rejoicing and simple, exuberant celebration, might be said to have been Buberesque; but the more I saw of the family, the more rooted in traditional Jewish rituals and inward, or Scholemish, their life appeared. What made them different from other Orthodox Jews was not simply a conglomeration of charmingly pious customs that outsiders could readily imagine transformed into a kind of Hasidic *Fiddler on the Roof*. It was the way they approached these rituals, their wholehearted adoption of the Lurianic mythos and the teachings of their leaders (and their dedication to the study of these things), and their passionate attachment to their Rebbe.

Curiously enough, the Hasidic Tale, which is considered by so many to be *the* authentic distillation of Hasidic life, is a relatively late Hasidic literary genre. The earliest collections of such Tales appeared in 1814, more than fifty years after the Besht's death, and as the scholar Joseph Dan points out in his introduction to his recently published compilation of works from the "classical period" of Hasidism (1780–1811), most of the stories in later collections were not even written by Hasidim. The reason the "authentic" literature of the classical period has not been read by most people, of course, as Dan readily admits, is that virtually all of it belongs to that class of writing called the "exegetical homily . . . characterized by the structural features and internal conventions of the sermon" and "really impossible to translate." Had the Tales never been published, therefore, the world would have had little chance to learn anything about Hasidic life.

When the Besht died, in 1760, the movement he started had begun to attract followers from every corner of Eastern Europe, among them some of the most promising students of his day. These intellectuals and teachers were attracted to the Besht's mystical ideas and brought them to the masses, for the first time in Jewish history, in a graspable form; without their presence, it is doubtful that the movement would have gone anywhere. This fact is frequently glossed over in histories of Hasidism. While the Besht's great rapport with the humble and unlettered is rightly stressed, and it is true that many a shoemaker and tailor came to his home, in Miedzybosz, to hear him preach, there is little basis for the widely held belief that the Hasidim were some kind of early flower children. The Besht did not exclude scholars from his circle, he merely made room in it for the nonscholar. Furthermore, while dancing, singing, and liquor may have added considerable intensity to Hasidic rituals and the Besht, according to his grandson, allegedly used snuff whenever he wanted to "go to the worlds above," altered states produced by exotic mushrooms (or anything else from the abundant pharmacopoeia of drugs employed throughout history by spiritual depth plumbers) have never been a feature of the Hasidic menu. Nor were his followers drawn only from the ranks of the desperate and displaced; many of them, according to Rabbi Jacob Joseph of Polonnoye, a disciple who wrote down many of the Besht's sayings and eventually (in 1780) published them, had "relatively stable social positions" which they put at risk by adopting the Besht's ideas.

The Besht was considered *the* prototype of the *zaddik*, a "righteous" man who, as one religious source put it, "has reached the ideal of communion in the highest degree and therefore appears before God as 'one of his own.'" The

great Hasidic leaders have all been considered *zaddikim:*
holy men who mediated between God and more ordinary
mortals to help them obtain earthly blessings and guide
them toward a more spiritual life. The kabbalistic concept
of the *zaddik* had been around for several centuries before
the Hasidim arrived on the scene, but it was they who in-
stitutionalized it and gave it special importance and though
neither the Besht in particular nor the Hasidim in general
were the first Jewish leaders to focus on concern for the
poor and unlettered, joy in worship, love for all Israel and
a closer communion with God, they were the first to for-
mulate a doctrine that would give the *zaddik* a crucial
role in the everyday life of his followers. Spiritually, the
zaddik was considered to be on a higher rung of the ladder
than most ordinary people, but since the whole Jewish
community was bound together, the Besht envisaged him
as a man who was obligated to step down from his exalted
position and intimate contemplation of God to better care
for the spiritual and earthly needs of his people. Belief in
the power of the *zaddikim* not only had far-reaching effects on the Hasidic movement and on the relationship its
adherents had to their leaders but in the final analysis
might be said to be the single factor that distinguishes Hasidism from all other Jewish movements.

After the Besht's death, his disciples established centers
of Hasidism throughout Eastern Europe. These leaders, or
zaddikim, were considered models of Torah living and
today, through dynastic inheritance, their descendants
(actual or spiritual) are considered holy men in a special
way. Buber called the *zaddikim* "helpers" and saw nothing strange about their position. Scholem believed that at
the beginning of the Hasidic movement the closest possible communion with God was the ideal sought equally
by every Hasid but that as the movement developed and
it became clear that most ordinary Jews had neither the
aptitude nor the time to try to concentrate on reaching the

highest kabbalistic realms of communion with God, this
goal was expected to be achieved only by the *zaddikim*.
For most Hasidim, he thought, the very different "adhere
to your sage," that is, attach yourself to and follow a
zaddik, replaced the earlier goal—a speculation supported
in a curious way by the moral of Moshe's story about his
great-grandfather Isaac and the third Lubavitcher rebbe
("Just go about your business, I'll worry about the heavenly intervention side of things"). Many religious authors
tend to skirt this subject a bit nervously. One such author, describing the attitude of the Besht's followers toward him, said that they "*all* but worshipped" him. (Italics
mine.) A provocative article written several years ago by
the scholar Arthur Green in the *Journal of the American
Academy of Religion* displayed no such skittishness. Mr.
Green linked Mircea Eliade's idea of the *axis mundi*,
"man's central principle for the organizing of sacred space"
(in all religions), with the tradition of the *zaddik* in Judaism. He points out that Jews have historically denied
that they have any priests. The rabbi is a scholar, legal
authority and teacher, not a holy man. "Every Jew," he
notes, "had equal access to God through Torah and prayer."
Green believes, however, that after the destruction of the
Temple the Jews yearned for a central "holy space" to
focus on and that this space was eventually found in the
physical persona of the *zaddik*. "The fact is that the post-
exilic Jews maintained a highly complex and ambivalent
attitude toward their tradition of sacred space. . . . While
longing for a return to the Holy Land continued unabated,
the dispersed community of necessity had to have within
it various means of more ready access to the sacrality
which its great shrine had once provided. Israel wandering
through the wilderness of exile was to find that it still had
need of a portable Ark of the Covenant. One of the ways
in which this was provided was by a transference of *axis*

mundi symbolism from a particular place to a particular person: the *zaddik* or holy man as the center of the world."

As Green points out, the *axis mundi* principle is, of course, a central component of Christianity. It is true that the place where the Besht lived, the places where the early Hasidic leaders lived, and the place where the Lubavitcher Rebbe lives today are places of pilgrimage, and although most Hasidim would deny it, Green may be right when he speculates that the *zaddik* is the closest thing Jews have to a "Hellenistic god-man or quasi-divine hero." Depending on their bent, Hasidic leaders have either emphasized, exploited, or downplayed their special role. The Lubavitcher leaders have traditionally deemphasized it, stressing instead their role as teachers and social innovators.

The most famous of the Besht's disciples was Dov Baer of Meziritch, a gifted Talmud scholar who eventually systematized his mentor's teaching and synthesized it with the philosophy of Isaac Luria. Like many of the Besht's disciples, Dov Baer, who is frequently referred to as the Great *Maggid*, was not always a believer in the joyful expression of his faith. His early days were spent as an ascetic. In time, however, his excesses of self-mortification made him ill and he was compelled to take to his bed. According to one of his contemporaries, he sought a cure from the Besht, who succeeded not only in curing him but in making him his foremost disciple.

Unlike his teacher, Dov Baer did not travel about much (partly because he was never very robust) and was not perceived by the common people as one of them. Nonetheless, he was widely respected as a teacher and was charismatic enough to become the movement's leader, despite some strong opposition, after the Besht died. (The Besht's only son, Zevi, was considered too retiring to assume the role of leader.) Housebound as he often was, he

drew scores of distinguished men to his side and attracted
many new disciples from the intellectual and wealthier
classes. These followers did not come and go, as most of the
Besht's students had, but remained with him, transferring
the center of Hasidism from the province of Podolia in
southeastern Poland to that of Volhynia in central Poland.
In a sense, his was the first Hasidic court.

In the eighteenth century, the most famous center for
traditional Torah study was the Lithuanian city of Vilna,
and its undisputed leader was the stern and widely admired *Gaon* (the Hebrew word for great scholar), Rabbi
Elijah ben Solomon. Vilna was the center of the opposition
to Hasidism and the *Gaon* was its most vituperative
spokesman. Led by Rabbi Elijah, the rabbinical authorities of Vilna contented themselves at first by merely de-
nouncing the new "sect," and hoping it would go away.
But after the Baal Shem Tov died and the Hasidic light
failed to dim, opposition began to take a more serious
form. In 1772, the year Dov Baer died, a strong ban was
pronounced against the Hasidim by the communal leaders
of Vilna and Brody and others were issued in the years
1781, 1784, and 1796. The new bans meant that the Hasidim were in fact excommunicated. The members of the
"sect" were now called heretics; other Jews were forbidden to eat their meat or drink their wine; and "intermar-
riage" with any of them was forbidden. "Had I the power,"
declared Rabbi Elijah, "I would have punished these in-
fidels as the worshippers of Baal were punished of old."

Even excommunication did not seem severe enough
punishment to him. A month after the 1772 decree of excommunication was published, a letter originating in
Vilna was circulated throughout the Jewish communities
of Eastern Europe. It charged that the Hasidim "meet together in separate groups and deviate in their prayers from
the text valid for the whole people . . . They are the
same who in the middle of . . . prayer, interject obnox-

ious alien words [that is, Yiddish] in a loud voice, conduct themselves like madmen, and explain their behavior by saying that in their thoughts they soar in the most far-off worlds. . . . The study of the Torah is neglected by them entirely and they do not hesitate constantly to emphasize that one should devote oneself as little as possible to learning and not grieve too much over a sin committed . . . Every day is for them a holiday . . . When they pray according to falsified texts they raise such a din that the walls quake . . . And they turn over like wheels, with the head below and the legs above . . . Therefore, do we now declare to our brethren in Israel, to those near as well as far . . . All heads of the people shall robe themselves in the raiment of zeal, . . . for the Lord of Hosts, to extirpate, to destroy, to outlaw and to ex-communicate them."

Severe as such censure was, it did little to slow down the growth of the movement. As the number of Hasidic groups throughout Europe grew, each group developed into a dynastic court, and differences began to appear among them. Some courts became known for their rationalistic bent (the Lubavitchers), some for their miracle-working (the Belzers), some for their mysticism (the Bratslavers), some for their wealth (the Rizhyn-Sadgoras).

When a rebbe died, one of his sons usually became the new rebbe. But when one reads Hasidic tales about the rebbes, it becomes clear that popularity and chance have played equal roles in the selection of who would assume the leadership. "The essential dictum of the choice," Mintz observed, "is the closeness of the successor to the Rebbe, for their intimacy in life ensures the transfer of piety and power and the maintenance of traditional patterns. Often a son-in-law, a nephew, or a close disciple of the deceased Rebbe is named. . . . When the Lubavitcher Rebbe died in 1950, the two candidates were the Rebbe's sons-in-law. Rabbi Menachem Mendel Schneerson had the strongest supporters and was asked to become the Rebbe, while his brother-in-law remained head of the Yeshiva." Only the Bratslavers, who never chose another leader after their great *zaddik*, Rabbi Nahman, died in 1810 (and for that reason are sometimes referred to as the "dead Hasidim"), have gone against the tide and remained leaderless. Belief in the rightness of dynastic leadership remains unshaken among Hasidim today, though naturally enough, history has provided instances that might give them pause about the inviolability of the tradition. Baruch of Miedzybosz, one of the Besht's grandsons, for example, lived the luxurious life of an Eastern potentate and even had a court jester to help while away his idle hours. Menahem Mendel of Kotzk (1787–1859), a Polish *zaddik*, was a misanthrope who declared "the whole world is not worth a sigh." For every story that casts the *zaddikim* in a bad light, however, there are hundreds that bear witness to their goodness, holiness, and piety, and each group, of course, gives special importance to the writings of its revered leaders, past and present.

Hasidic chroniclers invariably boast about the miracles their masters performed, the calamities they averted, the barren marriages they made fruitful, the sick they made well, the good works they inspired, and the valor with which they defended themselves against their enemies. But they do not, except in very rare instances, tell us anything about their leaders' self-doubts, false turns, or outright mistakes. Thus, any "history" of Hasidic leaders must of necessity be considered mythic and taken with many grains of salt, and the factual realities of their lives must be left to the imagination. This is easier said than done: more often than not, one feels a strong sense of irritation and frustration when reading these texts. The great rebbes' thoughts about God are always made abundantly clear, but what they thought about themselves, each other, their families, friends, or the neighbor whose horse kicked

down their fence is loftily ignored. Nowadays biographers
may err in the other direction. Nonetheless the modern
reader rebels against this dismissal of the quotidian. One
longs, almost salaciously, for a bit of gossip, a description
of furniture, a weather report. In vain. The diet that readers of Hasidic "biographies" must learn to sustain themselves on is one of moral philosophy and fable.

The power and authority of the rebbes have always
been strengthened by the belief that many of them have
lived in earlier reincarnations as sainted Jewish leaders.
Reb Asher, a Stoliner rebbe, was believed by his followers
to have inherited King David's soul. A leader of the Apter
Hasidim announced one Yom Kippur that he had been a
high priest in Jerusalem; and Moshe Teitelbaum, a Satmarer leader, once revealed to his amazed followers that
in earlier lives he had been a sheep in Jacob's flock, and
had participated in the Exodus and witnessed the destruction of the tablets. He also said that in his third reincarnation he had witnessed the destruction of the Temple in
586 B.C., but he declined to say who he was. When it was
suggested that he had been the prophet Jeremiah, he did
not deny it.

In contrast to many of their fellow Hasidim, the Lubavitcher rebbes have from the beginning stressed the practical and rational aspects of serving God, although mysticism plays no small part in the stories told about them or
in their world view. The story of the birth of their founder,
Schneur Zalman, for example, is steeped in mystical symbolism. According to Hasidic belief, most souls have been
sent back to earth in order to, as Nissan Mindel, Scheur
Zalman's Lubavitcher biographer, puts it, "make amends
for wrongs or omissions in a life that had once, or even
more than once, been spent on earth." New, untainted souls
are a great rarity, but the Besht is said to have had a mystical premonition that Schneur Zalman would be one, and
that he would "disseminate the Hasidic way with selfless

dedication, preparing the way for the arrival of the Messiah." For motives which are obscure, the Besht played no part in the boy's upbringing, and did not even permit his father to bring him along when he came for his annual visits to Miedzybosz. The only explanation he ever gave for shunning him was the enigmatic "he is not destined to be my disciple. He belongs to my successor."

Schneur Zalman was born in 1745, in Lithuania, then a part of Poland, in the town of Liozna. He did not meet Dov Baer until he was twenty. By then he had been married for five years and lived in his wife's town of Vitebsk, not far from his own hometown. According to his teachers, he had quickly surpassed them, so he decided to take temporary leave of his wife and friends, as was the custom among young scholars, and seek a new mentor elsewhere. In Vitebsk, as in most of the rather conservative, strongly anti-Hasidic towns of Lithuania, most young men who pursued their studies elsewhere went to Vilna, the capital, to study under the tutelage of the *Gaon*. Much to the dismay of his wealthy father-in-law, who supported his life of study, Schneur Zalman decided that he would rather study in the distant town of Meziritch with the Hasid Dov Baer, whose reputation as a Talmud scholar was excellent and whose new views intrigued him. It gives one some idea of the measure of distaste aroused by the Hasidim to learn that when he announced that he was determined to study with them, his father-in-law cut off all financial support. Nonetheless, he and his wife managed to raise money and he left for what he promised would not be more than a year and a half. The visit was very nearly far shorter. Dov Baer seemed at first unlikely to live up to his new student's expectations. He and his circle devoted so many hours to prayer and to preparations for prayer that there seemed to be little time left for study. Convinced that this form of worship was alien to him, he decided to leave, but, having forgotten some of his be-

longings in the study house, he returned, and found Dov
Baer there, explaining some point of law to his followers.
Listening to him, the young scholar was greatly impressed
by the master's passion and erudition and afterward had
his first mystical experience while listening to his mentor
tell a story that was rife with kabbalistic references.

The doctrines that underlay the story were that God
was unknowable even to the purest celestial creatures;
that the raison d'être of creation was man, a body and a
soul firmly planted on the earth; and that the true purpose
of man was to obey the divine law. Schneur Zalman spent
much of his life expounding these doctrines, but he wrote
about them in greatest detail in his famous religious guide,
Likutei Amarim (Collected Essays), more popularly
known as the *Tanya*, after the first word (in English it
means "it has been taught") of the Hebrew text. When he
returned home to Vitebsk a year and a half later one of his
friends asked him what he found in Meziritch that was so
much better than what most of his friends had gone to
Vilna for. He replied, "In Vilna you are taught how to
master the Torah; in Meziritch you are taught how to let
the Torah master you."

According to his Lubavitcher biographers, the next few
years were years of poverty and isolation for the young
scholar and his wife, but their horizon brightened in 1767
when Dov Baer asked him to become the local teacher in
his old hometown, Liozna. Three years later, Dov Baer
suggested that his youthful disciple, who was then only
twenty-five, revise and update the Code of Jewish Law
(the *Shulchan Aruch*), the standard text referred to by
Jews on questions of law, that had been composed more
than two hundred years before by Joseph Caro. As one of
his admirers later put it, "This was an enormous . . .
task, requiring extraordinary erudition and mastery of the
entire Talmudic and Halachic [legal] literature as well as
a boldness to arbitrate and make decisions in disputed

cases involving the opinions of the greatest masters of
Jewish Law up to his time." Except for one section, which
was published anonymously during his lifetime, the Code
was not published until after Schneur Zalman's death.
Known as the "Rav's *Shulchan Aruch*" (to distinguish it
from Joseph Caro's), it has since become the Lubavitchers'
standard Code of Law.

When Dov Baer died, the leadership was to have
passed to his son, Abraham, but he felt unequal to the
role and refused to accept it. Leaderless, the *Maggid's*
disciples decided among themselves to journey to various
parts of Eastern Europe to carry on their work. Schneur
Zalman drew the thankless mission of trying to win over
that hotbed of anti-Hasidism, Lithuania. Despite strong
opposition he succeeded in drawing a large part of the
population into the Hasidic fold, and helped establish a
seminary that was to attract some of the most gifted
young scholars of the day. Sometimes, traveling to distant communities, he concealed his identity to avoid
the hostility of his opponents. On one occasion, he decided to journey to Vilna with a friend to attempt to
persuade Rabbi Elijah that his opposition to the new
movement was based on groundless fears. The two men
appeared at the rabbi's door twice, hoping for an audience,
but they were refused each time. When several highly regarded members of the community tried to intercede on
their behalf, Rabbi Elijah left town and did not return
until after the two Hasidim had departed. Recently, opposition to the Hasidim had hardened because of rumors
that some of the *Maggid's* disciples, Rabbi Abraham of
Kalisk and his friends, had been seen somersaulting and
dancing wildly in the streets and mocking the *mitnagdim*
in the synagogues (they were) and that a certain Hasidic
leader had been seen at a feast on a solemn holy day holding a female on his lap (also true, except that the female
was his baby granddaughter). On the few occasions when

Hasidic books appeared they were publicly burned. Book
burnings were recorded in Vilna, Brody, and Bohemia. In
1783 a public debate or "disputation" was finally arranged
between Schneur Zalman and venerable leaders of the
mitnagdim. The old Talmudists expected to trounce the
Hasidic leaders by overwhelming them with their knowledge, but, according to one witness, as many as four hundred Talmud scholars who attended the debate were impressed enough by what Schneur Zalman said to become
converted to Hasidism, and many of them followed him
back to Liozna to join his community.

In the decades that followed, Schneur Zalman became
the de facto leader of all Belorussian Hasidim. Handwritten copies of his religious guide, the *Tanya*, began to appear all over Eastern Europe. What the *Tanya* offered was
nothing less than a synthesis of the mystical and rational
currents of Jewish thought, as well as a highly original,
complex kind of mystical psychology holding that by
searching the depths of their own souls men would come
to understand all the dimensions of the world. As the author says in his foreword, the *Tanya* was written for "seek-
ers" and the "perplexed." They were not the sophisticated
perplexed for whom Maimonides wrote his *Guide* six centuries earlier, who were torn between the contradictory
claims of philosophy and faith, but the just plain confused
perplexed, untroubled by doubts about their faith but unable, in his words, "to perceive the beneficial light that is
concealed in books."

Schneur Zalman was the founder of what came to be
known as Chabad Hasidism—the word *Chabad* is an acronym of the Hebrew words for wisdom, understanding, and
knowledge (it became known popularly as Lubavitcher
Hasidism only after its leaders moved to the town of Lubavitch years later). He stressed the intellect far more than
the Besht had. Like him, he recognized the importance of
pure faith and simple emotional attachment to God, but,

unlike him, he also focused on the importance of intellectual comprehension of that attachment. The *Tanya* stressed
a practical mysticism and a system of contemplation that
gave every Jew a chance to transcend his own existence.
It postulated the presence in each individual of two souls:
one, the "animal soul," from which proceeds all of what
is called "human nature"; the other, the "Divine soul,"
which exists before it enters a body, survives it after death,
and enables humans to rise above their "natural" inclina-
tions in the service of God. Forged copies of the *Tanya*
written by its enemies also occasionally made an appearance. They invariably contained heretical passages that
caused great uproar in the religious community. So, in
1796, Schneur Zalman published his book officially. Its
popularity only added fuel to the opposition, however, and
two years later he was formally denounced by some of
his enemies among the *mitnagdim* as a traitor to the tsarist government. Among the trumped-up charges leveled
against him by his accusers was the fact that he was sending money to the government in Palestine. The accusation
was based in part in truth; throughout the eighteenth century Hasidim had migrated to Palestine and counted on
their East European brethren for financial support. But
in 1796 Palestine was ruled by Russia's enemy Turkey.
Russia and Turkey had been at war from 1787 to 1792 and
Russia was still on uneasy terms with Turkey, fearing her
expansionist aims in the Mediterranean. As the *mitnagdim*
knew only too well, Tsar Paul I was uneasy about the loyalty of the Polish nationalists who had so recently come
under the wing of the Russian eagle. He was easily per-
suaded that the Hasidim were dangerous rebels who were
sending money to a hostile foreign power. Schneur Zalman
was arrested and incarcerated in St. Petersburg's Peter-
Paul fortress.

According to Hasidic legend the black carriage that
picked up the rebbe at Liozna to carry him to St. Peters-

burg was still on the road the following day, which happened to be a Friday. Several hours before sunset, the
rebbe asked the officer in charge of the military escort to
stop and wait until after the Sabbath to complete the journey. The officer refused. Minutes later, the story goes, one
of the carriage axles broke. A blacksmith was summoned
from a nearby village and it was fixed. They proceeded on,
but a short time later one of the horses teetered to the
ground and died. A fresh horse was brought but to the officers' astonishment, straining as they might, the horses were
unable to make the carriage budge. The officer in charge,
convinced that mysterious forces were at work, relented
at last and agreed to stop at the next town; but the rebbe,
fearing that they might not reach the next town before
sunset, refused to go another foot. In the end, they
camped by the side of the road just where they had
stopped, and continued on Saturday night without further incident.

In St. Petersburg the *alter* (or old) rebbe, as the Lubavitchers usually call him, was questioned closely, but his
interrogators could find no way to justify any of the
charges brought against him. Fifty-three days later (a
number which happened to correspond exactly with the
number of chapters in the *Tanya*, as his followers noted
with satisfaction), the tsar released him.

When the rebbe was released and taken to what he
thought was a fellow Hasid's apartment in St. Petersburg,
he was shown by mistake to the apartment of a militant
opponent of Hasidism who happened to live in the same
building. The man was civil enough to offer his guest
some tea but could not resist the opportunity to deliver a
violent harangue against the Hasidic movement. The
rebbe's friends waited in vain for several hours. When
they finally found him and took him to the right apartment he said, according to one witness, "What a relief it
is to be out of that man's house. Believe me, throughout

my imprisonment . . . I never felt as bad as during those three hours which I spent in the house of that *mitnagged.*"

Much to the dismay of his opponents, the rebbe's incarceration only succeeded in winning more adherents to his cause. Even Jews who had been totally apathetic to Hasidism became sympathetic to the martyred leader when he was denounced by his fellow Jews, and many who had been skeptical about the rebbe's uniqueness saw the hand of God at work in his release and hastened to join the fold. The anniversary of the release, which happens to fall six days before the holiday of Hanukkah, is celebrated by Lubavitchers annually.

Two years later, the rebbe was once again denounced, arrested, and required to defend himself before an imperial court. This time, however, he was given the opportunity to confront his accuser, a disgruntled rabbi from Pinsk whose star had been eclipsed by the local Hasidim. The two men debated the charges before a committee of the Senate for many hours, but no one, alas, could understand a word they were saying, since the debate was conducted entirely in Yiddish. Afterward, the two rabbis were compelled to submit a written report, in Russian, reviewing what they had discussed. During the rebbe's second period of detention, Tsar Paul was assassinated, and the new tsar, Alexander I, who was determined to win the approval of all his subjects, even the Jews, released the rebbe within a few weeks of his assumption of power. After his release the rebbe journeyed to the town of Liadi, in Belorussia, to establish another Hasidic center. He remained in Liadi for the last decade of his life, ministering to the spiritual needs of his followers and trying to better the economic conditions of Russian Jews, chiefly by establishing a fund to help poor families in overcrowded cities to move to towns and villages in the country.

When Napoleon launched his Russian campaign, the rebbe sided with Russia, unlike most of the Jews of Eastern

Europe, who were impressed by the 1807 Treaty of Tilsit, which gave Jews the same rights enjoyed by all the other citizens of Napoleon's newly created principalities. His choice was dictated chiefly by his distaste for French morals and by his lasting loyalty to Tsar Alexander, his former liberator. When Napoleon approached Liadi in August of 1812, the rebbe, who was then sixty-seven, was forced to flee. For five months he and his family stayed just ahead of the advancing French army, but the journey was a difficult one and the winter, of course, unusually harsh. In the end the hardships proved to be too much, and he fell ill and died.

At the time of Schneur Zalman's death, the Hasidic community was larger than it had been a generation before, but it was far from stable. It was threatened not only by foreign enemies but internal strife as well. Many Hasidim, especially the less educated folk of the southern provinces, considered Schneur Zalman's followers overly concerned with scholarship and self-analysis and insufficiently passionate, a charge that is still leveled at the Lubavitchers by other Hasidic sects today. All Jewish communities, of course, were beginning to feel the pinpricks of the *Haskalah*, or Jewish enlightenment, the secularizing educational movement from Western Europe that eventually was to sound Hasidism's death knell as a social force.

There have been six Lubavitcher rebbes since the death of its founder, and all but two of them, the present Rebbe and the fifth, have been imprisoned. Rabbi Dov Baer (1773–1827), the second leader (usually referred to as the *mittler* or intermediate rebbe), was Schneur Zalman's son. Sometimes, though not often, he is referred to as Dov Baer Schneuri. (Schneuri means Schneur's son and eventually evolved into Schneerson, the surname used by later generations.) In 1814, perhaps because of unhappy associations with the town his father had been forced to flee, he changed the seat of the dynasty from Liadi to

Lubavitch (City of Love), a town on the River Dnieper.
Lubavitch continued to be the seat of the movement until
1916. In 1826, the rebbe was imprisoned, like his father,
on a trumped-up charge: sending rubles to the Sultan of
Turkey. He was released after a while but died not long
afterward. The third Lubavitcher rebbe, Menachem Mendel (1789–1866), Rabbi Dov Baer's son-in-law, was a more
original scholar. He is almost invariably referred to as the
Tzemach Tzedek (Hebrew for "Blossom of Justice"), the
title of his popular Talmudic responsa. Many Hasidic masters (as well as other Jewish writers) came to be better
known by the titles of their books, a phenomenon that no
Hasid finds less than fitting. Menachem Mendel was the
first Lubavitcher to use the surname Schneerson. It struck
me as moderately odd that he should assume the surname
of his father-in-law, but I learned subsequently that he was
entitled to use it for an entirely different reason: he was
also Schneur Zalman's grandson.

Widely admired as his erudition was, the *Tzemach
Tzedek* was doubtless better known in his own generation
for thinking up an ingenious scheme for keeping untold
numbers of Jewish children out of the Russian army. In
1827 Tsar Nicholas I published his cantonist edict, which
introduced the legal conscription of children. Theoretically, the edict applied to children twelve years of age
and older. The Jewish communities were supposed to
supply a quota of ten children per thousand people. Christians had a smaller quota and various helpful exemptions.
When the authorities discovered that most Jewish communities could not or would not supply their quota, the
infamous catchers were sent to the communities to find
children, often as young as seven or eight, and deliver
them as cantonists to government officials. Children thus
caught were sent either to special schools or to live with
peasant families until they were eighteen. Then they were

sent to military barracks to serve as soldiers for twenty-
five years. This not only removed children from their families for a greater part of their lives but threatened to forever alienate them from their culture. Sometimes the
catchers could be bought off, but most Jews were too poor
to be able to afford bribes.

At what was apparently considerable personal risk,
since what he was doing was certainly treasonous, the
Tzemach Tzedek formed a secret society dedicated to
freeing the kidnapped children. Known as the *Techias
Hameisim* or "Resurrection of the Dead," its members kept
track of the children who had been caught, and gathered
funds to pay government officials for their ransom. The
officials would return the children to their families, tell
their army liaisons that the children had died, and then
issue death certificates to their families. The children still
had to be hidden, usually with relatives or other Jewish
families in some distant town, but eventually they would
return to their own families, bodies and beliefs intact.

When the *Tzemach Tzedek* died, in 1866, the leadership
passed to his son, Rabbi Shmuel (1834–1882). The fourth
rebbe's tenure coincided with a particularly vicious period
of anti-Semitism in Russia—one in which Jew-baiting, riots,
and pogroms were commonplace and cabals against the
Jews were known to spring from the highest government
circles. Because of his friendship with various noblemen
and foreign dignitaries, the Rebbe was often successful in
quelling a bit of the anti-Semitic fervor in the government
and protecting Jews in troubled towns and villages.

The fifth Lubavitcher rebbe, and once again the son of
the previous one, was Rabbi Sholom Dov Baer (1860–
1920). He was known chiefly for his zeal in organizing
yeshivas throughout Russia and generally upgrading the
level of religious education for isolated Jews, such as those
who lived in the Caucasus. It was during the fifth rebbe's

tenure, in 1915, during World War I, that the seat of
the dynasty moved from Lubavitch to Rostov, because
the German army had moved perilously close to Lubavitch.

The next Lubavitcher leader was Rabbi Sholom Dov
Baer's son Joseph. Before Rabbi Joseph I. Schneerson
(1880–1950), the sixth rebbe, assumed the leadership in
1920, the year his father died, he had already toiled on his
father's behalf for many years as his personal secretary.
He headed the Lubavitcher yeshivas, which trained many
of the religious scholars of prewar Europe; he helped expand the Lubavitcher programs for aiding poor Jews and
settling them in rural areas where they could be self-suffi-
cient; and he, too, traveled extensively as a troubleshooter
for beleaguered Jews. Before the Revolution, he was arrested four times by the tsarist government for "interfering" on behalf of his coreligionists in various towns and
villages throughout Russia. After it, when poverty and
hunger worsened everyone's lot, the recently chosen
leader of the Lubavitchers found that his flock had an
added burden to their woes—the anti-religious *Yevsektzias*
(the Jewish branches of the Communist Party, which
were later dissolved by the Soviet government) who saw
the Hasidim as enemies of the new state. Aided by the *Yevsektzias*, the government fought to undermine the still in-
fluential Hasidim by acts of intimidation and harassment.
In 1921, doubtful of the continuing tenability of the
Lubavitcher yeshivas in Russia, the rebbe founded a new
yeshiva in Warsaw which he foresaw would before long
replace the Russian ones as the hub of Lubavitcher teaching. He also organized the first Chabad (the name Chabad
is still frequently used for official purposes) communities
in the United States and Canada. His fears were, of course,
well founded. One morning in 1927, when the rebbe was
praying in his synagogue, some men from the secret police
rushed in and arrested him. According to one story, he was

asked at gunpoint at police headquarters to give up his religious activities. When he refused, his interrogator brandished his gun and said, "This little toy has made many a man change his mind." The rebbe is reported to have answered, "This little toy can intimidate only that kind of man who has many gods . . . and but one world. Because I have only one God and two worlds, I am not impressed by this little toy." He was sent home soon afterward, but arrested again later in 1927 and this time given a death sentence and placed in solitary confinement in Leningrad's Spalerno prison. Released again at the last moment, thanks to the intervention of a number of foreign statesmen, he was temporarily banished to the Urals. When he returned, he lived briefly in a tiny village outside Moscow. Then, again with the help of foreign dignitaries, he obtained permission to leave Russia with his family and voluminous library and settle in Riga. Shortly afterward, he journeyed to Palestine and in 1930 he visited the United States. On his American tour he appealed everywhere for support for the Russian Jews, and even met briefly with President Hoover at the White House, where he discussed the plight of Russian Jewry. When he returned, he moved to Warsaw, which had become the new center of Lubavitcher life.

When World War II broke out, most of Rabbi Schneerson's friends and followers urged him to leave, but he remained in Warsaw and during the siege of the city and its surrender to the Germans managed to help hundreds of European students find their way to safer zones and his American students to find safe passage back to their country. In 1940, however, his followers finally convinced him that the world he and his ancestors had built was being obliterated and that the only hope of patching together anything of what was being destroyed lay in the New World. With the help of the U.S. State Department, he was offered safe conduct to Berlin and arrived in New York on March 19, 1940. Hundreds of his followers, many of whom were recent emigrés themselves, were on hand to give him an emotional welcome. A short time later he moved to Crown Heights, where some of his court had already established a beachhead, and remained there for the last ten years of his life. Although he had been weakened by his ordeals he worked hard to launch programs to help Jewish refugees settle in America and to revitalize his tattered movement. Many of the institutions that have helped the Lubavitchers thrive began under his tutelage: the monthly *Hakriah Vehakdush* (The Reading and the Holiness), the official organ of the movement until after the war, when it ceased publication; *Machne Israel*, the movement's social service organization; the Lubavitcher yeshivas in Brooklyn, Worcester, Pittsburgh, New Haven, and Montreal; the still thriving *Merkos L'Inyonei Chinuch* (Central Organization for Jewish Education); several girls' schools, including Beis Rivkah, which most of the Lubavitcher girls of Crown Heights still attend; the Kehot Publication Society, which is the world's largest publisher of Hasidic texts and also publishes the Rebbe's discourses and speeches; a special Shabbos program led by young people that enables non-Hasidic children to spend Shabbos with a Hasidic family; a Chabad village (Kefar Chabad) near Tel Aviv in Israel; and a special program to reach the Jews of North Africa, especially in Morocco, which was more fully realized by the next (and present) Rebbe, after the sixth rebbe's death in 1950.

Rabbi Menachem Mendel Schneerson, the seventh leader of the Lubavitchers, and the son-in-law of his predecessor, was born in 1902. He and the previous rebbe share the same last name because they share the same lineage. They are both descendants of different sons of Rabbi Menachem Mendel, the third Lubavitcher rebbe. He is the son of a famous kabbalist, and the great-grandson of his namesake. Like his predecessor, he was born in

Russia and early in life was admired as an *illui*, a Torah prodigy, but unlike any of his predecessors, or indeed any other Hasidic leader, he allowed himself to tread on secular soil long enough to attend the University of Berlin and the Sorbonne, where he received a degree in engineering. Non-Lubavitcher Hasidim tend to tut-tut about this educational deviance from the norm, but his followers are quick to point out that though the Rebbe's piety is beyond reproach, his modern outlook and grasp of the realities of the secular world are probably the key to his having attracted thousands of sympathizers to a movement that forty years ago appeared moribund. Rabbi Schneerson married his predecessor's daughter, Chaya Moussia, in Warsaw in 1929 and the couple followed the sixth rebbe to America in 1941. Three years later, he received word that his father had died in a remote village in Kazakhstan in Central Russia. In 1939, the old rabbi had been arrested in his house in the city of Ekaterinoslav by the N.K.V.D. for his religious activities. He was taken away, imprisoned, then exiled to the little village, where he died at the age of sixty-six. This tragic event is said to have marked the seventh Lubavitcher rebbe for life, and many have speculated that it is one of the reasons that he has been especially zealous in succoring Jews throughout the world in times of crisis. It may also partially explain his insistence on not being scared out of the city, and remaining with his flock in a decaying section of Brooklyn instead of removing to a safe, sunny suburb. In fact, except for one trip to Paris after the war to fetch his mother, Rabbi Schneerson has never again left New York City.

According to Robert Steingut, the former New York City councilman and present Chairman of the State Workers' Compensation Board, the Lubavitchers chose to live in Crown Heights in the first place because of his grandfather. Mr. Steingut's father is Stanley Steingut, the former speaker of the New York State Assembly, and his

grandfather was Irwin Steingut, a powerful political figure of the nineteen-twenties and -thirties. In the mid-
thirties, Mr. Steingut said, a group of Orthodox Jews came
to his grandfather and asked him to help a group of desperate Russian Hasidim who were stuck in Poland and
were not being allowed to emigrate to this country. They
were Lubavitchers, the group's spokesman explained, and
their position was desperate. Shortly afterward, Irwin
Steingut called upon President Franklin Roosevelt, with
whom he had worked when Roosevelt had been governor
of New York, and with Roosevelt's help he succeeded in
getting the stranded Lubavitchers to the United States.
Steingut lived on Eastern Parkway at the time. "How do
you say 'thank you' to a politician like my grandfather
if you're a Lubavitcher emigré?" Mr. Steingut asked rhetorically, when I talked with him some time ago in his
office overlooking New York harbor. "You move into the
neighborhood." Mr. Steingut's parents also lived in Crown
Heights, at 1298 President Street, which happens to be
the house next door to the Rebbe's, and he grew up in the
neighborhood. He remembers the Rebbe as "an invariably
gentle, kind man who never acted disapproving or
preachy" with him or his family although their life style
differed radically from that of the Rebbe's followers.
Whenever they encountered each other, he recalled, the
Rebbe always acted interested in the minutiae of his everyday life and never seemed unduly upset on the many occasions when the Steinguts had to send a glazier over because Robert or his brother had knocked a baseball through
one of the Rebbe's windows. He rarely saw the Rebbe's
wife (few people do; she is always described as a "very
private" person) but remembers her looking "regal." Mr.
Steingut visits the Rebbe from time to time and is always
received with great warmth. Hesitating a bit, he said that
he has always felt that he and the Rebbe have a certain
special bond, and that it might have something to do with

the fact that he and his brother and sister were the only children that the Rebbe, who is childless, ever got to see in an ordinary day-to-day way over a long period of time.

It is common knowledge that the Rebbe assumed the mantle of leader of the Lubavitchers somewhat reluctantly; nonetheless, he has infused the role with a vigor and breadth it has not had since the early days of Hasidism. Having declared that the Lubavitcher motto, *Uforatzto*, "And you shall spread out . . ." (Genesis, 28:14), had an especially urgent meaning in the post-Holocaust world, the Rebbe set about opening Lubavitcher centers throughout the United States and in Argentina, Brazil, Venezuela, England, Scotland, France, Holland, Italy, West Germany, South Africa, and Canada. He created a Jewish Peace Corps that sent young students on summer vacations and young couples for several years to communities throughout the country to try to quicken the interest of Jewish groups in religious observance; he established the Lubavitch Women's Organization and the Lubavitch Youth Organization, which operates the so-called Mitzvah Tanks, and he created day-care centers in scores of cities, including such former religious deserts for Jews as Westminster, California.

Placing great faith in what he believes to be a desire for higher spiritual values among the young, the Rebbe has sent hundreds of emissaries to speak at colleges and universities. Today there are thirty-five Lubavitcher yeshivas in the United States and a hundred and seventy-five abroad. About a hundred Chabad houses in American college communities provide not only lodging but counseling, crisis intervention programs, drug programs, Shabbos and holiday services, and adult education classes. There are about a hundred Chabad houses in foreign countries, and last year thirty-five thousand children attended Lubavitcher summer camps around the world. Many of the seventh rebbe's projects have been carried off on quite a grand scale. In 1967, he initiated a *"tefillin* campaign" (*tefillin* are the small leather box and strap devices that religious Jews affix to their heads and left arms respectively for weekday morning prayers) during the Six Day War in Israel. Lubavitcher Hasidim went everywhere trying to persuade Jewish men to wear *tefillin* and the Rebbe's followers believe that it was the willingness of many of the Israeli soldiers to don the *tefillin* that won the war for Israel. Although his emissaries have been schooled to approach assimilated Jews with delicacy, the campaign literature distributed by his flock to anyone who appears interested in learning more about Judaism is phrased in absolutes: "All Jewish men and boys over thirteen should put on *tefillin* every weekday"; "Jewish women and girls from the age of three should light candles before Shabbos and on holidays"; "Jewish women should keep kosher homes and observe the Laws of Family Purity." One of the precepts the Rebbe urges his followers to focus on is to love their fellow Jews. This love, in the form of hospitality, encounter weekends, and lectures about Hasidic life outside the neighborhood, plays a large role in the community's sense of itself.

Rabbi Schneerson also supports once-a-month kindergartens for children who live far from synagogues; he has sent representatives armed with prayer books and *tefillin* to the jungles of Panama; he has sent a *mohel* (a man who performs ritual circumcision) to a tiny Caribbean island to make sure that a baby was properly circumcised; he has sent a rabbi to conduct religious services for a handful of Jewish soldiers posted in Alaska; and he has sent ambassadors to keep the embers of Judaism burning in minuscule Jewish communities in Japan, India, Burma, Afghanistan, and the Philippines. All of these activities are supported entirely by charity and occasional fundraising events. The Lubavitchers' annual budget for 1984 was "around" fifty million dollars, according to a spokesman for the group.

If you ask anyone who sees a lot of the Rebbe how he spends most of his time, as I did one of the young aides who works in the office at Lubavitcher headquarters, the answer you will probably get (spoken in a somewhat exasperated though not unkind tone of voice) is the one I did: "Well, he's a *zaddik*, so he does what *zaddikim* do; he learns, he studies, he *davens.*" If there were an international union of *zaddikim* scrutinizing the Rebbe's day in terms of clocked *zaddikim* man-hours, however, an on-site inspection would certainly result in an impressive report. Every day, up to three mail sacks are delivered to the Rebbe at his office in 770, and he is reported to open and peruse every letter himself—a task that is simplified somewhat by his fluency in ten languages. There is a six-man secretariat, composed of rabbis who have been close to the Rebbe for many years, that helps him answer his correspondence and also helps with the day-in, day-out business of running the various Lubavitcher institutions and organizations. He used to grant audiences to anyone who wanted to talk to him, on Tuesday and Thursday evenings from nine o'clock until way past midnight, but partly because his health no longer permits it, and partly because there got to be a waiting list of several years for interviews, he no longer has them. Today, the various matters he might have discussed with members of his court or visiting luminaries in person are discussed in epistolary form. This has not meant a shorter workday; when he leaves his office (around seven o'clock in the winter, nine or ten o'clock in the summer) he is invariably carrying a large manila envelope filled with letters and unfinished business, which he works on at home. He is rumored to sleep only three or four hours a night. According to one member of the secretariat, he receives a salary, but it is "small" and meant only to cover household expenses and the like.

Critics of the Rebbe have faulted him for assuming too active a social posture and not allowing his flock enough time for spiritual inwardness. The Lubavitchers insist that the two are interconnected. The Rebbe has also managed to instill a spirit of Messianic urgency in his followers. Jews have traditionally believed that the Messiah will come after a great cataclysm and, following his father-in-law's lead in assuming that the Holocaust was just such an event, Rabbi Schneerson has laid great stress on the possible imminence of the Messianic era.

Behind the zealous efforts of his followers to bring more and more Jews into the fold is the assumption that if more people follow God's precepts, the earth will eventually become, in the Rebbe's words, "a more habitable place" for the Messiah. Thus, each Jew drawn closer into the fold, each Sabbath candle lit, each weekday prayer enunciated, each dip into the ritual bath brings the world that much closer to the era when all mankind will live in a world without war, suffering, or cruelty. Should that day ever arrive, the Hasidim believe, some (they themselves, for example) will simply be readier to live in such a world, in the same way that a rigorously trained athlete is readier for the Olympics. Without putting too fine a point on it, the Lubavitchers are not reluctant to say that it just so happens that Rabbi Schneerson meets admirably the scripturally ordained requirements Maimonides codified in his *Book of Judges* for the Messianic role: that is, that he be descended from the family of King David (the Rebbe is descended from the *Maharal* of Prague—Rabbi Judah Loew ben Bezalel, ca. 1525–1609—who was believed to be a descendant of David); that he occupy himself with the commandments; that he meditate upon and scrupulously observe all of God's precepts; and that he be able "to prevail upon Israel to walk in the way of the

Torah and to repair its breaches." According to Jewish tradition every generation has its potential Messiah. Moses was one, but the Israelites, by worshipping idols, prevented him from fulfilling his destiny. With their "We Want *Moshiach* (the Messiah) Now" posters and bumper stickers, outreach programs, "Call-a-Hasidic-Lecture" hotline, and impassioned street proselytizing, the Lubavitchers sometimes seem like a team of Messianic advance men. If the present generation does not live to see the paradisaical era, they appear to be saying, it won't be because we didn't work the precincts.

CHAPTER FIVE

Sheina

U NLIKE most city women, who walk to their local shops, Sheina drives her light blue, air-conditioned Cutlass Supreme (the license plate is inscribed with the word MITZVOT) to her neighborhood markets, a habit left over from her days as a midwestern suburbanite. She also owns two dishwashers and three ovens (one for meat, one for dairy foods, and one for foods that are neither), a freezer, a washing machine and dryer, a Cuisinart and a Betamax, which she and Moshe bought chiefly so that they could tape the Rebbe's occasional televised talks. (In the last few years, in order to reach more people, the Rebbe's talks, which last for many hours and are spoken in Yiddish, have been broadcast on cable TV.) Sheina's robust good looks and stylishly tweedy clothes are rather midwestern American, too, and it is easy to imagine the reminders of various Lubavitcher duties pinned to her kitchen bulletin board reminding her instead to meet a

friend for golf, sew tutus for a school play, or buy cheese
for a cocktail party.

On a warm spring afternoon not long after I had spent
the Sabbath with the Konigsbergs, I asked Sheina how
she first became interested in Hasidism. We were sitting
in her breakfast nook, a round, sunlit, cheerful room filled
with plants, magazines, and newspapers—the *Algemeiner
Journal* (a Yiddish paper), the weekly *Jewish Press,* and
the *New York Times.* On the windowsill sat some twenty
charity boxes for various Lubavitcher and other causes.
Jewish recipe books filled a corner bookcase.

"I guess I started thinking seriously about spiritual
matters in 1968. A cousin of mine—of my ex-husband's,
actually—whom I was quite fond of was sending her kids
to the same camp I was sending mine to. The camp was
in New York State, and since we all lived in Michigan we
had to take a plane East; we planned to travel together.
Well, my cousin and her daughter and her sister and her
sister's boy left, but I left with my children a bit later. On
the way to the airport, we saw that there had been a terrible accident. A train had collided with a car, and everyone in the car had been killed. It was my cousin's. That was
the turning point of my life. I just couldn't accept their
deaths. Later that summer, when I was visiting my children at camp, I met a woman who was driving back to
Michigan and wanted company, so I went back with her.
She spoke to me about the psychic Edgar Cayce and reincarnation. When I got back home, I went to the library and
read everything I could about Cayce. In the back of my
mind there was always the thought that none of it had
much to do with Jews. Perhaps this was some kind of
modern idol worship? But the concept of reincarnation
seemed to answer many of my questions."

"Did you ever discuss the idea with a rabbi?" I asked.

"Well, yes, I did. I asked the rabbi at the synagogue my
family went to what Judaism had to say about reincarna-

tion and he said, 'Some people believe in it.' But he didn't, and he didn't much want to pursue the subject. He didn't understand that I was not just making chitchat and he didn't have any useful direction to send me in. So I just went about inquiring about spiritual matters in my own way, like people do nowadays. I studied Yoga. I never had any sense that I could benefit from just serving God the way Jews had for centuries, but I *was* becoming a more spiritual person. I even spoke about reincarnation at some public gatherings. One day in 1970 I got a call from someone who belonged to a psychical society, asking me to speak at one of her meetings. I told her that I really wasn't interested in chasing ghosts, but I ended up going, and I brought along a tape of a psychic's reading of me. As it happened, a reporter from a local paper was there, and the next day there was a story on the front page that really savaged me and all the talk about reincarnation. Oh boy, how it embarrassed me! Some people made remarks, too, about how Jews shouldn't be fooling around with Edgar Cayce. I still cringe when I think about it. But I feel that all that embarrassment was pushing me in the right direction. That week I paid a condolence call, and at the house I was visiting an obviously religious woman— she was wearing a wig—came up and asked to be introduced to me, and I thought, uh-oh, someone else to disapprove and scold me for doing these un-Jewish things. I said, 'You're going to tell me that Jews don't believe in reincarnation and that I shouldn't be wasting my time with such foolishness.' 'Not at all,' said the woman, and introduced herself and said that she was a Lubavitcher Hasid. '*We* believe in reincarnation. It's a part of Jewish tradition. The kabbalah speaks about it and so does the *Tanya.*' Somehow, I knew at once that my search was over. I said, 'God has sent you to me.'

"The woman told me that she was trying to start a local Chabad House and that a Lubavitcher rabbi was coming

to town soon to help organize things. I told her that I'd
like to help them with the project and pretty soon I became friends with a number of Lubavitcher people. They
were an extremely diverse group, from every economic
bracket. In my own circle of friends, although there were
a few exceptions, everybody was fairly well-to-do. Everybody had everything, and it didn't seem to mean anything.
Their lives centered around country-club matters, and vacations, and, in the case of the men, on their business and
real-estate deals. My new friends didn't care about economic status. They were spiritual students, all of them, and
the liveliest people I'd ever met. Oddly enough, for all the
talk I'd always heard about the separation of the sexes in
Hasidic communities, I was impressed by the friendliness
of the husbands and wives toward each other. They were
skeptical people in many ways, too, not at all like the fanatics people always made Hasidim out to be. It was in
one way a terrible period in my life. After nineteen years,
my marriage had fallen apart. I was often lonely and I suffered a lot from self-doubt. Before long, my activities with
the Lubavitchers became the focus of my life, and I became immersed in learning about Jewish matters from a
Hasidic perspective. I realized that I had never really bent
my will to the will of God. I decided to try to do that."

"I'm not sure I know what you mean by that," I said.

"I decided that I wasn't going to have a religion of
convenience. I wasn't going to try to evade the commandments by finding rationales for not doing them. The ritual
bath, for example—most Jews think the idea's absurd.
Even many members of Orthodox synagogues don't go
to them. Nobody talks about it, probably because it's a
private kind of ritual, unlike keeping a kosher home.
Rabbis tend not to talk openly about it. Parents don't
speak of it. People feel it's an archaic custom. In fact,
bathing in the *mikvah* is one of the central rituals of
Judaism. According to Jewish law, a community is sup-

posed to build a *mikvah* before it builds a synagogue. People say that there just aren't enough baths around, but you can always find one if you try hard enough. Anyway, I felt convinced by 1973 that if I wanted the kindness of God I had to stop shilly-shallying. I was accustomed to eating in good restaurants. I stopped doing that. I didn't go to public places where there was mixed swimming. I stopped turning on the lights on Shabbos. My old friends thought I'd gone off the deep end. But I had enough faith to know that what was happening to me was for the best."

"How did your children react to the changes in your life?"

Sheina looked out the window. "Well, you know my children were formed by that time. They were teenagers, and they didn't like my new way of life at all. They were aware, too, that people were laughing at me and I think it hurt them. Now the girls are married and have their own families, and my youngest—my son, Chaim—is twenty, and they accept the fact that this is the way I want to live. But at the beginning they were quite bitter about it. They said I was 'brainwashed.' I think many of the parents of young people who become part of the Lubavitcher community feel the same way. It's as if religious feelings have become sort of an aberration or neurotic symptom. But I was never put in seclusion, like the Moonies, or removed from everyday life. I came to this life because it seemed a lot more meaningful than the one I had been leading. After my husband and I separated, there was a period of about a year and a half when I was rather isolated. The children were with me, but many of the people I knew were put off by my new way of life. For one thing, I was forbidden by Jewish law to date until I got divorced, and living in the suburbs and not being married or willing to date makes you persona non grata. Most of the assimilated people who had been my friends just sort of forgot about me. Then, in the fall of 1973, the Lubavitcher rabbi who

had come to live in Bloomfield Hills suggested that I find
a way to have a 'Shabbos house,' in the city—a place
where I could be with other observant Jews on Shabbos
and be part of a community. My parents helped me to
find a place, and when I began to spend Saturdays in that
house in Detroit my whole life changed. My days of isolation were over. The following year, a second Lubavitcher
rabbi came. He and his wife and children had hardly
settled in when they were evicted. Their landlord said
that he objected to so many people coming and going on
Saturdays. We thought that he was just inventing a reason
to get rid of them because he thought that Hasidim were
peculiar but the rabbi didn't fight the eviction because
it wasn't that great a place. Anyway, they needed a
place to stay in a hurry, so I invited them to stay in my
Shabbos house. It had more than enough room, even when
I was there on Saturdays, and, of course, it was empty all
week. So they accepted, and before long we became sort
of an extended family. I was tremendously impressed with
their close-knittedness."

"Were your children there, too?"

"Sometimes my children stayed with me, sometimes
they didn't. I was sad that when they did come they didn't
really want to participate in the religious rituals. I wished
that they had been raised in the kind of passionate way
that I saw was part of a thoughtful religious upbringing.
But I was resigned to the fact of their independence. I got
divorced in 1974, and toward the end of that year the
second rabbi—who knew Moshe from Crown Heights, and
knew me very well because he'd seen so much of me by
then—thought it was appropriate to make a *shidduch* [an
arranged marriage]. I agreed, and here I am."

"What was your courtship like?" I asked. "Did it seem
strange?"

"Well, it certainly was not something I did lightly. But
it didn't seem strange, because by then the ordinary forms

of courtship had begun to seem strange to me. Besides,
I trusted the rabbi's knowledge of people, and I was right
to. Moshe flew out to meet me in December, and four
months later we were married. I saw him three times, and
by the third time we'd decided that we suited each other.
We saw very quickly that we could make a good life together," she said, smiling, "and we have."

Sheina went on to explain that Moshe had already rejected several candidates proposed to him in the years
since his wife died; he had not really been ready to re-
marry. But the Rebbe had warned him about prolonging
his mourning too long, and when the Bloomfield Hills
rabbi had told him about Sheina, he had had the feeling
that this was going to be a good match. Contrary to popular opinion, Hasidic men and women frequently reject
various candidates proposed to them by would-be match-
makers. Before he had flown out to Michigan, Moshe had
written to the Rebbe to tell him of his plans. After he and
Sheina met, they both wrote to him, as is the custom, to
say that they had "found favor in each other's eyes," and
asked for a *brachah*, or blessing. When the Rebbe wrote
and gave them the go-ahead, Sheina flew to New York,
where she stayed with a friend and talked to Moshe for
many hours over a long weekend.

Sheina's acquiescence to the idea of an arranged marriage and acceptance of the Hasidic form of courtship
was, of course, the most radical step she had taken in her
new life. Somewhere along the line, she had jettisoned the
dearly held, if ill-defined, contemporary belief in romantic
spontaneity, proven sexual compatibility, and tried-and-
tested ability to get along in a day-to-day way as the basis
for marriage. Her acceptance of a man who had always
been Hasidic was also unusual. *Baalei teshuvah* tend to
marry other *baalei teshuvah*, it being generally assumed
that adjustment to Orthodox life will be easier if it is
mutual. But Sheina was ready for total immersion when

she met Moshe, and the fact that he was an old-line Hasid merely added to his allure. (It is also uncommon for members of highly respected Hasidic families with blue-chip lineage—*yiches*—like Moshe's to marry *baalei teshuvah*, who are considered somewhat tainted by their knowledge of the secular world, so Moshe's acceptance of Sheina was a bit unusual, too.) Like the other transformations in her life, Sheina regarded the *shidduch* as another link to a world which would change the way she saw herself as a private person. As she recalled those days, it became clear to me that just as she had accepted the various rules that governed how she prayed, when she prayed, how she dressed, what food she ate, and what her ethical conduct should be, she accepted (and even liked) the restrictions and protocol of Orthodox courtship. In fact, they seemed to have appealed to her precisely because they were at odds with modern customs and practices. She sensed and was grateful for the fact that while everything was demanded of Orthodox men and women in terms of fulfilling their religious duties, far less was demanded of them than is demanded of most modern husbands and wives. The success or failure of any marriage depends on many complexities, of course, but most outsiders have observed that Hasidic husbands and wives seem surprisingly content, partly because they are so passionately dedicated to the same suprapersonal goals, partly because they do not expect so much from each other. There are few Hasidim who expect their mates to be unfailingly exciting lovers, forever youthful admirers, or amateur therapists. If the excitement level has been minimized in Hasidic courtships by relegating Eros to the back seat, so have the subsequent disappointments.

"How many good marriages do you know of in the secular world?" Sheina asked me when I questioned her about the passivity of her role in the initial *shidduch* arrangements. "How successful are people at choosing for themselves?" She looked at me defiantly. "Not very, I think."

After their New York meeting, Sheina and Moshe wrote once again to the Rebbe, and when he sent his blessing for the marriage he suggested that Sheina's children meet Moshe. At the time, Moshe and his five children were living in a small two-family house on Lefferts Avenue that, according to Sheina's daughter Tracy, whom I met on one of her infrequent visits to Crown Heights, was dark, cheerless, and ugly. Tracy, a healthy looking, pretty blonde with porcelain-pink skin, said that that first encounter with Moshe and New York Hasidic life was hard on everybody.

"Mom had warned us about Moshe's white beard, and we could see that he was a nice man, but the boys treated us like *we* were weird, and their life seemed so airless. They looked like they never had any fun. My brother Chip—Mom calls him by his Hebrew name, Chaim, by the way, but nobody else does—was sent here for a while to study, but it didn't really take because he missed the freedom of his life back home."

Tracy said that her sisters and brother were and still are convinced that, despite their mother's protestations, she was exchanging a good life for a narrower one. She thinks her mother is "just not the same person" she grew up with, and though she loves her, she cannot fathom why Sheina should have made a "commitment" to Hasidic ways. Tracy considers herself "reasonably religious." She lights candles on the Sabbath, keeps a kosher home, and intends to send her two children to Hebrew day school. But she also has non-Jewish friends and interests that have nothing to do with religion. On the other hand, when I pressed her for examples of the sort of interests or activities that her mother had given up that seemed to diminish the quality of her life, she could think of only one—tennis. (When I told her this, Sheina smiled gently at first, then bit her lip, then gave way to a fit of unsuppressible giggles. In be-

tween gasps of laughter, she said, "You can play tennis you
know. Nothing against it in the rules. Mindy around the
corner plays. Hee, hee. Just haven't had the time.")

After Sheina and Moshe were married, they wrote to
the Rebbe again to ask where he thought they should live.
The frequency with which the Rebbe's followers write
him—he is said to receive more than five hundred letters
a day—and the crucial role he plays in all his followers'
important life decisions have frequently been mocked by
outsiders who object to the Rebbe's special status. The
Lubavitchers do not much like to talk in a personal way
about the subject. On the one hand, their belief in their
Rebbe's supernatural powers and his ability to know what
will be good and what will be bad for them is absolute.
On the other, since they pride themselves on being a fairly
rational group, their own almost childlike dependence on
the Rebbe's clairvoyance is a subject they tend to avoid.
Their reticence disappears, however, when they are asked
to talk about other people. Then they are delighted to re-
count the many miracle stories told about their leader:
how the Rebbe's medical advice (sometimes running contrary to the considered opinion of noted doctors) saved
lives; how during World War II, people who traveled
when the Rebbe advised them not to were killed by tor-
pedos; or how the Rebbe's *tefillin* campaign won the Six
Day War, and so on. The powers of a rebbe are so great,
Hasidim believe, that they continue to exert some influence even after death. The Lubavitcher Rebbe visits his
predecessor's grave at least twice a month, it is said, to
enlist his former father-in-law's spiritual assistance in answering the many prayers he receives asking for his help,
and has been known to place reading material on the grave-
site before leaving the cemetery. In general, the present
Rebbe, like his predecessors, declines to make much of his
role as a performer of miracles. But he does not reject
the idea of the miraculous. None of the Rebbe's followers

would think of disregarding his advice. Even when that advice seems arbitrary, it is accepted. For example, when Moshe told me that he had wanted to be a teacher when he was a young man but changed his plans when the Rebbe told him that he ought to be a metal engraver, I thought that the Rebbe had at least given him a good reason for this advice. Later on, I found out that he had not really offered any reason, but Moshe followed his advice anyway, and claims that he is happy with his work and never gave his change of plans a second thought. When I told him that I found that pretty amazing, he said that *zaddikim* could see things that the rest of us could not.

Although they were a rarity, self-mocking Jewish jokes occasionally made their way to the Crown Heights study halls. One that I heard more than once from some of the younger Lubavitchers reflected a certain self-consciousness about the letters written to the Rebbe.

QUESTION: "How many Lubavitchers does it take to change a light bulb?"

ANSWER: "Two. One to change the bulb, the other to write the Rebbe about it."

When the Rebbe suggested that Sheina and Moshe live in Crown Heights, Sheina was more than willing. She had begun to think of Crown Heights the way the Transcendentalists thought of Brook Farm, and she couldn't wait to move there. On the other hand, it was already spring, and she did not want to disrupt her children's school year, so Moshe took a two-month leave-of-absence from his job and moved out to Michigan until the summer. Bubbe looked after his children while he was away and the children in Michigan adjusted with varying degrees of difficulty to their exotic new stepfather. Sheina's new husband caused titters everywhere he appeared. She could not have caused more of a sensation if she had brought home an Eskimo in mukluks. But Moshe took the scandalized glances in his stride, and Sheina gradually grew accustomed to them. They moved to Crown Heights together in 1975, and Sheina says that the little utopia she discovered in Brooklyn exceeded her expectations and that each year her life has become more rewarding.

That evening, the Lubavitchers were having one of their gatherings, or *farbrengens*, at the synagogue, and Sheina was eager for me to attend. The Rebbe is the only speaker at the *farbrengens*, and he talks extemporaneously and for many hours. Some of the gatherings have been known to last all night. Sometimes they are announced days in advance, sometimes only a few hours' notice is given. When the word gets out that a *farbrengen* is going to be held, everybody telephones somebody else, and in an amazingly short time, the whole community knows about it. I looked forward to the *farbrengen*, which was scheduled to take place at nine o'clock. It would be my first chance to see and hear the Rebbe for myself and also to see the Lubavitcher community assembled in one place. The Rebbe spoke in Yiddish, I had been told, but in deference to the many visitors who came to hear him a simultaneous English translation would be available. Walking along Eastern Parkway toward the synagogue, we bumped into Mendel and Shmuel. They had been having an animated conversation before we had arrived on the scene which our presence somehow stifled. We walked along together for a while, but without their father, who had gone on earlier, they seemed uneasy in Sheina's company (and downright uncomfortable in mine) and when we arrived at the synagogue they bounded toward the men's entrance like puppies released from the leash.

The mood of those milling around the synagogue in the evening was buoyant, and the sidewalk in front of the building was packed. As the Lubavitcher movement has

expanded, so has their synagogue. "770" is really three separate buildings that have had their adjoining walls knocked
down to make more worship and office space.

All Orthodox synagogues have separate women's and
men's sections—a practice initiated in ancient times by the
priests of the Temple, some say, because they thought that
the congregants would otherwise be distracted from the
religious ceremonies. Whether the priests' plan proved
to be effective then I cannot say, but the women's gallery
of the Lubavitcher synagogue, which is upstairs, would
surely have given the priests some second thoughts. There
were about four thousand people crammed into the synagogue—a space that, estimating generously, ought to have
comfortably sheltered two thousand. About a third of
those present were women, but the area consigned to
them seemed hardly large enough to contain half that
number. To enter the women's gallery—two windowless,
airless balconies blocked off from the men's section by a
black Plexiglas panel—one simply allowed oneself to be
swept forward by a tidal wave of female Lubavitchers of
all sizes, shapes, and ages that flowed through the narrow
women's entrance. Once inside, the lucky found seats, but
most scrambled atop the narrow back ledges of six stepped
rows of wobbly wooden pews, teetering this way and that
to find a spot that would afford a glimpse of the Rebbe, who
had not yet arrived. It was a scene that seemed inspired
equally by Hieronymus Bosch and the Forty-second Street
IRT station at rush hour. Sheina quickly found "her" spot,
a minuscule stretch of bench in the front corner of the
gallery, and somehow tucked us both into it. From this
vantage point, if you craned your neck down toward the
four-inch span that separated the black screen and the
rim of the balcony, there was a clear bird's-eye view of
the dais and its long table covered with white cloth, where
the Rebbe always spoke. Below, a black sea of Hasidim
swayed back and forth. Above, a tremendous din. Down-

stairs, little boys raced between the men's legs and around
the dais, and small girls drowsed on their fathers' shoulders.
Upstairs, innocent-looking teenage girls and delicately
powdered old ladies mingled with plump young mothers
and innumerable babies. A large contingent of grandmothers, their arms moving like steam shovels, popped
small morsels of food into the mouths of restless toddlers.
The smell of sour milk and wet diapers was faint but per-
vasive. Knowing that the Rebbe's talks usually went on for
hours, mothers came forearmed, and plastic bags filled
with apple slices, pretzels, granola bars, and peanut butter
sandwiches were much in evidence. Ignoring the confusion, a few gallant souls, eyes tightly shut, attempted
to pray. Sheina exchanged a few hugs and hellos with
people nearby, and settled down with a brightly colored
needlepoint wall decoration (a Hebrew alphabet) that
she was working on.

Then a regal white-bearded figure with a brisk almost
military gait and kindly, penetrating blue eyes entered
the room, and, except for the lip-smacking sound of suck-
ing babies, it fell completely silent. The Rebbe. Like
most of the other men, he wore a wide-brimmed black
fedora, long black coat, black trousers, and white shirt.
Unlike most of them, he wore a tie, also black. Taking
a seat in front of several rows of whitebeards assembled on the dais, he gazed placidly at his followers and
began speaking in the manner of a teacher picking up the
threads of a discussion with his students. No audience-
grabbing anecdotes, no pink lights, no uplifting chorale.

The Rebbe, who is in his early eighties, spoke for more
than four hours, in a voice that never wavered. The children dropped off one by one, but the rest of his followers listened raptly until the end. I listened carefully, too,
to the translated version of his talk, but most of what was
said went by me in a billowing, gray cloud of words. The
quality of the translation was so poor, the Yiddish accent

of the translator so thick, and the nature of the discourse
so elusive that the few intelligible phrases I caught—"a
truly free man is one who studies Torah," "we should dis-
associate ourselves from idolatry, from things that are
foreign to Jews"—were unlinkable. The Rebbe spoke without ever consulting a note, pausing every half hour for a
few minutes to rest and to hold up a minute wine-filled
Dixie Cup and toast his flock. The men also toasted him.
Each of them held a paper cup aloft and waited until
the Rebbe looked and nodded in his direction before
downing the wine. During these brief breaks, the men
sang beautiful Hasidic songs that were thematically related to the Rebbe's discourse. Late in the evening, while
scanning the sea of pale faces downstairs during one of
these interludes, I happened to catch a glimpse of Moshe
singing—hat pushed back on his head, eyes closed, mouth
curved in a slight smile. He looked as if he were crooning
a lullaby to a baby.

I have attended many *farbrengens* since then. Many of
them have been well translated (the translations of the
Rebbe's talks that are broadcast on cable TV, for example,
are models of clarity), broad ranging, and thematically
graspable. But one has to learn how to listen to them, and
for anyone with a secular background this really means
acquiring a religious one. Like so many Jewish texts, the
Rebbe's talks are not aimed at the uninitiated nor are they
readily accessible to those with a mere passing familiarity
with the subjects touched upon, although his followers
insist that the Rebbe can be understood on different levels
by everybody. For a non-Yiddish-speaking layman, the
constant references to Talmudic sources, persons, and
principles, the Yiddish phrases that no translator, however
deft, could even attempt to anglicize, and the nonsequen-
tial didactic style of the Rebbe's discourses can be daunt-
ing. During the first two or three *farbrengens* I attended,
I found myself straining my ear constantly to the earpiece

of the little transistor trying but failing to make out through the thicket of Hebrew and Yiddish references more than an occasional "thus," "so," "and," or "obviously." One year and many hours' immersion in Jewish texts later, I left the *farbrengens* feeling that I had understood about half of what the Rebbe had been talking about.

After the *farbrengen*, Sheina found Moshe outside the synagogue, deep in conversation with a friend. They were discussing the Rebbe's talk in the glowing terms music lovers might draw upon to express their appreciation for a virtuoso violinist's particularly stirring performance of a familiar but much loved piece of music, the music in this case being the Torah. Like true music lovers, they were delighted by the new dimensions that they had discovered in a familiar melody and marveled at the player's subtlety and ingenuity. While they continued their discussion, I asked Sheina if the crowding and disorderliness of the women's gallery ever bothered her. I was sure that she was well aware of the fact that most of the modern world disapproves of the separate women's gallery; indeed, she gave me a sharp look before she answered.

"Of course I wish that it were roomier. I don't like it. But it just doesn't matter that much to me. Despite what everybody believes, the synagogue is not the center of Jewish life. The home is, and I don't think you'll find many women in this community hiding in the shadows in their homes. I never think, 'Ah, now I am going to the synagogue, where I will focus all my religious feeling.' There's a place for religious feeling in everything I do. The rituals I perform and the prayers I say as I go about my daily life keep me from becoming blasé about it. They *force* me to think about the sanctity of the ordinary facts of my existence."

I said that many people thought that Hasidic women were limited by their role as priestesses of the home, much as the Victorian woman's pedestal prevented her from entering the larger world or seeing herself as anything but a household goddess.

"But we're not on pedestals, far from it," she said, as we joined a procession of Hasidim strolling slowly homeward. "Moshe has always played a big role in his children's upbringing—far bigger than most of the fathers I used to know—and since we're both committed to the same ideals, all the practical things I do are part of what he does. We're both equals before God; therefore we're equals, period. Victorian men probably believed that their professional lives gave them some sort of edge on their wives, but that's not how we think about things. Moshe's profession isn't the center of his world; his relationship to God is. His family life, the kind of children he has raised, and the degree to which all the little everyday things in his life are imbued with godliness are what matter to him. And what does being the priestess of the home really mean? It means setting the tone of the place where all the really practical bridges to a religious life are built. A lot of what we do is done in private, but in our lives 'private' does not mean 'inferior.'"

An interesting elucidation of this argument is offered by an Orthodox scholar, Moshe Meiselman, in *Jewish Woman in Jewish Law*, a heated defense of the way Jewish law treats women. Meiselman claims that "the high points in the lives of the major male figures of the Bible occurred in private" (for example, God spoke to Moses privately on Mount Sinai, Jacob wrestled with the angel without any witnesses, Abraham's binding of Isaac was enacted before no one) and that the Old Testament phrase "The entire glory of the daughter of the king lies on the inside," which is usually cited as an example of Judaic chauvinism, is merely "a statement of the private nature of the female role and . . . a panegyric on the private nature of the religious experience in general."

Meiselman compares Jewish heroes and heroines with their Greek counterparts and contrasts the story of Agamemnon and Iphigenia with that of Abraham and Isaac. "While Abraham sacrificed Isaac to God, for God, and before God alone, Agamemnon sacrificed Iphigenia for Greece and in the presence of Greece. The essence of the Greek heroic act lay in its public appeal and public nature. There was no glorification of inner heroism, but only of public display and public approval.

"Far from the shores of Aulis was the Jewish hero. To the Jew, moral victory for both man and woman is what one does for God and before God, the source of all value. Jewish tradition frowns upon public display; for the moment a human acts in public, his motivation can be tainted by unworthy considerations. . . . An important aspect of the religious-moral act is its privacy, far from the approval of the crowd." As further evidence of the depth of this belief, Meiselman cites the Jewish maxim "The world is maintained in each generation through the merit of thirty-six hidden saintly persons."

But if women and what they represent were so highly esteemed, it seemed odd that men continued to thank God, in their morning prayers, that they were not born women. Rabbinical authorities steadfastly deny that this is a put-down of women, of course. It is merely a way for men to express thanks, they say, for God's giving them the opportunity to perform many commandments that women are excused from. But why was it that the morning prayers of women had no parallel expression, since men were also excluded from various female tasks?

As the months went by, however, my own starchy notions of how the apparent inequality of Jewish women in Jewish law probably affected them were modified considerably by the obvious strength of the Konigsbergs' marriage and by what appeared to be a remarkably energetic, mutually supportive community of women, an almost

Amazonian society that was too busy to pause to reflect
upon its distance from the world of men. Many of the
women held jobs outside the neighborhood or took special
courses (usually religious or work-related ones) at institutions outside the neighborhood, and they seemed to be
as eager as their menfolk to discuss and dispute any
religious matter, large or small. Sheina often deferred to
Moshe on philosophic questions, but then she was a relative newcomer to Jewish ideology and Moshe had been
studying it all his life. Every night after dinner, he repaired to his religious texts, and it was not unusual for him
to be up until 2:00 A.M. studying. Moshe himself constantly
deferred to various authorities "who knew more about such
matters." Like many an old-fashioned European Jewish
wife, Sheina helped her husband in his work. But she was
hardly the self-effacing drudge, nor was Moshe an im-
practical head-in-the-clouds scholar. They both worked
hard. Like any metal engraver, he toiled long hours at his
shop. Sheina did a lot of artwork, including designing
medals, for him. As a young woman, she had attended art
school briefly, and the upstairs halls were covered with
enthusiastically eclectic pictures attesting to that period
of her life. While taking a course at the Parsons School
of Design a few years ago, she had discovered she had
a gift for calligraphy, and enjoyed sketching designs.
"Look here," Moshe said one day, and brought out a port-
folio of Sheina's metal designs to show me. He could not
have been prouder of the little collection if they had been
a signed set of sketches by William Morris. Sheina works
most of the time in their basement, where there is a pro-
fusion of books and papers, as well as a pantograph (a
device that copies designs onto metal on a predetermined
scale). When she was not working, she was invariably
busy with some community project, with preparations for
the next religious holiday, or with preparations for the
steady stream of guests that filled the upstairs bedrooms.

In her spare time, she was studying Yiddish and graphic design.

Any casual observer of the Crown Heights community could see that there was a certain brittleness in the way men and women treated each other, and that there were a fair number of women about who looked exhausted and ground down. These women had a dull, dead look in their eyes and walked with a kind of listless shuffling gait. But most of the Lubavitcher women sped around like intergalactic missiles, and the great majority of those I was to encounter seemed, like Sheina, to be as occupied with worthy projects as Eleanor Roosevelt, as hospitable as Welcome Wagoneers.

The cauldrons of chicken soup were there, of course, but the women did not seem shackled to them. Had they by force of character and unrelenting busyness worked their way around the system or was the system misrepresented? Most nonobservant Jews and a fair number of observant ones believe that Orthodox Judaism is hopelessly unfair to women. A widely cited condemnation of the way Jewish law treats women appeared some years ago in an article called "The Jew Who Wasn't There," by Rachel Adler; it was reprinted recently in a collection of essays entitled *On Being a Jewish Feminist*, edited by Susannah Heschel. Miss Adler's article focuses on the six hundred and thirteen positive and negative commandments that Jews are supposed to fulfill. According to Jewish law, women are excused from fourteen of the positive commandments, among which are the reading of the *Shema* (Deuteronomy 6:4-9 and 11:13-21, and Numbers 15:37-41), a basic statement of Jewish belief reiterated by men every morning and evening in their prayers; learning and teaching Torah; and putting on *tefillin*. The law doesn't say that women cannot do most of these things but that they are not obliged to do them. Two schools of thought exist as to why women should be exempted from performing these and other time-bound duties. One is that women were to be excused from doing anything that took them away from their life-sustaining obligations at home; the other is that men require extra obligations because of their innate aggression and the contact they have with the secular world. According to the latter view, men must remind themselves more frequently of their spirituality. Not so women, who, as one nineteenth-century rabbi put it, "have greater fervor and more faithful enthusiasm for their God-serving calling," and therefore less need to be reminded of it.

A good many religious women, Miss Adler among them, scoff at all this as sophistry. They believe that the exemptions are major impediments to a full religious life and that they rob women of the basic tools of spiritual expression. "In other words," Miss Adler writes, women "have been 'excused' from most of the positive symbols which, for the male Jew, hallow time, hallow his physical being, and inform both his myth and his philosophy."

Plunging into even murkier waters, Meiselman claims that the fact that women are disqualified as witnesses in a religious court is "one of the areas of Jewish law most misunderstood by feminist critics." The charge Adler, among others, makes—that their disqualifications put them in the same category as deaf mutes, the insane, minors, pigeon racers (pigeon racing was a form of gambling in Talmudic times), and other unsavory individuals—is, he says, "absurd." He points out that kings were also not allowed to testify and speculates that since "ability to testify and obligation to testify are interdependent in Jewish law," women, like kings, were simply disqualified. A king, busy with affairs of state, will not readily be free to testify so he was excused from his duty lest he failed to carry it out. Similarly, women, with their family obligations, will frequently find it difficult to attend court proceedings, and they, too, are excused from doing so.

(Meiselman points out that until quite recently women in secular courts could disqualify themselves as jurors simply by stating that they were women.) In practice, women do appear in religious court in many instances, but not much faith is placed in their ability to get the facts straight. In criminal cases, their testimony is not considered sufficient grounds for conviction. In religious divorce proceedings, too, a woman is not considered free unless she receives a *get* or religious divorce from her husband, a law that has frequently been used to bully women in matters of child custody or finances. Civil courts have tried to intervene on behalf of women in some of these cases (mostly by trying to coerce husbands into giving *gets*) but according to Jewish law only *gets* given because a religious court convinces a husband to accede to its ruling are considered valid.

On the other hand, a woman cannot be compelled to accept a *get* and this discriminatory attitude toward women as witnesses and in divorce proceedings does not, as is generally thought, embrace the entire corpus of laws regarding women. In monetary matters, for example, a Jewish woman enjoys the same rights as a man, and her legal standing is generally the same. Furthermore, as Meiselman points out, "[a woman] may enter into any contract she wishes (a right denied to her under common law), acquire and dispose of property . . . be a litigant in all cases of contracts and damages—precisely in the same manner as a man." Even Adler concedes that "for centuries, the lot of the Jewish woman was infinitely better than that of her non-Jewish counterpart. She had rights which other women lacked until a century ago. A Jewish woman could not be married without her consent. Her *ketubah* (marriage document) was a legally binding contract which assured her that her husband was responsible for her support (a necessity in a world in which it was difficult for a woman to support herself), and that if divorced,

she was entitled to a monetary settlement. Her husband
was not permitted to abstain from sex for long periods of
time without regard to her needs and her feelings. In its
time, the Talmud's was a very progressive view. The last
truly revolutionary ruling for women, however, was the
Edict of Rabbenu Gershom forbidding polygamy to the
Jews of the Western world." Rabbi Gershom's edict was
pronounced in 1000 A.D.

Many of the arguments justifying the Jewish laws regarding women lose their credibility, of course, when
they are advanced to people who live in secular society.
Moshe and Sheina have rejected most of the values of that
society (except those that can be fitted to the ancient
framework) and, buttressed on all sides by like-minded
fellow Hasidim, they serve God in a spirit of dedicated
communality. They present to the world not only a coun-
terculture but a counterreality, which turns most modern
notions of sexual politics, self-expression and cultural ad-
aptation upside down. But few Jews live in anything like
that kind of world. What of Freud, individuality, and all
the detritus of modern culture?

Apologists like Meiselman are quick to point out that
assumptions about status are unrelated to the *intent* of
most Jewish laws, but whether intended or not, has not
the apparent favored status of men as scholars and wor-
shipers been interpreted by generations of semireligious
Jews as conferring upon women an inferior role? Was it
not inevitable that the Jewish woman's traditionally exalted position as household goddess would become per-
verted, in a despiritualized context, to the butt of the
familiar Jewish-mother joke; and equally inevitable that
the proud young Talmud scholar who, in Europe, was offered food and shelter by total strangers on the Sabbath
when he studied away from home would, in a culture that
inherited the memory but no context for such rituals, become the equally familiar (if less joked about) Jewish

Prince? Why did so many Jewish readers feel as implicated as they were amused by *Portnoy's Complaint?*—a fun-house mirror held up to these two archetypes?

It has been argued by some, most persuasively by David Bakan in his book *Sigmund Freud and the Jewish Mystical Tradition*, that however Freud's theories have been interpreted or misinterpreted by the generations that followed him they were "a contemporary version of, and a contemporary contribution to, the history of Jewish mysticism" and that "Freud, consciously or unconsciously, secularized Jewish mysticism." At the very least, the kabbalist and the psychoanalyst shared a common belief in the power of a vital world beyond the veil of reality. Furthermore, if one accepts the amusing view of John Murray Cuddihy in his lively *The Ordeal of Civility: Freud, Marx, Lévi-Strauss, and the Jewish Struggle with Modernity*, that Freud, the traditional Jewish outsider and iconoclast in the goyish Viennese scientific world, overcame forever (symbolically at least) the isolation of his people by declaring that the libidinous secret selves of the gentiles were exactly like those of the Jews, then the boundaries of the diaspora are hard indeed to see in all but the most retrograde anti-Semitic cultures. Cuddihy suggests that "Europe's psychological pariah, the 'Yid,' becomes in this way everybody's social pariah, the 'id.' . . . Freud overcame the . . . opaqueness of the . . . society of the gentile by installing an id-'Yid' in the personality system of each of its members," converting all gentiles into "honorary Jews."

Such blurring of distinctions, as well as the modernist stance on the equality of the sexes and individual freedom, is regarded in Hasidic circles as misguided at best, a perversion of God's will at worst. Sheina remarked to me as we were walking home from the *farbrengen* that she thought that the need (apart from the economic need) of many modern women to have careers often reflected pressures they felt from society to prove themselves, rather than their own inner wishes. "The same thing applies to the separation of the sexes at 770. The reason people look at us in dismay is that they are applying Christian standards where they are not applicable. We are not striving for togetherness in shul. My relationship to God is private. It's not where I sit that counts but the spirit of my prayer. I don't worship once a week and then go home and that's it for religion for the week."

"But surely not all the customs or rules that are obeyed carry the force of law," I said. "Jews have always bowed to changes in custom."

"Changes in custom, yes, but not changes that violate the teachings of the Torah. Conservative and Reform synagogues can hire women rabbis and consider it a change of custom. But the Torah forbids women to touch the Torah when they are menstruating, so how can you have a woman rabbi officiating if she can't touch the Torah? Moshe told a story the other day about a little boy who was playing chess with his father that applies to what we're talking about. The father had just set up the chessboard and the little boy said to him, 'Why must the board always be just like that? Why couldn't we move the kings and rooks over here, and the pawns over there?' And the father answered, 'We could do those things, but then the game wouldn't be chess anymore.'"

CHAPTER SIX

The Mikvah
(Ritual Bath)

I T is probably safe to say that no aspect of Orthodox Jewish life has so piqued the curiosity of interested outsiders as the so-called Laws of Family Purity, the rules that govern sexual relations between all Orthodox men and women. Men and women in this context means husbands and wives. There are no Jewish sexual laws that apply to unmarried men and women, except those that forbid sexual congress between them and those that help ensure that transgressions will not take place. Like most people, I knew that Orthodox married women did not cohabit with their husbands while they menstruated and for a week afterward. I also knew that they immersed themselves in a ritual bath—a *mikvah*—at the end of this time and that the immersion officially ended what I had heard described as their period of "uncleanness." To the extent that I'd thought about it, which wasn't much, it all sounded like some unwholesome misogynist ritual from the pages of *The Golden Bough*.

There are three categories of Jewish law: "judgments," "witnesses," and "decrees." Judgments are the moral and ethical laws that are supposed to enable people to live together in harmony by not killing, cheating, stealing, and so forth; witnesses are the rituals and holidays that remind Jews of the central truths in their lives; and decrees are those laws, like the rules pertaining to food, for which no explicit reason is given but which are supposed to be obeyed as commandments of God anyway. The last is the category into which the ritual bath falls. Jews are simply supposed to observe the decrees whether they understand them or not. They are the customs most vulnerable to scorn and rejection, of course, and they have in fact been rejected by most of the Jewish world, including many people who may accept other demands or restrictions on their lives. Thus, it is rare to find a *mikvah* (the word is used both for the bath and the bathhouse) in modern cities and towns, even those that may boast a sizable Jewish population.

I had always been dimly aware that converts to Judaism were required to immerse themselves in the bath, but I didn't understand why, and it came as a surprise when I learned that Hasidic men regularly immerse themselves before the Sabbath and on other occasions as well, and that pots and pans and cutlery manufactured by a non-Jew are also immersed before religious Jews use them in their homes. In the Bible, the original consecration of Aaron and his sons as *Kohanim*, or priests, involved immersion, and before the high priest entered the Holy of Holies (the chamber in the ancient Temple where the Ark, containing the stone tablets from Sinai, was kept), he always immersed himself. Neither Aaron nor the high priest were considered impure or unclean. Rather, they underwent a change of status. The same is true for the

convert who enters the *mikvah* because it is a place of
spiritual cleansing and rebirth. According to tradition, a
convert is actually a Jewish soul that happened to get
caught in a gentile body, and immersion in the *mikvah*
merely frees that soul to go about its business.

Aryeh Kaplan, a popular young Orthodox rabbi who died
several years ago, conducted study groups in which he tried
to convey (among other things) the beauty of the *mikvah*
in mystical terms. His reflections on the subject can be
found in a slim, closely argued volume called *Waters of
Eden: the Mystery of the Mikvah.* Kaplan discusses the Hebrew words *tumah* (usually translated as unclean though
it can also mean impure) and *tahor* (usually translated as
clean though it can also mean pure) as they are applied to
those who immerse themselves in the *mikvah,* and he
stresses the misunderstanding the more common translation has caused. Neither the men who bathe in the *mikvah*
before the Sabbath nor the postmenstrual women are considered dirty in the way most people imagine. Men shed
whatever taint they may have acquired in their weekday
workaday world when they immerse themselves before the
Sabbath; women purify themselves as an acknowledgment
of the holiness of sex. The Talmud says that all water has
as its source the primordial river that flowed out of Eden,
so when someone immerses himself in the *mikvah,* "he is
reestablishing his link with Eden." Kaplan likens the
mikvah itself to a womb. "The womb is a place that is
completely divorced from all concepts of . . . uncleanness. A baby enters the world in complete purity, and there
is no way in which he can be defiled while in the womb.
Thus when an individual enters the *mikvah,* he leaves all
uncleanness . . . behind and emerges as a new, purified
person."

I was interested in knowing what Sheina thought about
the *mikvah,* but reluctant to discuss what seemed like
such a private matter with her. As it happened, the sub-

ject came up naturally one day. Sheina and a friend had
for years talked about trying to replace the crumbling old
women's *mikvah* on Albany Avenue and Union Street with
a better equipped, more modern one, she told me. Eventually, they had interested the women of the neighborhood
in making a new *mikvah* a community project, and, after
months of discussions, planning, fund-raising (and of
course the obligatory go-ahead from the Rebbe), the *mikvah* was finally on its way. Sheina wanted to show me how
it was coming along. The new *mikvah* was being built in
a gutted brownstone next door to the old one. There were
actually going to be three baths in the new building, all
built to extremely rigorous religious specifications. They
looked like small swimming pools, something like the in-
door pools that are built next to saunas in Scandinavia. Like
all *mikvahs*, they were fed by two sources of water; in each
of the baths, two hundred gallons of rainwater commingled
with ordinary city water. It is this rainwater that gives a
bath its legitimacy as a *mikvah*. Gleaming tiles covered the
walls, dressing rooms and showers were being installed,
and rolls of carpeting leaned against the walls. The Lubavitcher laborers, wielding trowels and hammers, looked
like displaced MIT philology professors. They greeted
Sheina cheerfully and spoke to her about the progress of
their work. Sheina had been more or less in charge of seeing that things went along smoothly from the beginning
of the project and it was apparent that she was immensely
proud of the new *mikvah*. As we left, she glanced up at
the old building (the plans called for its being gutted and
incorporated in the new complex, but its baths were still
in use until the new ones were completed) with its somber "Ritualarium" lettering etched above the doorway and
said, "We want people to like coming here. It's a beautiful
ritual, and we think it deserves a welcoming setting."

"I'd like to know a bit more about how it affects you,"
I said.

Sheina said that she had a doctor's appointment in Queens (for months she had been waging a valiant battle, with the help of a nutrition expert, to shed some pounds, but as soon as she lost a few, a particularly lavish Sabbath meal would render the previous weeks' efforts meaningless) and another one later on at the neighborhood *sheitl macher* (wig-maker) but that she would be happy to continue the discussion if I could come along for the ride. I agreed, and as we drove along Eastern Parkway past miles of decrepit, once elegant buildings and boarded-up brownstones, Sheina talked about the Laws of Family Purity.

"You know, I suppose, that according to Jewish law women may not have sexual relations or any physical contact whatever with their husbands while they menstruate and for a week afterward. This may seem unnatural and a strain on a marriage to outsiders, but I think it is fair to say that no Orthodox couple I've ever known thinks of it that way. In the first place, it's a time when couples stress all the other ways that they have of communicating with one another, and secondly, most people find that abstinence whets their sexual appetite so that the boredom that many marriages suffer from has no chance to develop."

Contrary to popular belief, Hasidim are not discouraged from enjoying sex and have as part of their inheritance a wide variety of quite specific Talmudic and post-Talmudic exhortations to enjoy the act of love, complete with Masters-and-Johnson-like suggestions as to how to go about it. One can only assume that they respond to these tracts as scrupulously as they respond to all the other advice of their sages. Much of the literature on the subject has as its theme the obligation of husbands to give their wives pleasure. This excerpt from the *Epistle of Holiness*, by Rabbi Moses ben Nahman, a thirteenth-century mystic, is illustrative: "Therefore, engage her first in conversation that puts her heart and mind at ease and gladdens her . . . Speak words which arouse her to passion, union, love, desire and eros . . . Never may you force her, for in such union the Divine Presence cannot abide . . . Win her over with words of graciousness and seductiveness . . . Hurry not to arouse passion until her mood is ready."

"I don't know if it's the separation or the beauty of the ritual, maybe it's both, but I feel like a new bride every month," said Sheina. "How many married women can say that?"

"Why are the rules so strict about *all* physical contact between husband and wife in this period? Why, for example, are you not even allowed to pass a table utensil to Moshe?"

"The prohibition against men and women cohabiting while a woman menstruates comes from the book of Leviticus. But our rabbis spelled out the ways such a prohibition could best be carried out in the Talmud tractate 'Niddah' [the word *niddah* means removed or separated] and in the Code of Jewish Law. Most of the customs are there for the same purpose, to keep the flames of passion [Sheina used this expression without the slightest note of irony in her voice] banked for a while. Nowadays, the casual touch of a woman's hand or the gesture of sitting on a woman's bed [another prohibition] would probably be considered ridiculously unstimulating to a lot of people. But to men and women who don't take casual physical contact for granted, the most ordinary acts can be erotic. We have an extremely low divorce rate in this community; no one's really counted but I would say it is less than five percent. I know that people think that it's low because of the social stigma attached to divorce, but that isn't it at all. I really believe that marriages are stronger here, certainly sturdier than most that I've seen in the outside world."

After leaving the doctor's office we drove back to Crown Heights and parked the car near the apartment building where the wig-maker's shop, a tiny two-bedroom apartment, was located. The proprietress, a small talkative woman who had been born in the Carpathian Mountains, led Sheina over to a chair and wall mirror and brought out various red wigs for her to try on. A sleepy-looking, rosy-cheeked young woman who had just arrived from Paris to attend her brother's wedding was also trying on wigs. When the women removed their wigs, they both looked strange and there was something about their ungroomed short-clipped hair that I found extremely unsettling. It was, I realized almost instantaneously, the way the two roughly shorn heads evoked concentration camp photographs. In fact the true mood of the room, with its gold-and-white filigree wallpaper, drawn window shades, soft golden light, wigs mounted on stands and happily chattering women was suggestive of an Offenbach operetta. Every wig had its own style name, and the women referred to them familiarly: "I think I'd like to try 'Cleo' this time"; "You know, you'd probably look very good in 'Jet Set'"; "There, doesn't 'Charlie Girl' bring out her eyes beautifully?" The wigs cost from sixty to seventy dollars, Sheina said, and some had to be brought in about every four months for recombing.

The young woman from France, who knew Sheina, told her that she and her family had found French anti-Semitism particularly hidebound, and they felt their differentness from the people around them much more acutely there than they did in New York because the French made much more of a fuss about it. French children, she said, were always laughing and pointing at her children. She expressed regret, too, that for all the elegance of the French Jews there was no *mikvah* there as up-to-date as the one that was being planned for the Crown Heights community. She said she couldn't wait to use the new one.

Sheina gave me a knowing look, and after we'd left the shop and were walking to the car, she said, "You see, I'm not kidding, we *enjoy* the *mikvah*."

"You don't ever feel that it's a burden, or wish that it wasn't necessary?" I asked.

"Absolutely not. I really feel renewed and refreshed by it. I feel it connects me in a mysterious way to the Jews of all time. There were two found when they dug up Masada, you know—embattled as they were with the Romans the Jews somehow found time to build two *mikvahs!* But it's a hard experience to describe. Why don't you try it yourself?"

I said that I'd like to, perhaps after the new *mikvah* was finished.

The centrality of the *mikvah* in the lives of the Orthodox is sharply illustrated by a story Aryeh Kaplan recounts in *Waters of Eden* about an American friend of his who paid a secret visit to a religious family he knew in Russia. It is not against the law to practice one's religion in Russia, but it is a fact of life that Jews who do so openly invite the antagonism of the bureaucracy. Just before the American was about to depart, the Russian, whose name was Yaakov, beckoned to him and said, "Wait, I have something that I would like to show you." Taking Kaplan's friend over to a clothes closet and looking over his shoulder anxiously, "Yaakov opened the closet, moved aside a number of boxes, and carefully lifted up a false floor. Under the floorboards there was a staircase, leading to a small pool. 'This is the city's *mikvah*,' he proudly announced, 'over forty families make use of it.' . . . No religious facilities could be built without express government permission. Otherwise it was subject to the direst penalties. Besides, the house was government property, and if caught, he would face a long prison sentence for 'defacing' it. Gradually—almost cautiously—he began to tell how the *mikvah* was built. All the work had to be done in the utmost secrecy.

No one, even his closest friends and neighbors, could know what he was doing. Only a small amount of digging could be done under the house each day, so that the dirt could be disposed of without arousing suspicion. Small quantities of cement—'for making minor repairs'—were purchased until there was enough to line the *mikvah*. A similar subterfuge had to be used to obtain pipes for the plumbing. In addition, the rigorous requirements of Jewish Law had to be satisfied. This is difficult enough under any circumstances, even if secrecy is not a paramount consideration.

"Not until the *mikvah* was completed did Yaakov dare tell anyone about it. At first, his closest friends shared the secret. Gradually, one by one, other families were invited to make use of the hidden *mikvah*. Most of them did not believe it possible—but they came anyway. Before long, Yaakov's 'top secret project' had become the community *mikvah*."

When Kaplan's friend asked Yaakov why he had exposed himself to so much danger to build the *mikvah*, he answered simply, "Without it, I could not live as a Jew."

But how does women's need to purify themselves before having sexual congress with their husbands relate to Judaism's concept of the holiness of sex? The argument is that when men and women cohabit, they may bring down a soul to the world, a new human. Kaplan points out that, biologically speaking, it would have been more efficient if the uteral lining were not shed each month, and notes that "there is no biological or medical reason why the uteral lining must be expelled and restored each month. There is no reason why the ovum has to 'die' only to be replaced by another egg. Most biologists look upon this as an unexplained inefficiency in the human reproductive system. To the primitive mind, which had no idea of the inner workings of the womb, the very idea that a woman should lose a portion of her vital fluids was both bizarre and frightening. They could not explain it logically . . . therefore they attributed it to some 'evil force.' According to most anthropologists, this is one of the main reasons so many taboos surround the menstruating woman in primitive cultures. . . . When we look at menstruation in the light of human imperfection in general, it clearly fits the pattern. As a result of Adam's sin, man lost the ability to perfect himself, both spiritually and physically . . . The clearest manifestation of this physical imperfection is man's mortality. Man wears out and dies."

Women, of course, inherited from Eve "pangs in childbearing" (Genesis 3:16), and, by extension, a reproductive system that was designed to remind her of her fall and expulsion from Eden. Thus, she cannot enter into sexual relations, one of the holiest of human activities, until she ritually purifies herself, just as the high priest did before entering the Holy of Holies.

To those who stand at some remove from the central myths of the Bible, this explanation may not seem so different from the taboos imposed on women by those primitive minds who attributed women's imperfectability to an evil force. But to the Hasidim, who believe that the Bible is the revealed word of God, it is a logical one, and one that makes bathing in the *mikvah* a crucial part of their lives.

Sometime after my visit to the unfinished *mikvah* with Sheina, and after the birth of my second child, I returned to pay a visit myself. It is about a forty-five minute subway ride from Lower Manhattan, where I live, to the Kingston Avenue IRT stop. After Brooklyn Heights, mine is the only white face on the subway car. It is sundown (the prescribed time for taking a *mikvah*) when I surface and, as usual, there is a large group of bearded, black-hatted, somberly dressed men milling in front of 770, which is just across the street from the subway exit. The neighborhood still seems dreamlike, but the faces above the beards have begun to look more individualized to me; the

perceptual trick seems to be to read them from the nose
up. Union Street, where the *mikvah* is, cuts into Kingston
Avenue, and as I walk down it toward the *mikvah* I find
myself trailing behind a black teenage boy bopping down
the street with an enormous radio that is blasting out
reggae music. Formalizing the occasion, I imagine that the
music is a kind of fanfare for the ritual I am going to experience, and that the boy and I form a kind of procession.
The farther away we get from Kingston Avenue the more
deserted and rundown the street gets. Across the street
from the tan brickface *mikvah* building, which glows
faintly in the fading light, is a large deserted apartment
building with broken windows. There are no windows at
all in the new *mikvah,* and the old ones have been ce-
mented over. A fancy brown canvas canopy arches over
the front door, giving the entranceway the appearance of
an elegant salon. I am buzzed into the building, ascend a
flight of stairs and give eight dollars to a Slavic-looking
attendant who tells me that she can't remember ever having seen me before. At the *mikvah,* many women shower
and bathe in preparation for the ritual immersion itself.
I explain to the attendant that I have already bathed at
home so she leads me to a dressing room with only a shower
in it. The shower has a sliding frosted-glass door, there is
burgundy, white and gold deco paper on the walls, and a
beveled diamond-shaped mirror over a Formica dressing
table. There is also a wig stand, a bright red Clairol Son
of a Gun 1400 hundred-watt hairdryer, a long cream-
colored terry cloth bathrobe, and a pair of brightly colored
rubber slippers. The attendant shows me a tan intercom
and tells me to pick it up when my preparations are completed and tell the *mikvah* lady that I'm ready. As I close
the door, I notice several other women flitting down the
corridor. The *mikvah* is considered an extremely private
ritual, and there is no socializing here, none of the affec-
tionate banter that is so prevalent in feminine Hasidic so-

ciety. Women generally go to the *mikvah* alone, and even
Sheina, who was always eager to act as my *cicerone* to
landmarks of Jewish Orthodoxy, had not offered to accompany me to this one. The lower half of the dressing room
is covered with gleaming off-white tile. I had always imagined *mikvahs* to be rather oriental: vaporous dim places,
chaste seraglios. Nothing could be further from my pre-
conception than this sleek Swiss spa.

The toilette one makes in preparation for the *mikvah*
is elaborate. Having read about (and followed) the complicated preparations before I came, I was not surprised
to see a small tray filled with Q-Tips, cotton balls, tissues,
shampoo, baby oil, toothpicks, bleach, alcohol, soap and
Adwe New Fluoride Formula Kosher toothpaste. It is considered extremely important that the waters of the *mikvah*
touch every part of a woman's body; even minute particles
of matter that prevent this from happening make the immersion invalid. The kinds of matter that might (literally) gum things up have been spelled out in excruciating
detail by rabbinic authority. "A splinter," for example,
"which protrudes from the skin, or even if it does not pro-
trude the skin but nevertheless is on the same level with
the outer skin *must* be removed." Even particles of food
that get caught in one's teeth are considered impurities,
so a little box of dental floss is provided. But then again,
the floss might get stuck, so, taped to the little plastic box
is the typed message "Don't floss if your teeth are tight
together." Most of the people who come to the *mikvah*
already know everything there is to know about preparing
for it. As a precaution, however, a lengthy checklist has
been taped to the wall. Among other things, it suggests
that "Rabbinic advice should be sought for temporary
fillings, root-canal work or capping in progress, nits in the
hair, stitches, casts . . . unremovable scabs, unusual skin
eruptions." It is further suggested that one ask oneself,
"Have I cut finger and toe nails and removed dirt in crev-

ices (bleach helps)? Removed all foreign bodies: false
teeth, contact lenses, paint and makeup, nail polish, arti-
ficial nails, Band-Aids, bobby pins . . . ?" The list goes
on, and suffice it to say that no crevice or orifice of the
body is neglected.

Scrubbing myself in the shower, I remember the woman
who commented on the "dirtiness" of the Hasidim and
laugh out loud. The last words on the checklist are "Now
you are ready for the great *mitzva* of *Tevilah* [immer-
sion]." A French version of the list has been taped below
the English one (many French-speaking Jews have been
visiting the community recently). With characteristic Gal-
lic grace, the French version adds a little coda to the
English one: Now, it says, you are ready to perform the
great *mitzva* of *Tevilah* "*avec joie et assurance.*" I ring
for the *mikvah* matron. I do not feel "*joie et assurance.*"
I feel nervous. I find myself wishing my mother were
here. Then, one of the kindest most benign faces I have
ever seen appears smiling at the door, and my worries
evaporate. The woman, who is middle-aged and wears a
dark wig, tells me as she leads me through the climate-
controlled corridor that her name is Brachah. Brachah, of
course, means blessing. These Lubavitchers really know
how to do things. I tell Brachah that I've never taken a
mikvah before. She folds her hands over her stomach and
beams. "Well, then, we'll treat you like a *kallah* [a bride]"
and proceeds to explain some of the basics of the ritual
to me. Then she asks, enumerating the various items on
the checklist one by one, if I have remembered to do all
of them. I have not. I have forgotten to comb my wet hair
and I have forgotten my nose, which I proceed to blow,
rather showily. Then, after blotting my eyes with a linen
cloth to make sure no mascara lingers on my lashes,
Brachah leads me over to the *mikvah*. I take off the robe
and stand expectantly in the chest-deep warm green water.
Brachah tells me to keep my eyes and lips closed but not

too tightly and to keep my feet and arms apart, so that the
water will touch my whole body. When I go underwater
I instantly curl into the fetal position because of the position of my body. When I come up, Brachah places a linen
cloth over my head and I repeat the *mikvah* blessing after
her. Then, the cloth removed, I go down two more times.
The second time down, I see a little speeded-up movie
of all the religious people I know, performing this ritual.
I think of all the generations of people I have not known
who have considered the impurities of the world dissolv-
able. My grandmother floats by, curled up, like me, like
a little pink shrimp. I see her as she was in her very old
age, senile and mute, curled up in the same position on
her bed. The third time down, I think of my boys sus-
pended inside me, waiting to join the world. I look up
and see Brachah's smiling face through the water. I feel
good. As I am climbing out, Brachah tells me that some
people prefer to immerse themselves with their bodies in
a horizontal position, and asks me if I'd like to try it that
way. I try it, but find it less satisfactory. It's too much like
going for a swim.

When I finish dressing, I find Brachah and the other
attendant huddled together at the reception desk. I've
told Brachah that I live in Manhattan and that I came by
subway. "We don't think you should go home by subway," Brachah says. "It's really not safe to walk alone out
there now." It's only a little after eight, but I take their
word for it and call one of the local car services, Black
Pearl. (No city radio cabs will come to Crown Heights.
No yellow cabs cruise the neighborhood streets.) Five
minutes later, a blue Chevrolet station wagon pulls up. I
thank the women for their help, say goodbye, and climb
into the car. The driver is a garrulous, handsome Haitian.
Loud, monotonous music blasts out of the radio. Hanging
over his rearview mirror is an air deodorizer, which fills
the car with an overpowering sickly-sweet smell. Com-

peting with the air deodorizer is the sharp scent of his after-shave, which he keeps in a kit on the front seat. At a long red light, he splashes a little extra on. My ablutions have made me feel tender, almost porous, and the harsh smells are overwhelming. Is this how Moshe and Sheina feel when they traffic with the outside world? The driver tells me that his company is often called upon to pick up women at that spot, which he seems to believe is a kind of shrine.

"You're Jewish, right?" he says, shouting to be heard over the music. "You have a lot of rules you have to follow?"

I hesitate. I am not up to any discussion.

"Yes, I'm Jewish," I say, as I roll the window down and point my nose toward the fresh air.

CHAPTER SEVEN

Passover, Exile, and Exile Politics

I N March, for more than three weeks, sheets and pillows lay strewn about on the Konigsbergs' floor, the contents of drawers lay heaped on beds, and mops, sponges, and dustrags stood battle-ready in every corner. The family was getting ready for Passover, the holiday that commemorates the deliverance of the Israelites from their captivity to the Egyptians some 3,300 years ago. (Many Jews refer to the holiday by its Hebrew name, *Pesach.*) But the state-of-siege atmosphere in the Konigsberg house in the weeks preceding the holiday had little to do with the larger issues of freedom and redemption associated with the holiday; rather, it was inspired by the Biblical injunction to eat only unleavened bread (as the Israelites did when they departed in haste from Egypt) on the days that commemorate the Exodus and to be sure that "no leavened bread shall be with you . . ." and "No leaven shall be found in your houses" (Exodus 13:7, 12:19). To be sure that no leavened food (defined by Jewish law as anything that is made from a grain that has come in contact with water for more than eighteen minutes) or leavening agents, such as yeast, are lurking in stoves, cupboards, coat pockets, or under rugs, religious Jews have always turned their houses upside down in the weeks preceding Passover. In the Middle Ages, when Jews suspected of practicing sorcery were frequently stoned, the Jewish community's preparations for Passover aroused the deepest suspicions among the gentiles. It was believed that Jews kneaded blood into their unleavened bread and even drank it at the Passover table. To allay such suspicions, the rituals connected with Passover often had to be performed secretly, or abandoned.

Over the years, many Jews who celebrate Passover have slackened off in their zealousness about the holiday. They may throw out their store of bread, crackers, and breakfast cereal, for example, but leave the whiskey (which is made from grain) where it is. Corner cutting of this kind has no place in the Hasidic world. In fact, there can be heard in the protestations of Hasidic housewives that there scarcely seems to be enough time to accomplish all the dusting and scouring a not-so-subtle note of pride that the effort they are making to do the impossible is unstinting.

I spoke to Sheina on the telephone several times in the weeks preceding Passover. As the holiday grew nearer she sounded increasingly frazzled. She had been working from the top of the house down, she said, and by the time I paid her a visit, a few days before the holiday, she had reached the kitchen. Every year she removed the top of her electric stove and replaced it with a special Passover cooktop. Standing next to the stove, she was explaining to two somber and scholarly-looking Lubavitcher electricians that she wanted a new plug installed near the stove so that the process of changing the stove wires would

be simplified. There was a certain newfangledness about
the scheme that the men obviously distrusted, and they
listened to Sheina's instructions with expressions that
seemed to say "There's nothing unkosher about this but
our grandmothers certainly didn't need such things."
Sheina was wearing old clothes and bedroom slippers and
she had a faded scarf wound around her head. She looked
tired. Most of the neighborhood people covered their
kitchen countertops with wooden boards or aluminum foil
at Passover, she said, but she covered hers with heavy
Formica-covered wooden boards. She had just finished
putting the boards in place when the electricians arrived.
Earlier that morning, she had stacked all her pots and
pans in special kitchen cupboards and tied the cupboard
doors with string to make sure that no one would open
them by mistake. The Passover pots and pans, which are
stored in the basement the rest of the year, had been carried upstairs by the boys and put away in cupboards that
had been scrubbed and scrubbed again and lined with
new shelf paper. I helped Sheina push a large carton out
of the laundry room, a narrow cluttered space hidden
away behind the kitchen. A few errant non-Passover dishes
were tucked into the family's year-round ovens, which they
did not use Passover week, she said, because they felt that
even though they were self-cleaning, some minute crumb
of leavened matter might escape incineration.

I asked Sheina if all her neighbors were as scrupulous
as she was.

"Everybody has different ideas about how to do things
on Passover," she said. "The rule of thumb is, when in
doubt, do what your bubbe [grandmother] did. Of course,
our bubbes didn't have self-cleaning ovens. Some people
wouldn't hesitate to use ovens that had a self-cleaning device in them. We're probably more conservative than a lot
of people. Moshe is my bubbe in these matters. He worries
about the self-cleaning oven so we don't use it. We just

don't bake anything that week. We don't eat at anybody's
house during Passover, because we realize that these differences exist. And we don't eat things that many quite
Orthodox Jews eat."

"For example?"

"Matzoh ball soup, for example, which involves wetting
the matzoh . . . and all those things that never used to
be around but are available now and are supposedly kosher for Passover, like canned tuna and Passover cookies.
Some of the rabbis who have O.K.'d these foods we might
trust, some we might not, but the real issue is that we
think that the rituals lose their meaning if Passover stops
being a time when you do things differently. Somewhere,
I'm sure, someone is selling kosher-for-Passover chocolate
Easter bunnies . . ."

"What about the Passover matzoh in the stores?"

"We don't eat it. The way mass-market production and
distribution is, there's no real way of knowing that the
flour, or even the boxes themselves, haven't come into contact with water at some point, or that a little bit of dough
hasn't lingered in the machinery for too long. So we have
special handmade matzohs, called *schmurah* [guarded]
matzohs. People order them in advance from a local bakery that's set up just for the holiday. When we get our
matzohs from them, we know that what we're eating is
okay. We know that the flour has been watched and that
the dough has not been allowed to sit around for more
than eighteen minutes in some factory."

With Sheina's help, I telephoned the bakery to ask if
they would mind having a visitor. A breathless man on
the other end said, "Sure, sure. Come," and slammed the
receiver down with a bang.

A quarter of an hour later, I stepped across the thresh-
old of a small, nondescript storefront on Albany Avenue,
about six blocks from Sheina's house. There was no sign
on the outside, nothing that distinguished it from a num-

ber of forlorn-looking, decaying storefronts on the same
block. Once my eyes had adjusted to the dim light inside,
however, I felt like Alice at the bottom of the rabbit hole.
The room looked like the inside of a gigantic carton.
Every inch of it was covered with thick, brown butcher's
paper. Several booths, also covered with brown paper,
stood against the walls. The room was dark and shadowy.
Near the door, in one of the booths, a man was distrib-
uting large paper-covered parcels (the packaged matzohs)
to a slowly moving line of silent customers. In two adjoining rooms, where the matzoh was being made, bakers raced
back and forth like jackrabbits. To guarantee that the production process took less than the prescribed eighteen
minutes, it had been streamlined to Mach speed. It was
12:15. As it happened, I had arrived just in time to see a
fresh batch being made. In one of the paper-covered
booths, a water pourer, hidden except for his arm, stuck
a pitcher through a hole in the paper and poured water
into a flour-filled vat held by another man seated in a
chair. The second man kneaded the mixture with lightning-
quick gestures, then raced with it over to a long paper-
covered table in the next room, where twenty women
wearing babushkas stood with hands outthrust. The man
handed each of them a wad of dough. Almost as one body,
the women rolled the dough, scored it, and before their
hands were raised from the table a third man with a
long wooden stick took the newly formed matzohs away
and eased them into a coal-and-wood-fired brick oven.
It had taken the women thirty-eight seconds to roll
and score the dough. Several other men placed the baked
matzohs on another counter where they cooled briefly
before being stored in boxes. 12:24. From start to finish,
the matzohs had come in at an amazing nine minutes—
well under the limit. It had been like watching a wacky
nineteenth-century version of *Modern Times*. One of the
bakers, a small, keen-eyed fellow, his face flushed from

the heat of the oven, trotted over to me with a warm matzoh and asked if I'd like to taste it. It smelled delicious. As I bit into the slightly blackened, homely-looking wafer, the production line came to a dramatic halt. All eyes fastened on me.

I smiled and nodded in a manner that I hope exuded good will. "Mmmmm, uh," I murmured. It tasted like burnt cardboard.

The day of the first Passover seder, the meal that begins the eight-day ritual commemoration of the holiday, I arrived in Crown Heights in the midafternoon. On the way from the subway to the Konigsberg house, I witnessed the following scene: Two black men, one of them a bit high, approached two Hasidic men on the sidewalk. Just before they passed each other, the man who was high removed his cap and said mockingly to the Hasidim, "Gooooood Shabbos." It was a Tuesday. The Hasidim looked right through him. They said nothing. I was walking in the same direction as the black men. After the Hasidim were well out of earshot the sober man said to his friend, "Why you want to do that? You crazy?" "I'll tell you why. Because I've been passing those two muhfuhs on this street for five years and they always look at me like I was a fucking brick wall."

An Orthodox psychiatrist I encountered who treats a number of Hasidim (including some Lubavitchers) described their peculiar nonresponsive manner in the secular world as a kind of all-embracing denial mechanism. "All of us practice a certain amount of this as we go about the city," he said. "There's so much going on that's depressing and awful that most of us couldn't function if we didn't just edit a lot of it out. The Hasidim do this with secular society as a whole. It's outside their framework and they just can't—or won't—cope with it." I expressed surprise that Hasidim would even call upon him for help. "Well,

it's still not exactly a common occurrence; it's just beginning to be realized in those circles that emotional illness
is not the same thing as moral turpitude, or laziness. In
general, they are still wary of psychiatry, except when
they are in a very bad state. Actually, it was the Lubavitcher Rebbe who suggested that I might work with Orthodox patients; and of course I'm religious myself, so they
probably feel that I'm not going to lead them that far
astray."

The fact that psychiatrists were enlisted to succor Hasidim who suffered in some extreme way answered a question that had been bothering me for some time: Where
in the little harmonious kingdom of the Lubavitchers were
the sort of extreme, outrageous, foolish, touchy, driven
and, dare I say it, mad people that according to I. B.
Singer and other Yiddish writers this world has always
been teeming with? Obviously, they were being packed
off to shrinks. "Figments of an overwrought imagination,"
said one Lubavitcher man when I asked him what he
thought about characters of this sort in Singer's stories.
"Where are such people? Do you see any?" The rest of
us may read Singer's stories with delight and gratitude,
but to the Hasidim he is, like Gershom Scholem, anarchic
and worse, an irreverent teller of secrets.

The night before, Moshe and Sheina had searched their
darkened house from top to bottom for any lurking crumbs
or bits of leavened food. Armed with a feather, a wooden
spoon and a candle, the equipment used for this ritually
ordained treasure hunt, they peered into closets, turned
raincoat pockets inside out, used the feather to probe the
corners of drawers and bookshelves, and collected their
modest findings in the wooden spoon. Whatever they found
would be burned the next morning. Since most households
have been thoroughly scoured, it is unlikely that anything
will be discovered in this ritualistic search, so bits of bread
are customarily secreted throughout the house by some-

one beforehand so that it will not be in vain. Afterward, a "Statement of Nullification" is made that absolves the householder from guilt regarding any bit of grain that he did not see and destroy. It is declared "null and ownerless as the dust of the earth." By that time all the whiskey, canned goods, and packaged foodstuffs that the Konigsbergs owned had been "sold" to a gentile, as had their year-round dishes, glasses and silverware. A bill of sale had been drawn up and given to the Rov (the rabbi, generally known for his mastery of Talmudic matters, who takes care of the everyday religious needs of the community), who turned it over to the former custodian of his building. In fact, none of the things sold leave the house; they are locked away in cupboards. After the holiday, the Rov would "buy" Moshe's things back at a slightly higher price. It is not considered a token sale, appearances notwithstanding, because theoretically the "buyer" may do what he wishes with his property while he owns it. Jews have been selling their leavened foods at Passover since very ancient times, but the custom of selling them contractually began in Central Europe in the sixteenth century.

The Konigsbergs' normally tidy house had entered another dimension of cleanliness. The floors shone, the furniture gleamed, and the wineglasses reflected the light of the newly scrubbed chandelier. It was an hour before the seder was to begin. Sheina was surveying the table, stirring things, and peering critically at the dishes neatly lined up in the refrigerator. Bassy, humming something lively, was carefully placing a seder plate laden with romaine lettuce, a paste of chopped apples and nuts, an egg, a lamb shankbone and a piece of potato near three cloth-covered pieces of matzoh at the head of the table. Sheina handed her a cup of salt water to put next to the plate.

Moshe, his sleeves rolled up, his elbows deep in an enormous bowl of water on the breakfast table, was carefully washing lettuce. Taking the leaves out one by one, he held each leaf up to the light and examined it scrupulously. He greeted me with a somewhat quizzical, if tolerant, expression. Although he seemed to take my visits for granted, I sensed that he was not pleased that I was remaining an outsider, and had begun to think of me, I believe, as a kind of female Phineas Fogg. In point of fact, I felt similarly frustrated by what I at first interpreted as lack of candor but eventually came to see as a more all-encompassing mind-set in Moshe. Unlike Sheina, he never liked to discuss the particulars of his life. The self he liked to talk about was a communal self. This was in keeping, of course, with his view of himself as merely one among many, someone whose own ego has been submerged to serve a higher goal. Neither private preoccupations nor public accomplishments seemed to be all that important to him. One day I had asked him about his work. It was as if I had asked him to discuss the pipes that brought the water to his house. Who could be interested in such a dull subject? He grudgingly told me that his employees were all Hasidim but that his customers were not. Some of them were not even Jewish. But his work was "just something I do every day but Saturday," he said, and would not hear of my visiting his shop, which was tucked into an old apartment building a few blocks away, because "there is nothing interesting to see" and it had "nothing to do" with his life as a Hasid. The part of his past that he talked about the day we met proved to be the sum total of the personal data he felt comfortable discussing. After that, his posture toward me was that of an affable Ambassador-at-Large from the Independent State of Hasidism. He was unfailingly cordial, but his cordiality masked a profound guardedness. My "outsiderness" was a factor even in my relationship with Sheina. In a sense, she was always being the teacher and I the pupil. I was there, of course, to learn about her world but it still surprised me that she was so incurious about mine. Somehow, whenever I brought up subjects that had nothing to do with her world (my son's sweet singing voice, for example) she invariably brought them round so that they did ("Do you teach him Jewish songs?"). Within these boundaries a modest friendship developed. But even when Moshe and I talked about completely impersonal things, my "outsiderness" coupled with my gender seemed to get in the way of any frank or even relaxed discussion between us.

The more Crown Heights families I became acquainted with, however, the more apparent it became that this was not just a personal quirk of Moshe's; the protocols of Hasidic life precluded anything like the easy friendships that existed between men and women in the secular world. Such friendships were considered fraught with sexual possibilities, and were therefore frowned upon. This created a great gulf, of course, between masculine and feminine society which I found fairly appalling. The young Hasidic men seem particularly affected by it. On the one hand, they were being raised to adore their mothers; on the other, they were not allowed to transfer any of that affection to girlfriends when they became teenagers, as most young men do. You might occasionally catch one or two gazing furtively at a pretty girl, but they never flirted, and if caught looking they would affect a kind of lachrymose, indifferent air. Their studying engaged them mightily and most of their vanity (and allure) was connected with their scholastic accomplishments, but they did not as a whole look happy. Many of them looked depressed, many more, numb. Moshe's sons almost always drifted off whenever unfamiliar women or girls invaded their domain, and on the only occasion when my curiosity about their lives got the better of my tact and I asked them one or two questions about their lives, they lobbed the questions right

back ("What are your favorite subjects at school?" "So
what's a favorite subject?" "Apart from the Rebbe, who
are the people you most admire?" "What do you mean,
admire?") in classic Henny Youngman style.

"I'm looking for bugs," Moshe said now.

"Bugs?"

"That's right. You never know when one will find its
way into the lettuce patch." I nodded noncommittally,
not really understanding. Moshe allowed himself a small
sigh (Lubavitchers have to do a lot of explaining), then
added, not unkindly, "Bugs aren't kosher. I've found two
already. Aha, here's another," he announced gleefully.
"Oh, here's Miriam and Yehuda. Hello, hello." Miriam
was Moshe's oldest daughter and Yehuda was her husband. They had just come from Cape Town, where they
had been living for the past four years. Both were in their
late twenties. Six doe-eyed children, aged one through six,
trailed in alongside them. Miriam was pregnant. As she
and Yehuda led their little procession toward the kitchen
to say hello to Sheina, Yehuda smiled at me and said he'd
heard about me and wished me well. "Sometime I'll show
you something Miriam wrote when she was younger. She
has talent, too," he said. "No you won't, that's all nonsense,"
his wife answered quickly, looked flustered but pleased.
Both Moshe's sons-in-law had disarmingly sweet faces
and eyes that radiated strong intellectual curiosity. Like
Moshe, they both obviously found it easy to be friendly
in a detached sort of way, and displayed none of the skit-
tish fear of women that the young unmarried boys did.
Moshe wiped his arms on a towel and scooped up a little
boy and girl. They giggled. "Hi Feige, hi Yossi." Both children beamed at their grandfather. He beamed back. Miriam gave him a look of unqualified approval.

"I know what the things on the seder plate are for,
Zeyde [grandfather]," the little boy said.

"Do you? So tell me."

"The meat is for the lamb our people sacrificed in Egypt and ate the night they were freed; the egg, which we dip in salt water, is to remember the sadness of being slaves; the bitter herb is for the suffering of our . . . our . . . the Jewish people in Egypt; the *choroset* [the apple and walnut mixture] is for the bricks they used to have to make when they were slaves, and the potato is supposed to show that spring is coming."

"That's wonderful, Yossi. Where did you learn all that?"

"Well, Mommy taught me some, and my teacher did, but I also read it here," he said, showing his grandfather a little pamphlet. The pamphlet was published by the Lubavitcher Student Organization and explained the rudiments of the Passover rituals. It also offered a Passover crossword puzzle ("1. On *Pesach* God took the Jews out of ———"); a matzoh-ball contest—a thinly disguised checklist of things to do for Passover with prizes offered to all; and a Matzoh Maze.

"Zeyde, why are we speaking English?" the little boy asked his grandfather.

"Because that lady over there, who is our guest, doesn't understand Yiddish."

The boy, who had pale skin and short dark hair, looked at me curiously, but said nothing. Lubavitcher children are taught not to make disenfranchised Jews feel embarrassed. Miriam and Yehuda were talking to Sheina in the kitchen. Sheina held a little girl on her hip while she stirred something in a pot; the other children had faded into the corners. They were watchful, well behaved, and quiet. The children that I moved among, including my own, were treated like principals on social occasions that they were invited along on; these children were part of the crowd scene. Nobody fussed over them or worried about whether they were sufficiently amused. A great deal of fuss had been made about their education, and they were obviously well-loved and nourished, but they were not viewed as small adventurers on their way to some special, as yet undisclosed private destiny. They were little Jewish men and women en route to the same destination as their parents.

"Come and talk to Miriam," Sheina said to me. "She'll tell you about her life in South Africa."

Miriam and I sat down to talk on a quilted couch in the living room. She had her father's dark, luminous hooded eyes but her features were more angular than his. She was an intelligent-looking, bespectacled young woman who spoke (also like her father) in quick, staccato phrases. I asked her how she'd found herself in Cape Town.

"The Rebbe asked us to go. There's been a large Jewish population in Cape Town for some time. They're very conservative people, mostly business and professional people. They call themselves Orthodox, but really they're unobservant Orthodox, as a friend of ours once called them. Hardly anybody we met when we got there had any sort of Jewish education, so we tried to create an awareness in the people we talked to of who they were and what it means to be a Jew in religious terms. We followed the teachings of the Rebbe as best we could. We weren't there to force anything on anybody, but to help them grow."

"How did you know where to go, or whom to see?"

"We did what other Lubavitchers had done in other cities. We went to the university. We found out the names of various Jewish groups and we went to speak at their meetings. I spoke to Jewish women's groups. I didn't know at all how people would react to us; I never suspected that so many people would be receptive to the idea of changing their lives. I don't mean that we made miracles or anything, but a good number of people that we got to know did start to keep kosher homes and observe

the Sabbath, and a few, like Dovid—I think you met him—
really changed the course of their lives."

"Apart from your work, how do you like the country?
Were you affected by the racial tension there?"

"We love the country. It's very beautiful. And there's
a relaxed way of life there that's very much to our liking.
We didn't like the racism. Of course, things are not right
there, and it affected us on a personal level because the
African maid we had was from one of the homelands and
wasn't really supposed to be working in Cape Town. They
came to get her twice. It was frightening. Once they took
her away and put her in jail, and we had to be very secre-
tive about smuggling bail money to her and getting her
out. Another time, she was standing outside our shul and
she saw the police coming to get her. She was terrified.
My husband told her to hide in his office and just lock the
door. It was dangerous for both of them."

"Did you get involved in any broader way with the
politics there?"

"No. I don't think that Jews should do that, and I didn't
have any real answers to the problems there, anyway.
Liberals always have answers. For them, the solution to
any problem is always easy: follow liberal ideology—no
matter what bloodshed follows or what good the bloodshed does. When we first arrived in South Africa, we
found that many of the South Africans were wary of us.
Later, we found out that they had seen a lot of hotheaded
Americans arrive and make a lot of trouble, especially for
the people they had come to help."

"Do you prefer conservative politicians?" I asked.

"Well, as I said, we're really not political people, but
we do feel more comfortable with the politics of many
conservative politicians. We trust Reagan more than we
trusted Carter, because he's not so ready to make conces-
sions to the Russians just to make himself look good. But,

I don't know if my father or Sheina told you, we're not going back to Cape Town. I'm going to be teaching in the girls' school here."

"Why aren't you going back?" I asked.

"Cape Town didn't have a *mikvah*. So every month I had to fly to Johannesburg to use the *mikvah* there. I had to stay overnight, too. It's supposed to be a private ritual, but of course Yehuda always flew with me and we stayed with Lubavitcher friends, so it was obvious why we were there, which was embarrassing. It was disruptive to our family, too, disruptive enough so that we decided to return."

"Did the Rebbe approve of your decision?"

"Yes."

Yossi, the little boy who had explained the symbolism of the seder plate to his grandfather, had been standing near us for some time, looking at me quite intensely. I smiled at him. He bit his lip, then blurted out,

"You should learn Yiddish."

"Yes? Why?"

"So you can tell secrets."

Yossi said no more but sidled over to his mother and rummaged in her handbag until he found a small magazine called *The Moshiach Times*. The magazine was the official organ of the Lubavitcher children's group, *Tzivos Hashem* (the Army of God). I had been told that the idea of a closely organized, formal children's group had come from the Rebbe. The format of the magazine, which is published in Crown Heights seven times a year, is not unlike *Ranger Rick* or any other children's magazine, except that the themes are religious and generally couched in paramilitary language. Sheina subscribed to the magazine so that any children who came to the house could browse through it, and I had glanced at a few copies on previous visits. The magazine encourages children to work their way up through the ranks of the Army by zealously performing their religious duties. In every issue there is a page with a list of "New Officers"—children who have performed their religious duties well enough to earn a new rank. There are girl officers as well as boy officers on the list and children of both sexes depicted on the cover. The Rebbe made it known that he wanted no sexual bias in this quarter, and, according to one story I'd been told, on one occasion even admonished the woman who drew the cover illustrations because she had not included any girls in one of them. There are reportedly seventy thousand children in the Rebbe's juvenile army. The "Field Report" on the first page of Yossi's issue listed *Tzivos Hashem* bases in twenty-eight states, though most of the new officers appeared to hail from Brooklyn, New York. One article, called "Meet the Major," was an interview with the Army's highest-ranking officer, Major Moshe Neuberger, a boy who looked about nine or ten. The major said that he had "joined up with a bunch of friends," had quickly advanced in the *Tzivos Hashem* battalion in his summer camp, and that he "worked very hard learning Torah by heart." Other features of the issue were a short tale, under the heading (in Gothic print) "Heroes of Olde," about the third Lubavitcher rebbe; a comic strip about Super *Neshama* (*Neshama* is the Hebrew word for soul), alias Klar Kentowitz; a "Top Secret" mission (to learn extra Torah during the Passover vacation) from "Agent 613"; and a short story, set in Austria in 1957, about a religious boy who saves a train by spotting a fire he would not have noticed if he had succumbed to the temptation of going to the dining car like everyone else, to eat its unkosher food.

I asked Miriam if she ever read the classic fairy tales to her children, or any other secular books. She said she didn't, because she wanted the villains and heroes her children grew up with to be Jewish ones. On the coffee table in front of her was a small pile of gaily illustrated books. These were the sort of books that she read to her children at bedtime, she said, handing two small books to me. One was called *The Double Decker Purple Shul Bus*, the other *The Three Little Goats Who Went Shopping for Shabbos*. Like *The Moshiach Times*, the books were short on fancifulness, long on proscriptive moralizing. There was not the slightest chance that any child reading them would be led down the customary fairy-tale garden path to terror, unease, malice, or plain uncapped fantasy.

While Miriam and I had been talking, the rest of the guests had arrived. They included Bubbe, Dovid, and an ex-inmate of Allenwood Prison Camp with his wife and son (who were to spend most of the evening gazing at their hosts in awe). Mendel came in, accompanied by a slim young man with a neatly trimmed beard and well-cut vested suit who looked vaguely familiar. I asked Sheina who he was. She grinned and said, "Don't you know? Look again." I looked. It was Shmuel, transformed into a thin person. He had shed at least thirty pounds since the last time I had seen him. As we all assembled around the table I told him how well he looked and that I had hardly recognized him. He looked directly at me, for the first time since I had met him, and smiled.

"I, uh, just changed my eating habits."

"He eats like a rabbit now," Mendel said, clapping his brother affectionately on the shoulder. "No *kugel*, no *cholent*, just rabbit food."

I noticed that the two Iranian girls weren't there and asked Sheina about them. She said that they had moved to Pennsylvania, where a relative of theirs lived. They hadn't left a forwarding address and so far had not written or called to let anyone know what had become of them. Miriam and Bassy brought Bubbe over to meet me. Bubbe was so pale that most of the other pale people in the room seemed ruddy in comparison. She spoke very little English, I was told, but when Bassy explained to her in Yiddish who I was, her eyes managed to convey

interest and curiosity. She looked frail and not especially
well, and Miriam and Bassy guided her to her place between them at the table with great solicitude. Sheina had
told me that Bubbe's husband had died of starvation in
Russia during World War I but that she had somehow
found her way to Canada with her daughter (the children's
mother) and son.

Sheina showed Bubbe great deference, too, and seemed
not at all discomfited by the fact that her marriage to
Moshe had not caused any realignment of Bubbe's position in the family. All the bubbes' and zeydes' places in
their families were secure, of course, because though personality conflicts were as common in the Hasidic world
as anywhere else, the values of the older and younger
members of the family were the same. There was no generation gap. There were no Lubavitcher homes for the
elderly. Old people stay with their families until they
die, unless they get so sick that they have to be hospitalized. Hasidic children rarely rebel against their parents; they rebel against secular society. The modern goals
of innovativeness, independence, and originality that play
a role in most adolescent rebellions have no place in this
milieu. There is no way of being just a little rebellious,
either. You are not just offending your parents if you
stray from the fold, you are offending your entire family,
your teachers, your friends, your neighbors, the Rebbe,
and God. Few are willing or able to take on that kind of
burden. According to several recent surveys made by the
American Jewish Committee, a substantial number of
American Jews have ceased practicing their religion and
have only the most tenuous sense of religious identity.
The Lubavitchers have been doubling their numbers every
decade since the nineteen-fifties. This is attributable, in
part, to their high birthrate and successful proselytizing
campaign (typically, the converts are fairly young, fairly
well-educated men or women, in equal numbers, with min-

imal religious backgrounds), but it also reflects the fact
that so few people leave.

The seder was the most impressively formal occasion
I was to attend at the Konigsbergs'. By and large, most
modern American seders are fairly slapdash affairs. The
ones I had attended when I was young, which I suspect
were fairly typical, were jolly family gatherings that were
about as evocative of the perils of the Exodus as *Hogan's
Heroes* is of World War II. The men donned yarmulkes at
the last minute, and stumbled over the unfamiliar Hebrew
words they were called upon to intone; there were always
sympathetic winks for the children from some "free-
thinker" grownup who was eager to let us know that he
thought that all this was pretty irrelevant, and there was a
consensus that everything should be hurried along so that
everyone could get down to the serious business of eating
and drinking. The Konigsberg seder was slow moving and
stately. The rituals were performed meticulously and rev-
erentially, and there was so much discussion of the meaning of exile in the modern world that the meal itself did
not begin until eleven o'clock, though we had sat down
at eight-thirty. All present agreed that Jews were in a
permanent state of exile, and would continue to be until
the Messiah came, and that all attempts at assimilation
were futile and misguided. "Jews can never really become
a part of any other society," Miriam said, sipping from a
goblet of sweet kosher wine. "Even if they want to forget
that they're Jews, society can't forget it."

A perfunctory nod was made in the direction of politics.
Shmuel said that being in exile meant that the values of
the diaspora rarely meshed with those of the Jews. The
question arose as to whether President Carter had been
good for the Jews. Most agreed that he had not been,
because he sold out the Israelis at Camp David. The

Rebbe, who officially supports no candidate or party, is nevertheless known to hold strong views on various issues. Prime Minister Menachem Begin used to call on the Rebbe whenever he came to New York, but he never visited again after the Camp David Agreement, it was said, because he had displeased the Rebbe by yielding up what the Lubavitchers' leader believes to be the God-given soil of Sinai.

Even the most sophisticated members of the Hasidic world appear to regard all politics, all world events, from the point of view of this single issue. Unlike various Christian fundamentalist groups, the Lubavitchers steer clear of the larger political fray, regarding the political arena as too hopeless to merit their attention. But political opinions do surface, and when they do they are frequently startling. For example, shortly after the 1982 Beirut massacre, I attended a talk given by Rabbi Manis Friedman, director of the Beis Chanah Women's Institute, a Lubavitcher study center for women with little or no formal religious background, in Saint Paul, Minnesota. Rabbi Friedman, whom I had heard at several other Lubavitcher gatherings, is a young, amusing speaker who wears vested suits that are sometimes not black and has the knack of conveying complex Hasidic philosophy in easily digested, slightly slangy English. (It is his excellent translations which make the Rebbe's TV talks accessible to his English-speaking audience.) The events in the Middle East were unrelated to the main topics that evening (love and marriage) but someone brought up the subject of the events in Beirut anyway. Expecting a long and complex reaction from Rabbi Friedman, I was startled to hear the event summarily dismissed as yet another case of the world's anti-Semitic bias. "Why wasn't there a worldwide hue and cry after Ma'alot, or all the other times innocent Israelis have been killed by terrorists?" he asked. The sub-

ject of the alleged collusion of the Israelis or the morality
of the issues involved, never even surfaced.

Another concomitant of the Lubavitchers' view of themselves as permanent exiles in a strange land is their lack
of interest in and even cynicism about social change. "No
reshuffling of the furniture [i.e., socialism, communism,
or any other radical social movement] will ever change
things," Rabbi Friedman said that same evening. "You
have to bring goodness to the earth as you find it. Everything God created on heaven and earth is exactly as He
wanted it to be." In their efforts to communicate with
Jews of all stripes, this view translates into "let's also accept people for who they are" and has enhanced the
Lubavitchers' reputation as tolerant and modern. In local
politics, it has often meant that the Lubavitchers have
lined up with sadly retrograde politicians who can deliver favors in exchange for votes.

Several years ago, a Lubavitcher businessman was suspected of renting exclusively to Jews in his federally subsidized low-income housing. When confronted with this
by local officials he responded that he was "only trying to
integrate the neighborhood," since eighty percent of the
neighborhood was black. A Lubavitcher group including
the same landlord petitioned their Congressman, Charles
Schumer, to get HUD to give them more federally supported housing units. "But they wouldn't agree to put up
a 'For Rent' sign," an aide to Representative Schumer told
me recently, "because they wanted to put their own people
in the apartments. When HUD made the rule that you
could only get into these subsidized houses by lottery, they
were furious, though to be fair, almost all the city community groups opposed the lottery because they all wanted
the people who *they* knew needed the housing to get it."

Seven years ago, the City Council president, Carol Bellamy, issued a report that detailed various alleged abuses

of a Lubavitcher antipoverty and housing organization. According to an article that appeared in *City Limits* (a housing policy magazine) some time later, the report was the result of scores of rent strikes and complaints by tenants that were directed chiefly against one rabbi, David Fischer, who ran the organization and owned most of the buildings in question. The tenants of the largely four- and five-story walk-up buildings all had the same story to tell. The buildings, "located in the midst or at the fringe of the Lubavitcher community, all tenanted by families, most of them Hispanic or black (one building . . . housed mostly older non-Hasidic Jews) all suffered a . . . cessation of essential services." All the buildings had gone downhill when they had been purchased by a new owner, and the owner invariably turned out to be Rabbi Fischer. In most cases, the cessation of services was the prelude to "offers . . . and sometimes threats" designed to get the tenants to move out. All of the buildings, it turned out, had been accepted for some form of government-subsidized renovation. While the Bellamy report gave the tenants some welcome moral support, it carried no legal weight, since the City Council is not a law enforcement agency. The report was submitted to various local, state and federal agencies for further scrutiny, but after several years it sank into bureaucratic oblivion.

In the Lubavitcher community most men and women are so dedicated to leading lives of irreproachable probity that any charge of impropriety made against one of its members is invariably met with expressions of incredulity and, usually, denial. When asked by Tom Robbins, the author of the *City Limits* article, about the allegations made in the report, Yisroel Rosenfeld, a Lubavitcher who is the executive director of the Crown Heights Jewish Community Council and the neighborhood's elected district leader, said that the allegations were never more than "a smokescreen" for local political interests who objected to the presence of the Lubavitchers in Crown Heights. "If they were really true, do you think he'd [the landlord mentioned in the report] be out walking the streets? Wouldn't he have been indicted?"

Robbins believes that the report was never pursued by the various government agencies who received copies of it because government officials are afraid of incurring the wrath of the Hasidim, who always vote as a bloc. Gordon Haesloop, the general counsel at the City's Department of Investigation, one of the agencies that was given the report, disagrees. Nothing came of the report, he says, because no criminal acts were found. "There were irregularities, and there was some discrimination. HUD denied the corporation's right to receive any more funds. Perhaps the situation was that the city was glad to have the buildings rehabilitated. If the city had pressured the Lubavitcher group to provide more services in all likelihood the landlord would have said, 'That's too expensive. You do it,' and abandoned the building."

"I'm a hundred percent sure that *some* people do things a hundred percent wrong in a Hasidic community," Moshe said when I asked him if he knew about the alleged wrongdoings mentioned in the Bellamy report. "Just like they do everywhere else. This is not a neighborhood of angels, just a place where most people are trying to live a spiritual life." But he said he had not been aware of the Bellamy report, and did not know if the facts reported in it were true or not.

In the nineteen-fifties, when upper middle-class and middle-class blacks began moving into the neighborhood, there was little friction between the Hasidim and their new neighbors. In the nineteen-sixties, when confrontational politics became popular and the Lubavitchers felt threatened by the growing numbers of poor blacks and crimes committed in the neighborhood, relations between them and the black community were at their nadir. In 1964, a group called The Maccabees was formed. Feeling insufficiently protected by the police, its members took turns patrolling the streets at night in cars that had radio contact with their headquarters, which would relay calls for help to the Seventy-first Precinct. The Lubavitchers called it a street patrol. Others called it a vigilante group. There were several incidents in which people allegedly caught committing a crime were allegedly beaten up by members of The Maccabees before the police got there. Several years later, in part because police protection had been stepped up, in part because efforts had been made by leaders of the black and Lubavitcher communities to work together to make the neighborhood safe, the group was disbanded. Nowadays, it is the blacks who are apt to complain that they do not have enough police protection, and they accuse the Lubavitchers of wangling more than their fair share of it.

Although they maintain a passing interest in world events, the Lubavitchers are uninvolved in national or international politics except as they relate to Soviet Jewry or the State of Israel. Over the years, they have waged an intensive campaign to help Jews leave the Soviet Union. One international expert in this field, noting the Lubavitchers' success in this area, said that "the Rebbe has a staff around him who are experts at statecraft. The way to get somebody out of Russia is to write to the President and ask him to intervene on that person's behalf. Somehow, there's a mystique about the Rebbe that moves people to do things, and it's not related to the voting power of the community which is relatively modest. A lot of people get mad at the Rebbe, because he is opposed to all confrontational politics, like demonstrations for Soviet Jews. But he opposes them because he thinks that those

tactics only harden the resistance of the Soviets. He believes in moving quietly and keeping the pressure on, and
his methods seem to work. It's hard to argue with success."

Even though the Rebbe does not endorse candidates or
political parties, the word somehow gets around at elec-
tion time that a certain candidate is favored and inevitably
all of the community's two thousand registered voters cast
their votes for the same person. A photograph of a group
of eminent Lubavitchers smiling at a certain politician may
appear in the newspaper, or, in the days when the Rebbe
granted audiences, people would somehow learn that a
candidate had been granted an unusually long one, and
nothing further needed to be said.

The Lubavitchers have their own town in Israel, Kfar
Chabad; they support scores of institutions there, such as
schools, camps, and Chabad houses; and soldiers in the
field have become accustomed to seeing the Lubavitcher
Mitzvah Tanks roll up to the front lines. But they do not
belong to any political party, and no Lubavitcher representative sits in the Knesset. Israelis tend to consider the
Lubavitchers their good Hasidim, and the Satmarers, who
are vociferously anti-Zionist and oppose most Israeli policies, their bad Hasidim. Toward the end of the seder I
asked Moshe if the stories that I had heard about Satmarer
Hasidim attacking Mitzvah Tanks, or vandalizing news-
stands that carried the pro-Israel *Algemeiner Journal*
(whose editor and publisher is a Lubavitcher), were true.
He sighed deeply and looked at his hands.

"I don't want to say anything against other Jews but I'm
afraid they are true. There are those who say that in the
last days of exile all these bad things—even the Holocaust—are a last step before the Messiah comes."

"The Holocaust?"

"Some people believe that the Holocaust happened
when it did and where it did because Germany was where
most of the Jews who had abandoned Jewish ways lived."

"Are you saying that that's why all those people died, because they incurred the wrath of God?"

"No. No one knows why they died. I'm just saying that some people believe that all those bad things happened for a reason. We may not know the reason, but there always is one."

CHAPTER EIGHT

The Satmarers
and
the Lubavitchers

Pinchas Korf, a neighbor of the Konigsbergs on President Street, is a mild-mannered man in his later forties who is known not only as a gifted scholar and teacher but as a kind of Hasid's Hasid. A friend who has known him for most of his life described him as being "full of heart and wisdom. If I were asked, who do you know who best lives up to Hasidic ideals, it would be Pinky Korf." The Hasidic community has such a lively word-of-mouth network that Rabbi Korf's abilities as a teacher were spoken of with admiration even among the young Satmarer students in Williamsburg. One of them, an eighteen-year-old student named David Kohn, asked Rabbi Korf if he would teach him Hasidic philosophy, specifically the *Tanya*. Rabbi Korf agreed to do it and they met at the boy's request at his father's frame shop and factory at the corner of Broadway and Union Avenue, in Williamsburg. After the first meeting, which took place in the spring of 1983, the young man telephoned Rabbi Korf and asked him if he would mind teaching him at his father's store again. Rabbi Korf said that he would prefer meeting at the boy's home but the boy said that his parents would allow them to meet only in his father's office. Rabbi Korf hesitated. He was worried about his safety in a Satmarer neighborhood and about calling attention to himself by sitting with the boy in so public a place. Only a few weeks before, a Lubavitcher Hasid who lived in Williamsburg and had been receiving visits from Satmarer students had been stoned and received death threats. That week *The Jewish Press* carried a story headlined "A Family Mourns In Williamsburg Because Son Becomes Lubavitch Hasid." The story, which described what every Hasid knows—the deep enmity the Satmarers feel for the Lubavitchers—quoted one Satmarer leader as saying, "It's worse than if he was to join the Moonies." Rabbi Korf also feared exposing his family to the same trials as Mendel Wechter's. Rabbi Wechter was a Satmarer Hasid who had chosen to study Lubavitcher texts to heal the rift between the two groups. When it was discovered that Rabbi Wechter's students were reading Lubavitcher books, his wife was fired from her teaching job at the Satmarer girls' school and the family began to get threatening phone calls. Eventually, they were forced to leave Williamsburg for Boro Park, but even after they moved protests were held outside their house, including one in which a hundred people pelted it with eggs and stones.

In late May, reassured by his student that everything would be all right, Rabbi Korf agreed to meet him in his father's office, and on the appointed day they sat down as usual to study. A few minutes later, six men burst into the room, sent the father and son into the next room, took the telephone off the hook, threw Rabbi Korf down on the floor, cut off his beard, beat him, and threatened to kill him if he ever returned to Williamsburg.

Lubavitcher officials, who had in the past played down Satmarer provocations, decided that this time things had gone too far.

"This was clearly a set up," said Yehuda Krinsky, a Lubavitcher spokesman, shortly after the incident. "When you teach nothing but hatred, there's no way that young people are going to act intelligently and morally. But we're not going to just sit back and take it this time."

A week or so later, a twenty-eight-year-old Satmarer official named Jacob Cohen was arrested and charged with participating in the attack on Rabbi Korf. The Lubavitchers asked the Satmarers to condemn the attack, but the Satmarers did not oblige them. A short while later, the Lubavitchers' *Beth Din* convened and placed a ban on all Satmarer products. Although the Brooklyn District Attorney was charged with prosecuting the case, the Lubavitchers also hired their own lawyers to oversee their interests.

Difficult as it may be to believe, the Satmarer–Lubavitcher feud can be traced to purely ideological causes. One of them is that the Lubavitchers have succeeded in capturing the imaginations of a large number of young Jews, among them some Satmarers. After years of disfavor, Orthodoxy has grown in recent years in America, and the Lubavitcher ranks have swelled with Jews from all walks of life. The Satmarers, unlike the Lubavitchers, do not proselytize, keep to themselves, and, like most other Hasidic groups, rely on their own high birthrate to keep themselves going. Though the number of known defectors has never been reckoned to be more than a handful, every loss is considered a grave blow.

But the deeper source of enmity between the two groups is their disagreement about the State of Israel. The Satmarers believe that a true Jewish state cannot exist until the arrival of the Messiah and that the existence of a democratic Jewish state that functions independently of Jewish laws is sacrilege. An ad that the American *Neturei Karta* ("Keepers of the City"), a group affiliated with the Satmarers, placed in the *New York Times* shortly after Egypt and Israel signed a peace treaty states their position succinctly: "Neither peace treaties nor payments, neither arms nor politics determine or even influence the attitude of the Jewish people toward the Zionist state which had the audacity to usurp the holy name of Israel. The prophets of old castigated any wrongdoing by the Jewish rulers of that time. What would they have to say about today's Zionist rulers who want to substitute their fraudulent manmade sovereignty for . . . the written and oral Law in Jewish life, who want to break the Divine Covenant with the Jewish people and replace it with a prejudiced and blind chauvinism?"

Extreme as it may sound, this view of Israel was in fact *the* view shared by most of the Orthodox rabbis of Europe before World War I. As the scholar Allan Nadler pointed out several years ago in the periodical *Judaism*, "Most of the leading Rabbis of Eastern Europe viewed political Zionism with deep suspicion if not outright contempt, for this movement was accurately perceived as yet another outcome of the dangerous . . . Jewish enlightenment, or *Haskalah*, whose goal was the radical alteration of traditional Jewish society in Europe. Those rabbis who ended up joining Zionist ranks were almost always relative unknowns in the rabbinic world and they never represented more than a small minority . . . The world's acknowledged leading Talmudists were almost without exception bitterly opposed to the Zionist plan to 'normalize' the Chosen People, for the Zionist dream represented a rejection of traditional Jewish values and its realization would mean the total destruction of traditional Jewish life in Europe." The rabbis' worst fears were realized, of course, not by Zionism, but by the Holocaust, which destroyed every semblance of traditional Jewish life and every Jewish

community as well. In the postwar world the presence of
a Jewish homeland and place of refuge made any notion
of anti-Zionism absurd. As Nadler wrote, "Orthodoxy's
ideological battle with Zionism was over—almost. One
lonely but determined sage of pre-War Europe adamantly
refused . . . to grant any legitimacy to the successes of
the 'heresy.' That was Rabbi Joel Teitelbaum [the former
Satmarer rebbe] who continued the old Rabbinic war with
Jewish nationalism as if nothing had changed."

Rabbi Teitelbaum died several years ago, but his
nephew, who took over the leadership, shows no sign of
temporizing his group's position. When the Belzer grand
rebbe, who lives in Israel, came to visit his followers several
years ago, the Belzers were terrorized by the Satmarers. It
was even rumored that the venerable rabbi's life had been
threatened, and Mayor Koch was called upon to intervene.
The Belzers are so fearful of Satmar violence that they
park the school buses that carry them en masse to their
Manhattan jobs in the black neighborhood of Bedford-
Stuyvesant rather than the Williamsburg section, where
most of them live, for fear of having them vandalized.

To those unacquainted with the philosophic reasons behind the Satmarers' anti-Zionism, and indeed to many of
those acquainted with them, the Satmarers' picketing of
pro-Zionist rallies, their anti-Zionist demonstrations outside
the United Nations, their attacks on pro-Israeli groups, and
their terrorizing of Lubavitcher teachers do not look much
different from the worst kind of anti-Semitic thuggery.
The Lubavitchers probably bear the brunt of the Satmarers' enmity because they are so visible: visibly religious
and openly helpful to Israel. They do not, in fact, consider
themselves Zionists. Ideologically, they agree with the Satmarers that only the Messiah can rule the Holy Land. They
are pro-Israel because, as Rabbi Krinsky put it, "We are
Jews and Israel is a land of Jews." Rabbi Krinsky, whom
I talked with in his modest, cluttered office in the back

reaches of 770, said that he thought that the Satmarers were as violent as they were because "they live in a philosophical void. The young people are not taught much Hasidic philosophy. They do everything by rote. Why do they burn the Israeli flag? Because first they teach their young to hate Zionism, then they teach them to hate Zionists, then they teach them to hate anyone who isn't like them. Our teachings are diametrically opposed to theirs. There is no Lubavitcher–Satmarer feud, as the newspapers are always suggesting. We have no quarrel with them. But dressing like a Hasid and going to shul does not make you a Hasid. Piety and adherence to the ways of the Torah do. Hasids don't attack other people. Hasids don't defame other Jews. In fact, according to the Talmud, the Second Temple was destroyed because of 'causeless hatred.' For thirty years, Lubavitchers walked as a group among the Jews of Williamsburg on Passover to show our solidarity with other Jews. But in 1977 we were attacked on their streets, so we don't do it anymore. And this hatred did not originate in America, either. I have a file going back fifty years that documents the Satmarers' penchant for violence." Reaching into a fat folder, Rabbi Krinsky pulled out a yellowed front page of a Yiddish newspaper published in Transylvania on the twenty-eighth of June 1935. The headline was "Rabbi Teitelbaum's Students Kill People. Teitelbaum Has 300 Jewish Hitlers Who Squash Their Opponents," and the story beneath it described the violent tactics used by Rabbi Teitelbaum to trounce the opposition when he sought to become Chief Rabbi of the city of Satu-Mare.

If the Lubavitchers are not Zionists per se, of course, their support of aggressive Israeli politics goes a bit further than they are wont to admit. As Nadler pointed out, "During the Yom Kippur war, the Lubavitcher Rebbe called upon the Israelis to take Damascus. The advice was presented not as his individual opinion, which is what it was,

but as his considered religious ruling—an expression of
Da'as Torah, the sacred view of Halakhic Judaism. Since
1973, the Lubavitcher Rebbe has been a vocal proponent
of West Bank annexation. He has also condemned the
Camp David Agreement and advised Israel to recapture
the Sinai, for he insists that the Torah absolutely forbids
the Jews to relinquish so much as one inch of the Holy
Land to 'idolators.' "

The Satmarers regard all manifestations of Israel's defense policy as contrary to their deepest beliefs. At his
rallies, at which a huge American flag usually covered the
wall behind the dais, Rabbi Teitelbaum frequently denounced the Zionist platform and particularly Israeli defense policies in the strongest terms. The only appropriate
method of international statecraft, he believed, was *Shtadlanut*—the form of diplomacy employed by Jewish lobby-
ists at the royal courts during the Middle Ages, and for
centuries the *only* form of diplomacy available to those
who represented Jewish interests.

Bribery, pleading, placation, and appeasement were the
tools of Jewish court diplomats, never confrontation. As
Nadler pointed out, "The entire Zionist platform, especially the defense policy of the Jewish State, constitutes a
radical departure from the philosophy and methods of
Shtadlanut," and was deplored by Teitelbaum. Rabbi
Teitelbaum also dismissed as unworkable all plans for permanent peace in the Middle East and regularly denounced
those who devised them. He had a plan of his own and it
was remarkably simple: "If the Zionists were only to give
up, there would be no more sorrows in Israel," he said.
"For now, too, . . . they would undoubtedly remove the
wrath of God and all of these hardships would vanish."

Oddly enough, it was the Zionists who saved Rabbi
Teitelbaum's life during the war. In the spring of 1944,
a famous Hungarian Zionist leader, Rudolf Kasztner, negotiated a deal with Adolf Eichmann, who was then the SS's

negotiator on emigration matters, in which some seventeen hundred Hungarian and refugee Jews (Kasztner had originally asked for one hundred thousand) were to be allowed to leave the country in exchange for goods, jewelry, and money. Initially the Satmarer rebbe's name was not on the list of those who were to be included in the "Kasztner transport" (as it came to be known), which was not surprising, since the list had been drawn up chiefly by Zionists. One night, however, Kasztner's father-in-law had a dream in which his deceased mother told him that if the Satmarer rebbe were not included among those in the convoy, all the people in it were doomed. When he told the Zionist leaders about his dream, they decided to include Rabbi Teitelbaum and his entourage in the convoy. At first, Eichmann reneged on his part of the bargain, which was that the train carrying the Jews would be seen safely to Vienna and then to Lisbon. Instead, the transport went to Bergen-Belsen where the passengers were detained. The Germans, through Heinrich Himmler, had demanded more money. After several months, Kasztner agreed to pay the Germans twenty million more Swiss francs, five million to be paid in advance, and the balance after the group arrived in Switzerland, its new destination. Once again the transport started off, but as the train drew near the Swiss border, to which two German officials had been dispatched, a cable arrived from Himmler demanding that all the money be paid before the train crossed over. Astonishingly, and for reasons that have never been made entirely clear, the train passed safely across the border in disregard of Himmler's orders. According to the Satmarers, Himmler's instructions arrived just as the train was approaching the border and the station master, a kind-hearted gentile, took pity on the convoy, admitted the train, and stamped the cable "received" one minute after it had crossed the border.

Although he owed his life to the Zionists, neither Rabbi

Teitelbaum's position nor his rhetoric betrayed the slightest sign of softening after the war. Another bizarre theory of the Satmarer rebbe's was that Zionism was the root cause of modern anti-Semitism as well as World War II. The idea was that the Zionists somehow whipped up Nazi anti-Semitism so that the Jews of Europe would be obliged to concede the need for a Jewish state. Further, Teitelbaum suggested (in terms that were indistinguishable from the rhetoric of the worst Jew baiters) that there was an international Zionist group that conspired to make sure that none of the free-world countries would accept refugees, so that fleeing Jews would have no possible haven but the Zionist state.

One of the few people in the Hasidic world who has suggested that the Satmarers and the Lubavitchers ought to consider a *rapprochement* is Mendel Wechter, the thirty-seven-year-old Satmarer scholar who was forced to leave Williamsburg when his neighbors learned that he was studying and teaching Lubavitcher texts. Rabbi Wechter tried to point out to those who would listen that since both groups actually shared the same religious view of Zionism, there was no real basis for the Satmarers' animosity. His efforts came to nothing, of course; worse, they seemed only to rub salt on a raw wound. The Satmarers blamed him for putting dangerous thoughts into their children's heads and encouraging students like David Kohn to lose their way. After Rabbi Korf was attacked, a Satmarer spokesman said that he saw the attack on the rabbi as "the result of a war being waged over the minds of young children and men. It's mind control and cultism at its worst."

Even though Rabbi Wechter had moved to Boro Park and now considered himself a Lubavitcher, he continued to be an irritant to some Satmarers. But most of his friends assumed that the distance he had put between himself and Williamsburg would make his foes forget him. Then,

three weeks after the attack on Rabbi Korf, a blue van
drove up to Rabbi Wechter's house at 6:10 A.M., just as
he was leaving for morning prayers. Five masked men
jumped out, shoved him in the van, drove him about a mile
and released him, but not before shearing off his beard and
removing all his clothes except for his underwear. In the
fracas, his ankle was broken and he had to be taken to the
hospital, where he was treated for lacerations of the back
and face as well as the broken ankle.

The incidents provoked a flurry of responses. The Satmarers denied that the attack had anything to do with anyone in their community and one of their spokesmen said
that he hoped that the attackers would be brought to
justice. The following week a four-column ad appeared
in *The Jewish Press* further disassociating the Satmarers
from the event and accusing the Lubavitchers of having
"heaped shame on all Jews [by] going to the non-Jewish
media" (all the local papers had carried stories about the
attacks) and "blowing these incidents out of proportion."

The Konigsbergs scoffed at the Satmarers' denials. So did
Rabbi Krinsky, who said that he knew that the attackers
were Satmarers because the men who cut off Rabbi Korf's
beard had warned him that Rabbi Wechter was next.
Krinsky told a reporter from *The Jewish Press* that "there's
a hit list," and that he knew who was on it. A meeting was
held on the Korf case in late June, but further motions were
postponed because the lawyers had not finished preparing
their cases. The meeting would have been fairly uneventful
had not a group of Satmarers attacked a *Daily News* photographer and damaged his camera. (When the trial finally
took place, a year later, Jacob Cohen was acquitted. Rabbi
Korf's young Satmarer student had signed an affidavit saying that Cohen had not been present during the attack and
again denied in court having seen him that day. When he
gave his testimony at the trial, he looked extremely uncomfortable and stared at his lap a lot. Pinchas Korf was certain

that Cohen had been the leader of his assailants and had identified him in a lineup. The Lubavitchers claimed afterward that they had good reason to believe that the boy himself had been threatened and also that he had been told that since it was not a religious court it did not matter if he lied.)

After the postponement, an "Open Letter to the Satmar Community" appeared in *The Jewish Press*, signed by Mendel Shemtov, a Lubavitcher businessman, which accused the Satmarers of saying that they would punish anyone who had participated in the acts of violence against fellow Jews but not acting on their promise. *Der Yid*, the Satmarer organ, had carried a story the previous week in which a Satmarer leader had said that the "severest measures will be taken against anyone who commits such harmful acts. It will not be tolerated that people commit criminal acts on their own . . . If we find out that those who commit these acts are from our community we will expel them . . ."

Echoing the skepticism of most Lubavitchers about this statement, Mr. Shemtov challenged the Satmarers to follow through on their promise. Brushing aside the fact that the arrested man had not yet been convicted, he pointed out that one of their number had already been "indicted and charged with three counts, punishable by imprisonment. The victim of the first beard-shearing clearly identified him as his assailant. If the Satmar leadership is seriously concerned with finding those responsible for such acts as they too label disgraceful, then they have the *Halakhic* and moral duty to have this individual summoned before their Rabbinic court and dealt with accordingly."

There the matter rested for a while, except that letters kept pouring into the office of *The Jewish Press* from advocates of both sides. After several weeks of publishing the letters, the paper posted the following notice on its front page: "In the interest of Shalom-Peace, *The Jewish Press* will refrain from publishing any further letters about the Satmar-Lubavitch quarrel. We received many letters on this dispute and to publish them would only fan the fires of hate."

CHAPTER NINE

Education

O<small>NE</small> balmy spring evening, Moshe, Sheina, and I met for dinner at Moshe Peking, a *glatt* kosher Chinese Restaurant on West Thirty-seventh Street. Moshe Peking was one of the few restaurants in the city they frequented. (Recently they have stopped eating there, because Moshe has no way of knowing whether some of the banned Satmarer products were being used in the restaurant's kitchen; even when he did frequent it he never ate any meat, because he will not eat any meat that has not been butchered by a butcher he knows.) The menu differed from that of an ordinary Chinese restaurant chiefly in its omission of pork and seafood dishes. Veal was substituted for pork in its "Moo Soo" dish, and kosher fish for shellfish in the "Pho-Nee Shrimp in Mock Lobster Sauce." But the food was good, the service cordial, and Moshe and Sheina seemed more relaxed than I had ever seen them. Toward the end of the meal, I asked, half jokingly, what Moshe thought the chief difference between men and women was. He answered unhesitatingly, "Women rule the heart, men the intellect." Sheina nodded in agreement.

Most Hasidic men and women probably share Moshe's belief, and its institutional nexus is that the education of boys is quite different from that of girls. From the earliest pre-kindergarten years, the boys and girls attend separate schools. Although the education of women is considered important, and Lubavitcher schools maintain high standards, it is probably fair to say that there is no serious expectation of turning out scholars of distinction from the girls' schools. The young girls learn about the Bible, about the religious holidays, and about the dietary laws. When the boys get old enough to learn Hasidic philosophy, they study it for about three hours a day; the girls study it for forty-five minutes. Both boys and girls attend school six days a week, Sunday through Friday, although Friday is actually a half-day because of the Sabbath. The boys are on this six-day schedule from the age of four on, but despite the fact that girls are known to mature earlier than boys, the girls do not attend school on Sunday until they are six. The high-school boys' day ends at 9:30 P.M.; the girls' day at 4:45 P.M. After high school, when most of the local boys go on to various yeshivas—mainly to the modern, spacious Lubavitcher campus in Morristown, New Jersey—girls who wish to pursue their studies attend "seminary" in another wing of the same shabby, overcrowded building they sat in when they were in kindergarten. Like the kindergarten girls, they, too, are exempted from studying on Sunday, and while their brothers (many of whom are on their way to ordination) are expected to be at their studies until about 9:30 in the evening, the second-year girls'-seminary students are finished with their studies at 12:30 P.M.

At Machon Chanah, the Women's Institute for Judaic

Studies, a Lubavitcher yeshiva for *baalot teshuvah* on Eastern Parkway, the day is longer and the workload more intensive; they begin at 8:30 A.M. and finish at 9:30 P.M. But
in their case the hours are long because, as one of the teachers put it, "They have so much catching up to do." I sat
in on a class there just after Passover. Perhaps the students I saw were not a representative lot, because most
of the student body had not yet returned from visiting
their families for the holidays and only a few students
were on hand, but the ones I saw seemed a little like
orphans. The teacher was a plump fellow with nervous
gestures and rumpled clothes who gazed into the middle
distance most of the time with an expression that might
have been interpreted either as profound concentration
or cosmic boredom. The class was reading and interpret-
ing a bit of Biblical text. The women stumbled quite a lot
over the Hebrew words of the text but they offered their
exegeses avidly and sometimes lengthily, trying hard to
win the approval of their distracted mentor. I talked to
a number of them at a lunch break in the basement. They
all appeared to have been dealt fairly bad blows in life by
one thing or another, and though they were all ages and
came from diverse backgrounds, an aura of almost preter-
natural fatigue hung over the group like a chill fog. The
dormitory that the younger *baalot teshuvah* live in is
on President Street, not far from the Rebbe's house.
A rambling, mahogany-paneled mansion, it is one of the
most elegant houses on the block. When officials of the
school set out to find a suitable dormitory, one of them
told me, the Rebbe directed them to spare no expense in
finding a cheerful, inviting house. The Rebbe takes a keen
interest in the school (which has been around since 1972
and is named after his mother) and in the well-being and
education of the *baalot teshuvah* in general.

I spoke briefly with the head of the girls' school, Beis
Rivkah, which is located on Crown Street, and with the

head of one of the local boys' elementary schools, The
United Lubavitcher Yeshivot, on Ocean Parkway. The
girls'-school principal stressed the ways the school prepared
its students for life, the boys'-school principal stressed the
school's high scholastic standards. However, while they
may feel different about their students' futures, both ad-
ministrators expressed their institutional aims in nearly
identical language: they wanted their charges to wake up
in the morning, eat, learn, and go to sleep like Jews. Both
schools have accredited academic programs, but secular
subjects are taught in the afternoon. The morning hours,
when the students' minds are freshest, are devoted to
religious studies. In Lubavitcher classrooms it is the
Rebbe, not George Washington, whose portrait hangs
above the blackboard. Token curricular nods are made
in the direction of fresh air and exercise, and some of the
boys have what is usually perceived as a kind of raffish
interest in national sports. ("Berel here knows all about
baseball. This kid is on the ball," the principal of the
boys' school said to me in one of the classrooms. "Berel,
tell this lady who has the highest batting average in the
American League.") But, talking to some of them, I discovered that even among the young, certain parts of the
American folkways, such as cheerleaders, varsity compe-
titions, idolization of actors, rock singers, or sports figures
were considered silly—*goyim naches* (Christian pleasures).

Watching a line of little boys following their redheaded
teacher to the cafeteria for lunch, I wondered, not for the
first time, why so many Hasidic children (and Hasidic
adults, for that matter) look pale and weakly. No one,
to my knowledge, has ever provided a satisfactory answer
to this question (or to the equally commonplace "Why do
Hasidim wear black?"). It may be because they spend so
much time indoors, like the little Russian-Jewish boys
described by Isaac Babel, who saw the sun only when
they crossed the street for their violin lessons. It may be

their diet, which is long on fats and carbohydrates and short on raw fruits and vegetables, or it may be because they exercise so little. I had also observed that many Hasidim seemed to marry their cousins, or people whose families came from the same part of Europe that their own ancestors hailed from, and I wondered if this amounted to an excessive inbreeding. A doctor I talked with at Albert Einstein Hospital, who counsels many Jewish couples who are concerned about bearing a child with Tay-Sachs disease, dismissed the idea. "I'm not sure that if they dressed and groomed themselves more like everybody else, they'd look all that different from other people," he said.

I was not permitted to visit any of the older boys' schools—although I was quite keen on seeing in action the traditional yeshiva pedagogical custom of having the boys study in pairs, constantly questioning and challenging each other—because the official in charge of such matters thought that a visit from a woman would be too "disruptive." But shortly after I visited the modern, well-equipped school for young boys, I paid a visit to Beis Rivkah. Bassy and Miriam were both alumnae of Beis Rivkah, and now they were teachers there. The Beis Rivkah school building is decrepit, drafty, and charmlessly old. Its dark, cavernous lobby calls to mind English bomb shelters. Most of the teachers are women. In one classroom I visited, however, an older man with a German accent was discussing feminism with a class of fourteen-year-olds. In a voice heavy with scorn, he was deprecating the average secular woman as a self-hating, insecure, lonely creature who felt compelled to prove her worth to the world by finding some meaningless work that would give her life definition. But were these women happy? he asked rhetorically, answering his own question with a derisive smile. Except for the one or two girls who were dozing, the girls shook their heads and answered his smile with knowing smiles of their own. The teacher was one of the most popular in the school, my guide had whispered to me as we entered his classroom.

Bassy had invited me to spend the morning in her class-room. On the way I looked in on Miriam's class in Bible history. As I entered, Miriam and the class were laughing about something. The girls were looking at her admiringly and I was struck by how animated her features were. At our last meeting Miriam had told me how much she en-joyed teaching, and said that she was supported immea-surably by the ready availability of any number of trust-worthy and competent women in the community she could leave her children with.

Bassy dimpled when she saw me in her doorway. Turn-ing toward her twenty-three five-year-old charges, she said, "Children, what do we do when an older person comes in the room?" The girls scrambled to their feet and shouted, "SHALOM!" After that, they sang a song, in Yiddish, about giving a charity penny to a little girl. Vi-king mariners could not have sounded lustier. They were almost bellowing, and when they went on to another song about the pleasures of doing good deeds (to the tune of "Frère Jacques") the singing became, if possible, even more enthusiastic. Bassy smiled benignly at them. The room was decorated with cut-out Hebrew letters, numbers illus-trated with symbols of Jewish life, and pictures of Biblical scenes. Semiopaque paper had been taped to the windows to keep the draft out. It was a shabby but cheerful room, equipped with most of the standard things (blocks, dolls, paints, and puzzles) that please young children. The girls wore dressier clothes than most young nursery or kin-dergarten children usually wear, but the slightly formal clothes did not appear to cramp their style.

Bassy asked the class, "What do we do every morning when we get up?"

"WE PRAY!"

"And how do we hold our hands?"

"TOGETHER!"

"What are we praying for? One at a time now, raise your hands. Yes, Chanah."

"We are thanking God for giving us our *neshama* [soul] back."

"Very good, children, very good."

The classroom routine was a curious mix of learning by rote, praying, lackadaisical play, and wildly unbridled singing. Bassy was far more tolerant of her pupils' high jinks than many a modern teacher would be. On the other hand, when the din got to be too much, she exacted instant silence by ringing an enormous wooden-handled brass bell, a device that most modern teachers would probably consider as outdated as the Rack.

While the girls were painting some plastic flowers, an elfin, dark-skinned girl wearing tiny pearl earrings and Mary Janes came up to me to examine a brooch I was wearing. She told me that she had attended a circumcision ceremony the day before.

"It wasn't my mother's baby," she explained. "My mother's not pregnant yet."

"Mine is," said a little red-haired girl standing next to her.

"So is mine," piped up another. And another. It emerged that at least three quarters of the children in the room had pregnant mothers or had recently welcomed a baby brother or sister to their homes. Chatting with them, I learned that most of their mothers had attended Beis Rivkah. When it was clean-up time, the girls vied for the privilege of washing the paint splotches off the tables.

"Let me, *Morah* [teacher], let me!"

Bassy worked only a half-day. The children would be with another teacher in the afternoon. As we walked the children down to the lunchroom, I asked the little girl with the pearl earrings what she would like to be when she grew up. She pretended to think about the question, then grinned broadly, "A mother." A chorus of "me too's" echoed down the hallway. As it happened, I'd asked the same question of a kindergarten class at the boys' school. None of them wanted to be firemen, policemen, or astronauts. The boys' equally unanimous answer was, "A father."

Walking home from school Bassy told me that Shmuel had gotten engaged to a girl from upstate New York, the sister of a friend of his. We talked a little about her own student days. She had enjoyed school a lot, she said, and did not agree with those, like Sheina's daughter Tracy, who said that being shut off from the world so much did young women harm. It seemed unimportant to her that she had not been allowed to dance, swim, play sports, or move about socially with boys.

"You didn't wish you could have seen boys more, when you were a teenager?" (She had just turned twenty.)

A bored shrug of the shoulders. "It was no problem. My friends and I had a great time. We didn't worry about whether the boys liked us or didn't like us. We didn't get depressed when a boy didn't call us up, and we didn't have to think, 'What should I be, who should I be?' We just studied what we had to study. I know that Tracy enjoys her life but I want different things from mine. The main difference is that mine is one of commitment, discipline and restraint."

I asked her if she ever did anything just for fun.

"Well, I play the piano a lot. I still give piano lessons to about eight girls, and there are the Lubavitcher girls' conventions that take place every year. They are big money-raising events that we put on plays for. Sometimes they're in New York, sometimes they're out-of-town. We stay up all night getting ready for them and we get a great feeling of closeness working hard together. Sometimes we went to hospitals . . . and I've been going to Lubavitcher summer camps, first as a camper, then as a

counselor, since I was seven. I've been to camps in upstate New York, in Michigan, in California, and in Israel.
I made good friends in camp."

"Were you paid when you worked as a counselor?"

Bassy seemed surprised by the question, as if the idea
had never occurred to her. "No, we worked as volunteers."

I had not been in the school when the science teacher
was there, but I wondered how the Lubavitchers, who believed that the world was created some 5,750 years ago,
handled the subject of evolution. I asked Bassy about it.

"We skip it," she said, as we walked up the steps of her
house. "We don't have to take the biology Regents; we
take, say, the chemistry one instead, so we don't put ourselves in the position of giving an answer that we consider
right but the Board of Regents would say was wrong."

"Are you ever troubled by the scientific evidence that
points to the earth's being billions of years older than you
are taught it is?"

"Not at all," she said, turning the key in the front door
lock. "Scientific theories are always being revised and
rejected. Who is to say who's right? Have you read the
Rebbe's letter about evolution? I think that would answer
your question better than I can."

Later that week I obtained a copy of the letter Bassy had
mentioned. It had been written twenty years ago by the
Rebbe to a friend who, unlike Bassy, was troubled by
being unable to reconcile what he believed to be scientific
truth about the age of the world with the Torah view of
such matters. Since then, the letter had become the Lubavitchers' polestar on the subject. The Rebbe begins his
letter, which has faint echoes of his Sorbonne days under
the tutelage of Cartesians, by saying that trying to "reconcile" science and Torah is a hopeless task since "science
formulates and deals with theories and hypotheses, while
the Torah deals with absolute truths. These are two different disciplines, where 'reconciliation' is entirely out of

place." He goes on to attack the world's docile acceptance of scientific theories as fact and points out that most known scientific theories are based on interpolation and extrapolation and that "all speculation regarding the origin and age of the world comes within the second and weaker method, that of extrapolation . . . It is small wonder (and this, incidentally, is one of the obvious refutations of these theories) that the various 'scientific' theories concerning the age of the universe not only contradict each other, but some of them are quite incompatible and mutually exclusive, since the maximum date of one theory is less than the minimum date of another.

"If one accepts such a theory uncritically, it can only lead him into fallacious and inconsequential reasoning. Consider, for example, the so-called evolutionary theory of the origin of the world, which is based on the assumption that the universe evolved out of existing atomic and subatomic particles which, by an evolutionary process, combined to form the physical universe and our planet, on which organic life somehow developed also by an evolutionary process, until 'homo sapiens' emerged. It is hard to understand why one should readily accept the creation of atomic and subatomic particles in a state which is admittedly unknowable and inconceivable, yet should be reluctant to accept the creation of planets, or organisms, or a human being, as we know these to exist. . . .

"In view of the unknown conditions which existed in 'prehistoric' times, conditions of atmospheric pressures, temperatures, radioactivity, unknown catalyzers . . . conditions, that is, which could have caused reactions and changes of an entirely different nature and tempo from those known under the present-day orderly processes of nature, one cannot exclude the possibility that dinosaurs existed 5722 years ago, and became fossilized under terrific natural cataclysms in the course of a few years rather than in millions of years, since we have no conceivable

measurements or criteria of calculations under those unknown conditions."

I was not surprised to learn that the Rebbe did not feel
that his argument was weakened by the fossil finds of our
century. But his interpretation of the meaning of fossil
evidence (which bears a remarkable similarity to that of
the nineteenth-century British fundamentalist minister
Philip Gosse, whom I doubt he ever read) must be one
of the boldest attempts ever made to fit scripture and geol-
ogy together.

"Even assuming that the period of time which the
Torah allows for the age of the world is definitely too
short for fossilization (although I do not see how one can
be so categorical), we can still readily accept the possibility that G-d created ready fossils, bones or skeletons
(for reasons best known to Him), just as He could create
ready living organisms, a complete man, and such ready
products as oil, coal or diamonds, without any evolutionary
process . . . The question, Why create a fossil? is no more
valid than the question, Why create an atom? . . .

"If the theories attempting to explain the origin and age
of the world are so weak, how could they have been advanced in the first place? The answer is simple. . . . It is a
human ambition to be inventive and original. To accept
the Biblical account deprives one of the opportunity to
show one's analytic and inductive ingenuity. Hence, disregarding the Biblical account, the scientist must devise
reasons to 'justify' his doing so, and he takes refuge in
classifying it with ancient and primitive 'mythology' and
the like, since he cannot really argue against it on scientific
grounds.

"If you are still troubled by the theory of evolution, I
can tell you without fear of contradiction that it has not
a shred of *evidence* to support it. On the contrary, during
the years of research and investigation since the theory
was first advanced, it had been possible to observe certain

species of animal and plant life of a short life-span over thousands of generations, yet it has never been possible to establish a transmutation from *one species into another*, much less to turn a plant into an animal. Hence such a theory can have no place in the arsenal of empirical science.

"The theory of evolution . . . actually has no bearing on the Torah account of Creation. For even if the theory of evolution were substantiated today, and the mutation of species were proven in laboratory tests, this would still not contradict the possibility of the world having been created as stated in the Torah rather than through the evolutionary process . . .

"Needless to say, it is not my intent to cast aspersions on science or to discredit the scientific method. Science cannot operate except by accepting certain *working theories* or hypotheses, even if they cannot be verified, though some theories die hard even when they are scientifically refuted or discredited (the evolutionary theory is a case in point). No technical progress would be possible unless certain physical 'laws' are accepted, even though there is no guaranty that the 'law' will repeat itself. However, I do wish to emphasize, as already mentioned, that science has to do only with *theories* but not with certainties. All scientific conclusions, or generalizations, can only be probable in a greater or lesser degree according to the precautions taken in the use of the available evidence, and the degree of probability necessarily decreases with the distance from the empirical facts, or with the increase of the unknown variables . . . If you will bear this in mind, you will readily realize that there can be no real conflict between any scientific theory and the Torah."

CHAPTER TEN

Frummies and B.T.s

A CONVOCATION of Lubavitcher women, The Lubavitcher Women's Group, *Neshei U'Bnos Chabad,* is holding its annual convention on a spring weekend. Some three thousand five hundred women from fifty states and a handful from Canada, Australia, South Africa, and Israel have come to Crown Heights to see one another and hear various speakers, including the Rebbe, address themselves to the theme "Reaching Above and Beyond." Speeches, coffee klatches, and meetings are scheduled from Friday through Monday, but the Rebbe's address on Sunday evening is considered the highlight of the convention.

By late Friday afternoon, swarms of women fill the streets. The men, who usually dominate the streets in the pre-Sabbath dusk, have disappeared. Small battalions of synthetically coiffed women in regulation Hasidic garb—knee-and-elbow-hiding conservative suits and dresses—scurry to the places that they have been bivouacked for

the weekend. Although there are few families that have
not opened their homes to the visitors, a large percentage
of the convention's population appears to have found its
way to the Konigsberg house and is preparing to light
Sabbath candles when I arrive. The table, resplendent
with two candelabra, a dozen tiny oil lamps, and brown
napkins folded in wineglasses, looks like the cover of *The
Jewish Woman's Outlook*, one of the magazines Sheina
subscribes to. Hasty introductions are made all around,
the candles are lit, and Sheina escorts her guests over to 770
for evening prayers, stopping on the way at her step-
daughter Miriam's to hear a welcoming speech by a young
Lubavitcher woman. Miriam's house is tidy but will receive no awards from the decorating board at *The Jewish
Woman's Outlook*. The general atmosphere is of a study
hall into which family furniture has been moved as an
afterthought. Small, motionless children, perched like ob-
jets d'art on the stairwell, watch the visitors trudge upstairs
to a room that has been filled with folding chairs. Miriam's
seventh child is due soon. She looks pale and tired, but
welcomes the women cordially and helps them find chairs.
The girl giving the speech is about twenty years younger
than most of the women in her audience. She is nervous.
Her speech, which extols the virtues of Lubavitcher life,
is listened to politely but without much interest.

At the synagogue, the left side of the women's gallery,
which affords the best view of the dais and the Rebbe,
has been set aside for visitors. Two large signs printed
with the words RESERVED FOR OUT-OF-TOWN GUESTS have
been taped to the black Plexiglas partition, further obscur-
ing the hazy view of the downstairs proceedings. By
Lubavitcher standards, the visitors' area is almost pleasant. The out-of-towners are a bit less avid than the home
crowd, and there is not too much shoving. By normal standards, the room is packed. As usual, about a third of the
women are standing on the backs of the pews, and all

seats and floor space are occupied. Many of the women
are reading from prayer books. Others are straining to
catch a glimpse of the Rebbe, either by squinting through
the plastic screen or by bending down and peering
through the space between the screen and the rim of the
balcony. The Rebbe is ensconced in the front right-hand
corner of the room, praying by himself. Somebody else is
leading the service. He seems to be totally absorbed in
his prayer book, oblivious to the thousands who chant and
sway behind him, their voices rising in a powerful ar-
rhythmic hum. The out-of-towners are quite distinctive
looking. In front of me is a group that according to Sheina
comes from somewhere in the West. They are thinner than
most of the other women, stand very straight, and wear
small jaunty straw hats. There is also a Russian contingent: recent emigrés. They wear outdated clothes, are
fairly stout, and look a bit bewildered.

As we walk back to the house after evening prayers,
Sheina is greeted every few steps by friends and acquain-
tances. Everyone seems to relish saying, "Good Shabbos,"
which is spoken with a kind of lilt and emphasis usually reserved in the secular world for "Happy Birthday!"

Back at the Konigsbergs', Moshe pours the ritual wine
into the kiddush cup and another Sabbath meal begins.
The guests include two young women and an older woman
from Toronto (the young women have recently become
baalot teshuvah; the older woman, a svelte, blonde di-
vorcée in her fifties, is the mother of one of them. She is
not religious and looks uncomfortable, as she will for
the duration of the weekend); the pretty Israeli-born
owner of a chic Manhattan cosmetics business and her
ten-year-old daughter; and a Montreal woman and her
daughter and son.

Moshe does not appear to be discomfited by the little
seraglio that peers down the long table at him. Mendel

does, and he mostly addresses himself to the young boy
from Montreal who is seated next to him. Shmuel and
Bassy are eating with other families. While we down
robust portions of gefilte fish and chicken soup, several
of the Canadian guests compare notes on the number of
times they or other Hasidim they know have been stopped
by guards at the Canadian–U.S. border and subjected to
elaborate questionings and car searches. The woman
from Montreal, who is attractive and good humored, says
that the last time she drove across the border she left all
her jewelry at home, took off her rings, and dressed in the
plainest clothes she owned so that she would look as color-
less and unobtrusive as possible.

"But my husband wore his hat and long coat and he
couldn't leave his beard behind, so of course they stopped
us, and turned the car inside out, and delayed us for quite
a long time."

"You think that they harass you because you're Jews?"
I asked.

"Well, yes. You'll be in a line of cars going across and
you will just know that you will not make it across without being stopped. It happens every time. It's a kind of
petty form of anti-Semitism, and of course you really can't
prove it . . . But there's nothing new about that kind of
thing. Minor bureaucrats have always jumped at the opportunity to harass Jews."

Her son, a rosy-cheeked fifteen-year-old with the merest
fringe of a beard, added: "I got fed up once and I said
to a guard, 'Do you hate the Jewish people? Why do you
do this? I'm going to write to the government and complain.' He just shrugged and pretended not to know what
I was talking about; but he stopped bothering me."

After dispatching a gargantuan third course of baked
chicken, spinach soufflé, noodle pudding and warm fruit
salad, Moshe sat back in his chair and sang a sweet, word-

less Lubavitcher melody, and then he and Mendel sang
another, gayer song, about how nice it was when Jews all
sat down together at the table.

Someone mentioned Jacobo Timerman's book about
Israel, which had appeared not long before, and asked
Moshe what he thought of it. Moshe's answer came from
between clenched teeth.

"It had no reality for me. The man is a Communist.
I knew it when I saw his book on Argentina and it was
apparent in his writing about Israel. Besides, he was a
guest of the Israelis. He hadn't been there long enough
to begin to understand what it means to try and keep
that country safe. His opinions about Argentina were
invented."

"You don't believe that the Argentinians vilified and
tortured him because he was a Jew?" I said.

"No, I don't believe it."

"Anti-Semitism in Argentina is an invention of the Communists," Mendel said with an ironic smile. "We have boys
here in the community from all walks of life in Argentina—farmers' boys, teachers' boys, industrialists' boys—
and all of them say that there is no anti-Semitism there."

"But how can you acknowledge that a benign country
like Canada might have anti-Semitic acts taking place on
its border and deny that a country like Argentina, where
as many as thirty thousand people have disappeared,
would have some anti-Semites in its secret police?"

Moshe shook his head vehemently. "You don't understand. Sure, the police curse at their enemies and call them
all kinds of names. If the enemies are Jews they'll call them
dumb Yids or whatever. But those are just names. The
point is I don't believe that man, whatever he says, because he is sympathetic to the Communists. The poor
Russian Jews have been living with Communism for a
long time. They know what it's like to be in a place where
morality and truth really mean nothing. All of us have

relatives or friends who have been persecuted by the Russians. They've been arrested, sent to work camps, even killed—for simply existing as Jews. Communists are God-less people. Their words are meaningless."

This was the first time I had seen (and only time I would see) Moshe stirred to anger. He was shouting and his face had turned red with rage. Sheina put her hand on his and said, "Sh, sh, don't get so excited," and he calmed down. But he continued to look at me fixedly, as if to say, "I won't say anymore for the sake of Sabbath calm, but be sure that this is a matter of considerable importance to me." Not long before this discussion, I had read the Timerman book about his experiences in Argentina. The details of his incarceration had seemed harrowingly authentic to me, and I found it astonishing that one obvious reality, the suffering of Russian Jews, could so utterly anni-hilate another, the suffering of Mr. Timerman. The broad, bright light that the Hasidim trained on their communal and inner life seemed to narrow to laser thinness when turned on the outside world—a circumstance that appeared to strain the quality of mercy hereabouts.

The Konigsbergs' Sabbath breakfasts are uncharacteris-tically spartan, come-when-you-will meals that consist chiefly of tea, rolls, and pastry. The tea cannot actually be brewed, but is prepared by diluting half-cupfuls of strong tea essence, made the day before, with water drawn from an urn that is kept on a metal plate over a low flame. Lily, the cosmetics-store owner, and her little girl and I were the first to arrive in the breakfast nook. The girl quickly dispatched a roll and juice, then dove to the floor to play jacks. Lily has small, delicate features and dresses with an up-to-the minute modernity that sets her apart from the more conservatively fashionable women of this circle. I asked her how she came to be a part of it. She smiled shyly.

"Very slowly. I came here at first because my husband became religious. But I refused to do any of the rituals without feeling sincere about them and that has taken a long time—years. Did Sheina tell you that I used to be a dancer?"

"No."

"Well, I was. But then I had an accident and couldn't dance professionally anymore. That was when I started my cosmetics business. A lot of my friends were dancers and singers and actors. And I still loved to go dancing. I also loved doing whatever I felt like doing on Saturdays. After all, I worked hard all week. For a long time I refused to give all that up. Now, the things that used to seem important don't seem important at all. Early on, the toughest hurdles were related to my work. We make up a lot of entertainers and it was extremely difficult to explain to them that we weren't going to be able to make them up for Friday and Saturday shows anymore. But the hardest step for me, believe it or not, was cutting my hair. I don't know why. I had always had long black hair and I was proud of it. For some, keeping a kosher home is difficult, others are nervous about the *mikvah*. All of us seem to have had one stumbling block that was somehow symbolically the last obstacle to fully entering this life."

Lily asked the two young women from Toronto, who had just joined us at the breakfast table with the mother, what their stories were. While they added another round of praise to the many that were heard that weekend about the satisfactions of religious commitment, the mother looked on in stony silence. We both went to the kitchen to get some tea.

"It's curious, isn't it?" she whispered to me as I filled her cup, "when I was young it was the old people who were religious and the young who were against it all; now the young are the zealots and we cannot imagine what they see in it all. My daughter thinks that I'll be won over

if I spend enough time here and get to know enough
people like the Konigsbergs, but this isn't for me. The
truth is that I'd give anything right now for a cigarette
and a nice poached egg."

Guests in various states of (modest) deshabillé wandered in and out of the breakfast nook, with cups of tea,
prayer books, and commentaries on Jewish history. There
was a whiff here of the languors of a novitiate, and another of the let's-all-be-jolly-together-chumminess of a pa-
jama party. When Sheina called everybody in to lunch,
Lily and the two Toronto girls trooped directly from the
breakfast table to the dining room table.

Five new guests, all women, were present at lunch: two
friends, a stockbroker from Manhattan and a social worker
from California; a young girl studying at Machon Chanah
and her mother, a woman of about sixty; and a svelte dark-
skinned beauty who said that she was a sportswear designer and the daughter of a Sephardic rabbi. Bassy was
with Bubbe; Moshe and the boys were elsewhere, too. The
lunch was copious, mostly cold meats and fish but including one hot dish, a steaming bowl of *cholent*.

The stockbroker had recently moved to Crown Heights
because she had been spending weekends in the neighborhood for a long time and "it was easier not to have to
constantly make the transition back and forth between
the two worlds," she told me. "I would return to the city
after spending Shabbos here each weekend and one day I
just said, 'I like where I came from better.' And I used to
love Manhattan."

"How did your colleagues feel about your move?" I
asked.

"Angry—and sort of rejected. I work mostly with men,
and I guess they just liked to think of me as one of the
boys. I played on the softball team; we socialized together.
When I said that I couldn't do those things anymore they
said they couldn't understand it. Really, they didn't want

to try. One afternoon one of the men in my office started screaming at me, in front of everyone. He said, 'How can you be doing this to yourself? You're such an intelligent, rational woman. Don't you know it's all a lot of hokum? How can you ally yourself with a bunch of badly educated fanatics?' He went on in that vein, screaming at the top of his lungs."

"What did you do?"

"I just waited until he was finished. I amazed myself. I have a terrible temper. But I saw that he had no real idea of what a religious life meant and that he was threatened by it. So all I said was, 'Sometime, when I'm in a position to, I'll invite you out to Crown Heights for a Shabbos.'"

"I'll bet he can't wait to do that," said Lizzie, the lively-looking, curly-haired girl from California, laughing. "It's really amazing how much hostility we encounter. Particularly from Jews. Our gentile friends are curious; Jews feel threatened by us."

"Moshe told me a good story about that," said Sheina, wiping her lips with a blue cloth napkin. "It takes place in the nineteen-forties, when it was more unusual than it is now to see a Hasidic man on the streets of New York. There was a Hasid on a bus wearing his dark clothes and broad hat and next to him sat a woman who kept giving him disapproving looks. She seemed to be trying to hold her tongue, but finally, she was unable to restrain herself. She whispered to him, in Yiddish, 'Why do you go about like that? You're giving Jews a bad name. You're in America now. Why don't you look like an American?'

"Well, the Hasid turned to her and said, in English, 'Excuse me, I didn't catch all that.'

"Hearing the English, the woman burst out, 'Oh, I'm terribly sorry, you must be Amish. I really admire the Amish people. Such high standards of morality! Such pride in tradition! And there's so much integrity in the way you refuse to conform to the ways of American culture.'"

Lizzie smiled. "I know all about Jewish antagonism to Jewish things. The only reason I'm here is that I went with some buddies in California to goad a Lubavitcher rabbi who was speaking at my college. You know in California everybody's pretty arrogant; we think we have the best of everything—nature, health, material comforts. So my friends and I tried to debunk the rabbi's ideals. But in the first place he wasn't goadable, and in the second the life he led sounded good to me. I didn't return to see him right away but eventually I went back, and here I am. I work in a hospital here now, and I'm learning more all the time about *Yiddishkeit* [Jewishness]."

"How do you think the women in this community who have always been religious regard you?" I asked.

"Ah, the *frummies* [*frum* is the Yiddish word for observant]," she said, casting a conspiratorial look at her friend. "Well, that depends on who we're talking about. Most of the people in this community are fantastically warm and kind, whether they are F.F.B.s—*Frum* From Birth—or not. But there is definitely a bit of tension between some of the *frummies* and the B.T.s—*baalot teshuvah*. Many *frummies* look down on us a little, I think, because we've been in the fleshpots of the world so long, and because we've supposedly got all these useless facts about heroic couplets and Mozart and the Chrysler building, say, at our fingertips, but we're often so ignorant of things they've known about all their lives—things that they learned in kindergarten, like Hebrew, or what holiday is for what, or what the reasons are for the rituals. On the other hand, the B.T.s may sometimes feel a bit superior to the *frummies*. We *are* better educated, at least in secular subjects, and we do tend to see the outside world from a less narrow perspective. I'm thirty, you know, and naturally they've tried to match me up with young men in the community—with disastrous results!" She giggled, and cast another glance at her friend, then added, "The fact that

many of the B.T.s have jobs that are not within the traditional spectrum also causes some anxiety around here."

"It's hard, too, sometimes to straddle both worlds," said
the clothes designer. "The values of each are so different."
Most of my nonreligious friends are as uninterested in the
details of my religious life as the people around here are
in my professional life, or for that matter in anything I
ever learned about nonreligious subjects."

"Well, I don't think women should have to have careers;
it's enough to bring up your family, lead a *frum* life, and,
if you want to, teach," said the young student at Machon
Chanah. Her voice had a strong defensive edge.

"What if a woman is born with, say, musical or artistic
talent? Should she try to develop it?" I asked no one in
particular.

"Not if it's going to interfere with religious ways," the
young girl snapped back at once, with considerable heat.
"My mother and I knew a woman who used to give
concerts. She was a fine pianist. But when she became
religious she learned she either had to stop giving concerts or put a screen up so that she wouldn't be seen by
the men, so she just stopped giving concerts."

"And wasn't that a shame," cried her mother, who was
plainly dressed and spoke with a particularly thick Yiddish
accent. "Why should God be against a woman playing
beautiful music?" She glanced briefly at me and raised her
eyebrows. I raised mine in a small gesture of solidarity. He
can't be! And men can play in front of women. Why? I was
in a concentration camp. If Jews can survive that and still
go on to play beautiful music, who can say that they
shouldn't?" The woman shook her head and looked around
the room for some sign of agreement from the other guests.
In vain. Most of the women stared at their plates. The rest
looked startled, and gazed unhappily at the woman the
way good children stare at the class cut-up. (Where had I

seen this happen before? A group of women politely disapproving of someone that they consider out-of-step. Someone very like this woman. It was a memory from childhood.
I was visiting my favorite aunt in Connecticut during a
spring vacation. An elderly religious lady who had come to
have tea with my aunt and some of her friends saw fit to
berate my aunt and the other women for abandoning their
Jewish ways. They had gazed at the woman with the same
polite forbearance, the same disapproval.)

"Women can't perform in front of men because it might
arouse the men, Mom, that's just the way men are," her
daughter said, looking embarrassed.

Her mother allowed herself a short barking laugh, then,
peering intently at the innocent, pudgy face of her young
daughter, she said, "You know so much. How do you
know what men are or aren't? You don't know. Landowska
was some kind of temptress? She drove the men in the
audience crazy? I'm sure she'd have been surprised to
hear it."

Lizzie came to the daughter's defense. "I guess the idea
is that a man can play in front of women because women
are more spiritual. Anyway, those are the laws, so we go
along with them. If people don't want to go along with
them they don't have to, but I guess the idea is that we
didn't make the laws, God did. We're supposed to accept
them all, even if we don't have a good rationale for every
one."

Later that afternoon, at the Brooklyn Jewish Center, a
cavernous behemoth of a structure once used by the entire
Jewish community but now used mainly as a yeshiva and
wedding reception hall by the Lubavitchers, several hundred women milled around in one of the spacious reception
rooms. The room was filled with tables laden with what a
printed program described as "light refreshments"—egg-
salad sandwiches, whitefish salad, fruit cups, and an assort-

ment of homemade cakes, all prepared by the neighborhood women to tide everybody over the interlude between
lunch and dinner.

The speakers, who began at about the time everyone
expected them to—three quarters of an hour late—addressed themselves chiefly to the community-project and
child-rearing aspects of "Reaching Above and Beyond."
Keeping home values spiritual, sending children to religious schools, and trying to uphold the high standards of
Hasidic life were among the topics discussed. They were,
of course, preaching to the already converted, and there
was a great deal of fidgeting. I saw Lizzie, who was sitting
a few rows in front of me, turn to her friend and roll
her eyes and yawn ostentatiously. The self-congratulatory
tone and repetitive black-and-whiteness of the speeches
had a very real soporific effect on me. There was nothing
wrong there, of course, that a lively rendition of Scott
Joplin could not cure, I found myself thinking, but just
as I started to get really absorbed in a kind of epic fantasy
in which all the assembled women kicked up their heels
in a cakewalk, joined not only by their husbands but by
much of non-Hasidic Crown Heights, the Barrio, Little
Italy, and Chinatown, my attention was caught by the
tone of voice of one of the speakers. She seemed to be
scolding the women for allowing their children to run
around 770 too much during services and the *farbrengens*.
Many of the women looked chagrined, a few looked
stricken, but the vast majority looked merely disbelieving,
even when the speaker capped her scolding with the
broad hint that her objection to the children's high jinks
were shared by an authority higher up. No one talked
about the speeches afterward, and by the time everyone
reached home to light the *havdalah* candle, most of what
had been said seemed to have already been forgotten.
Sheina was busy helping two girls who had stayed elsewhere for the weekend find a ride back to Manhattan, and

Moshe and Mendel retired to the corner to study together. Noses close to their books, they talked softly to each other while a steady stream of women flowed in and out the door.

The Sunday of the convention happened to coincide with Mother's Day, and—my family having expressed interest in having me on hand—I left the Konigsbergs' Saturday night and told them I would be back the next evening in time to hear the Rebbe speak. When they learned the reason for my departure they could barely hide their amusement. Unlike Hanukkah, Passover, Purim, Succoth, and the other religious holidays and festivals they observe with zeal, Mother's Day, Father's Day, Thanksgiving, Halloween, Valentine's Day, and, needless to say, Christmas and Easter are nonevents on the Lubavitcher calendar. The Jew who annually puts up a Christmas tree and thinks nothing of it is in their view a dupe of subtle cultural pressures that gradually convert him into a non-Jew. The nonreligious holidays seem merely irrelevant; they would no more think of adopting the customs associated with them than they would think of donning feathered headdresses and performing a rain dance.

At seven o'clock on Sunday evening, the conventioneers assembled at 770 to listen to the Rebbe speak. Three times a year, Lubavitcher women are invited to sit downstairs in the men's section: just before Rosh Hashanah, on Beis Rivkah's graduation day, and on the final day of the Women's Convention. On all three occasions, the Rebbe makes a special address to the women, and the men sit upstairs.

If I had had any illusions about the comfort and spaciousness of the men's section, these were quickly dispelled. I arrived seconds before the Rebbe was scheduled to speak. Standing in the doorway, with about twenty other latecomers, I couldn't spy even an inch of space that we could squeeze into. But I underestimated the skills of the crowd. Several mighty shoves carried all the stragglers into the room and many small jostles got us to the back wall, where I was securely pinioned between several plump, middle-aged matrons and an imperturbable older woman who held her sleeping granddaughter in her arms.

Minutes before I had arrived at the synagogue I had been caught in a sudden downpour. All the latecomers had been drenched by it and our damp clothes made things uncomfortable for everyone standing nearby. Unable to retreat even an inch, they became human blotters. Oddly enough, this did not seem to bother them. A red-cheeked, bespectacled woman behind me unfurled a handkerchief between us, but it didn't help, and she soon rolled it up in a soggy ball and stuffed it into her purse, giving me a "well, this-is-what-you-have-to-go-through-for-important-things" smile and patting me on the shoulder in a gesture of solidarity.

An excited murmur arose as the Rebbe entered the room through a side door and strode in his vigorous way up to the dais. He spoke for an hour and a half, in Yiddish, without notes, mostly about keeping the faith. Toward the end of the speech, the Rebbe touched on a point that had been discussed in passing all weekend: a petition he, like many clerics, was circulating urging that all public schools begin their day with a moment of silence. He was quick to point out that he was not advocating any kind of prayer, only that time be made available at the start of every day for "every schoolchild, regardless of religion" to think about the Creator, so that the rest of the day would be imbued with the spirit of these thoughts.

The Rebbe went on to say that he believed that children thus fortified would not want to harm one another or commit any of the unlawful, violent acts that plagued modern, secular schools. He was utterly convinced that the spiritual space made by a moment of silence would be filled, ipso facto, by a spirit of goodness. As I listened with one ear to the halting efforts of the translator on the little transistor that had been provided at the door and with the other to the Rebbe's singsong Yiddish, I fell under a kind of spell. A chorus of voices echoing from my childhood to the present trumpeted the news that a state-imposed pause in the school day was a bad idea, and from any rational point of view, I found the idea of the petition repugnant.

"All fundamentalists are alike," a friend had recently remarked. "They're never satisfied with simply having their own religious views, they have to impose them on everyone else." But somehow, this seemed like an inadequate representation of the Rebbe's message. He expressed his belief in the curative power of goodness so plainly and passionately that it could be felt in every corner of the room. For a few moments, my disapproval of the petition and my skepticism evaporated. To my amazement, I found myself wishing that things could be as the Rebbe wished them to be.

CHAPTER ELEVEN

Scenes from Days of Awe

W<small>HILE</small> most of the Jewish holidays are related to historical events, Rosh Hashanah and Yom Kippur, which are observed during the Jewish month of *Tishrei* (mid-September to early October on the Civil Calendar; Hebrew months are known by the names they acquired during the Babylonian exile), are purely religious. They are sometimes called the Days of Awe—awesome because all men's actions for the past year are supposedly judged on those days —and they celebrate God's supremacy in the universe and are considered especially holy. For a month before Rosh Hashanah the ram's horn, or *shofar*, is sounded at every weekday morning service to remind the congregants that a period of deepened soul-searching is approaching. Rosh Hashanah, the Day of Judgment, is a two-day holiday; Yom Kippur, the Day of Atonement, a one-day holiday and a day of fasting. Both holidays emphasize God's role as judge of all human actions. According to Jewish tradi-

tion, Rosh Hashanah ("head of the year") marks the beginning of a ten-day period in which God decides "who
will live, and who will die; who will be serene and who
will be disturbed; who will be poor and who will be rich;
who will be troubled and who will be exalted." But God's
final judgment is reserved for Yom Kippur, the Day of
Atonement, and during the period in between those who
feel they have transgressed and are penitent are offered the
opportunity to cleanse their souls. According to the Talmud, three books are opened by God on Rosh Hashanah:
the book of the wicked, the book of the righteous, and the
book of those in between. The righteous are promised a
good future life, the wicked are condemned to death, and
judgment on those in between is deferred until Yom Kippur
when God makes a final decision about their fate. The
metaphor of open and closed gates is frequently associated with the two holidays; on Rosh Hashanah the gates
are opened, on Yom Kippur they are closed. The *shofar*,
one of the oldest of the world's wind instruments, was
used in Biblical times to intimidate enemies, to declare
war, and to assemble the populace. It is the Bible that
prescribes that the *shofar* be sounded on Rosh Hashanah.
Maimonides said the *shofar* had the effect of awakening
those who were spiritually asleep. Symbolically, the *shofar*
also proclaims God's sovereignty, in the same way that a
fanfare proclaims the sovereignty of a newly crowned king;
it reminds Jews of the day that the Law was given at
Mount Sinai, when a *shofar* was sounded "exceedingly
strong."

On Rosh Hashanah the crowd at the synagogue was the
largest I had ever seen. The women's section was like a
living organism composed of hundreds of heads, arms,
legs, hats, scarves, prayer books and shawls. Sheina and I
had planned to meet there, but I could see that it was
unlikely that we would find each other, and I soon gave
up trying. There were some non-Hasidic-looking women

in the crowd outside the building. They stared at the mob
flowing through the door in disbelief and appeared to be
daunted by the solid wall of humanity that seemed to
block all access to the synagogue. Not I. Like an old hand,
I relaxed my body, took a step forward from the doorway,
where I had become landlocked, and let myself be swept
along by the crowd and hoisted by helping hands to a
tiny beachhead on the back of a pew.

With two thousand women pressed against one another
like sardines, you would imagine that a stranger, number
two thousand and one, would slip in more or less unnoticed. Not in this crowd. All the women within eyeshot
gazed at me curiously, and looked at one another with
quizzical expressions, as if to say, "Who can this be?"
Before five minutes had elapsed, two people had appointed themselves my guardians. One of them, an elegant older woman with pale green eyes, handed me a
prayer book that she produced from a plastic bag. It was
written in Hebrew. I whispered that I could not read it.
She unhesitatingly climbed down from the bench (she
was about sixty-five and negotiated this feat with some
difficulty), disappeared into the throng, and returned a
few minutes later, a triumphant smile on her lips, with
a Hebrew–English prayer book. As the service went along,
I often lost my place despite the English text, and was
out of step with the rest of the congregation. I never felt
lost for long, however, because my other guardian, a
small curly-haired blonde girl of about eleven, had appointed herself my text finder. All I had to do was look
up for a fraction of a second and she would lift my finger,
turn a page if necessary, and put it down on the right
phrase. This happened many times in the course of the
four-and-a-half-hour service.

In the late morning, the Rebbe blew the *shofar* in the
prescribed long and short blast manner. About halfway
through the ritual he seemed to falter and find it difficult

to make anything but a very weak sound. In the midst
of his difficulties a baby started to cry, and the sound
drowned out the sound of the *shofar*. It was a painful
moment. There were many furrowed brows, and the entire congregation seemed to be straining to somehow help
its aged leader (who had had a serious heart attack) get
on with his task. Perhaps he sensed it, because the last
notes he blew were pure and clear.

Nine days later, on the eve of Yom Kippur, at a storefront
on the corner of Albany Avenue and Eastern Parkway, hundreds of roosters and hens in metal cages clucked mourn-
fully. They had good reason to sound that way. Eventually
all of them would be purchased by Lubavitcher men and
women for the *kapparot* ("atonements") ceremony, a ves-
tige of sacrificial Temple rites that seems to have originated
among the Jews of Babylonia. The ceremony, which begins
with the celebrant reading selections from the Book of
Psalms and the Book of Job, involves waving a fowl over
the head three times (a rooster for a man, a hen for a
woman, both for a pregnant woman) while chanting the
words, "This is my substitute, my vicarious offering, my
atonement; this cock or hen shall meet death, but I shall enjoy a long and pleasant life." Afterward, the fowl is slaughtered. At the end of the day the slaughtered birds are
given to the local school cafeterias.

Sheina performed the ceremony at home. Mendel offered to bring her a hen in a box so she would not have
to face the scene at the storefront, which, from experience,
she knew she had little stomach for. Standing in her
gleaming modern kitchen, she held the struggling hen
gingerly in her arms, performed the ceremony, then hastily thrust it at Mendel, who took it back to the storefront
to be slaughtered.

Moshe had performed the same rite and later on had
also taken part in a flogging ceremony. Thirty-nine largely

symbolic lashes were administered to his prostrate body
by a fellow congregant in the synagogue. Immediately
afterward, he and Mendel left for Allenwood. Shmuel was
spending the holiday with his sister Chanah and her family
in Virginia, and Bassy was with Bubbe.

Religious Jews do not travel on Yom Kippur, and the
thought of any other Jew doing so makes them uncomfortable, so I asked Sheina if it would be all right for me
to spend the night at her house. She said that she would
be grateful if I did. She was going to be alone except for
one young woman guest from Montreal and a male visitor
from Israel, and Moshe had been a little concerned about
the propriety of her being alone in the house with a
strange man and a young woman.

This male stranger, who was about seventy years old,
hardly ever materialized, and slammed his upstairs bedroom door shut whenever he heard any of us come in the
front door. He appeared to have found some secret route
from the synagogue to his room and back and never seemed
to use the bathroom. We encountered each other only once,
in fact—late Friday night. Sheina and the young woman
had gone to bed. I was reading on the sofa. The front door
opened and the man, stooped, sallow, and wearing his
wide-brimmed hat, had gotten about halfway up the stairs
before he noticed me. For some reason, my presence
seemed to unnerve him. Flattening himself against the
banister, he stared at me in confusion. I greeted him in
as reassuring a tone as I could muster, but he did not return my greeting and fled up the stairs as if he had seen
a ghost.

Everybody fasts on Yom Kippur because of the Biblical
injunction to "afflict your souls" on the holiday. There are
five afflictions mentioned by Jewish sages—abstaining from
eating, drinking, lovemaking, washing or anointing the
body in any way, and wearing leather shoes (leather being
deemed especially comfortable). Numerological mysteries

are associated with those negative precepts, as they are in much Jewish theosophy. It has been pointed out, for example, that the five afflictions correspond to the five books of the Torah, which are meant to be accepted that day without the "curtain of our physical pleasures"; the five times the soul is mentioned in the Yom Kippur Torah reading; the five senses which man can use for evil or good; the five times the Temple high priest immersed himself on this holiday; and the five services held during the day.

Numerology was and still is an important component of mystical lore. Since every Hebrew letter has a numerical equivalent, Jewish scholars have always speculated endlessly about the numerological significance of their sacred texts. Certain numbers have dominated these speculations. The numbers three, seven, and nine, in that order, always have special significance in Jewish ritual. Incantations were traditionally spoken three times, mystical acts were supposed to be performed three hours before sunrise or three days before the new moon, and diviners could expect answers to only three questions at a time. The number seven, too, is frequently invested with mystical significance. "All sevens are beloved," says one text, and Judaism reflects that belief in many ways. Jacob had to work for seven years to win Leah and Rachel; a bride walks around the groom with her family under the wedding canopy seven times—a reflection also of the belief in the protective magic of the circle; seven blessings are said during the wedding ceremony and at the first meal after it; and for seven days after a wedding a *minyan*—a quorum of ten men together for religious worship—gathers each day with the new couple in attendance to repeat the seven blessings. But no more apt example of the ancient Jewish belief in the beneficial powers of the number seven exists, I think, than this Talmudic prescription for curing a recurrent fever:

"Take seven prickles from seven palm trees, seven chips from seven beams, seven nails from seven bridges, seven ashes from seven ovens, seven scoops of earth from seven doorsockets, seven pieces of pitch from seven ships, seven handfuls of cumin, and seven hairs from the beard of an old dog, and tie them to the neck hole of the shirt with a white twisted cord."

The number nine also has an honored, if lesser, place in Jewish mystical lore, owing chiefly to its being the square of the number three. Early Jewish writings barely mention it, but it appeared from time to time in the kabbalah of northern Europe. In medieval manuscripts it was written that demons congregated in groups of nine and in nut trees whose branches had nine leaves; if anyone saw a demon he was forbidden to mention it for nine days, and many cures were concocted from nine kinds of herbs. The use of the number nine was common in medieval Teutonic magic, and probably found its way into Jewish custom by way of German folk beliefs.

On Yom Kippur married men also don their *kittels*—long white linen robes in which they are married and buried and which are also worn on Passover.

Both men and women immerse themselves in the *mikvah* before the holiday, and Sheina had volunteered, along with a friend, to help Brachah pass out towels and see that everything went smoothly. There are a number of men's *mikvahs* in the neighborhood, all old and decrepit. But there is just one *mikvah* for the women. Ordinarily, this does not make any difference, since only a handful of women usually show up each day. But the day before Yom Kippur hundreds do, and Sheina came home exhausted but pleased at the many compliments paid the new *mikvah* by women who had come to it for the first time from other neighborhoods. "Even the Belzers couldn't help but admire it," she said. The Belzers' compliments were particularly satisfying. The Belzer rov had pronounced the Lubavitcher *mikvah* unusable a while back, because, he declared, the hole that let in the rainwater had been placed in the wrong position; the Lubavitchers had circumvented the problem by giving one of their *mikvahs two* holes—one on the bottom where they thought it should be, and one on the side, where the Belzers thought it should be.

That evening and the next day, the synagogue reached a new zenith of crowdedness. A significant number of congregants had paid sixty dollars for their seats, but the seat allocations had little meaning since no one was ever turned away at the door, as they were in many synagogues, and most people just squeezed into any space more than an inch or two wide and remained there for the duration of the service. Those who had paid, like Sheina, did not seem to resent the intrusion of the nonpayers. When I suggested that there didn't seem to be any real point in buying a ticket, she just shrugged and said it all went to charity anyway so it didn't matter. "Besides," she added, "I spend most of the day in a little neighborhood synagogue around the corner where it's more peaceful."

On Yom Kippur morning, for all the solemnity of the holiday, the congregation's spirits appeared to be particularly high. People practically tripped over one another in their haste to get to the synagogue. Even as the day wore on and people's energy levels dropped from lack of food and drink, the communal zeitgeist became, if anything, more charged. The singing grew louder and more animated, and the Rebbe, on his feet for much of the time, bore no trace of the fragility that was so much in evidence on Rosh Hashanah. He led the singing with rhythmic arm jabs and often clapped his hands. At several points in the service he was required to prostrate himself. Each time, he arose with astonishing alacrity.

Like everyone else, I remained glued to the same spot all day, except for a brief midafternoon adjournment. After the first few hours various members of the congregation—a woman in the front row who kept brushing invisible crumbs off her mother's shoulder, another in my

own row who kept her head buried in her hands, a bright-
eyed young man who rocked back and forth so violently
when he prayed that he annoyed all the men around him—
began to seem like old friends. As more time passed
and scores of prayers evoking the evils and splendors of
the world were read, a kind of survivors-on-a-ship-that-
has-passed-through-dangerous-seas atmosphere developed,
along with a mood of weary benevolence. By early evening, the congregation was almost breathing in and out in
unison. Many of the prayers, especially those that expressed awe about the intricacies of the world, seemed
like formalized versions of sentiments I had held all my
life (some of the nourishment my ancestors took from
these self-same waters had to have seeped through the
dam of secularization); others struck no sympathetic
chord. Like everybody else there, I felt grateful for the
possibility of transcendence in ordinary life, but unlike
them, I could not fathom, for example, how God in Heaven
could have less tolerance for the frailty of His children
than most earthly mortals had for the frailty of their own.
But if my rational self kept its distance from the flow of the
day, another part of me drifted along with it. For the first
time, I understood why the Hasidim did not mind sacri-
ficing their identities to their communal world; that world
was their identity and in the synagogue that day the congregation was so identifiable with God, his people, and the
Torah that, like the kabbalistic image of a supernal man/
woman larger than the universe, it seemed to expand to fill
all imaginable space.

Toward the end of the day, Sheina managed to squeeze
into her "reserved" seat next to me. Fresh waves of people
had begun to arrive and seemed determined to find
places. The pews trembled under the additional weight.
These late arrivals included mothers who had been at
home with small children all day (they brought the children along), older people who had gone home to rest for

a while, and those who, like Sheina, had slipped away to small neighborhood synagogues. But everybody wanted to be with the Rebbe when the gates closed. Could fifteen thousand people actually fit into the synagogue? Nobody seemed to be missing. Most of the congregation had been here since ten o'clock in the morning. It was now 7:30 in the evening. Downstairs, the men were so tightly packed that you could not make out any of them from the neck down. Like the women, they had become one body with thousands of heads. Upstairs, there was near pandemonium. Several women actually toppled from the pews. Territorial rights to a particular square inch of bench were hotly disputed. Neither candy nor juice (children are exempted from fasting) effectively hushed the small, tired children whose mothers beat their breasts with their right fists as they recited a long list of sins which they ask forgiveness for. The list included "lewdness," "desecrating the divine name," "immorality," and 'impudence"—transgressions which seemed almost ludicrously inapplicable to the lives of most of the people present. When there was a lull in the service, I mentioned this to Sheina. She shook her head, impatiently disclaiming her own innocence. "Nobody can say that they haven't been guilty of *something* on that list. Who hasn't been guilty of 'causeless hatred,' or 'a begrudging eye,' or 'obduracy'? Besides, you're not just asking forgiveness for yourself, but for the whole Jewish nation. Not every Jew is in shul today, you know." Sheina's answer called to mind the story of the pious man who told Maimonides that he was unwilling to utter the long list of sins at the Yom Kippur service because he knew he wasn't guilty of them and it was wrong to lie to God. Maimonides' reply was that if the man knew "the gravity of the service of God . . . and to what extent the service of God is required," then he would understand that not a day passed in which, to some degree, he had committed all of the enumerated sins.

In front of us, a tired-looking older woman was joined by her four daughters, all beauties, and their many children. To reach her, they had to climb, one by one, through, around (and, in the case of the children, under) an all but impenetrable wall of bodies. The daughters' cheeks were flushed and their wigs askew; the little girls' blouses had come out of their skirts. The older woman revived incrementally as each one of them arrived, and she put her arms around as many of the children as she could reach to hug. She popped a sourball into one child's mouth, straightened the nearest daughter's wig, retrieved a fallen bottle. Somehow, they all managed to squeeze into a space about as wide as a telephone booth. One last song was sung, with ear-shattering gusto, to the tune of "Napoleon's March." The crowd was so dense my back had begun to hurt from the pressure of so many elbows, knees and prayer books pressing into it from behind. To my right, a purple-faced Valkyrie loudly berated a terrified looking newcomer for blocking her view.

Suddenly the children stopped fidgeting and there was absolute stillness and silence. All eyes were fixed on the Rebbe, who was watching one of his followers blow the *shofar* for the final time. Shortly afterward, the service concluded, the doors opened, and everybody stepped out into the darkness of the everyday world.

CHAPTER TWELVE

Dissidents

WHEN the young stockbroker I had met at lunch at Sheina's the weekend of the convention described the peculiar feeling she had when she returned to Manhattan from Crown Heights, I had known just what she meant. Each time I left the neighborhood, I felt extremely disoriented. Though the subway ride back to Manhattan meant a return to normalcy for me, that "normalcy" included a great deal of confusion, indecision, and wrong turns that contributed to my conviction that my life was simply a gigantic puzzle that probably would not ever be completed. Needless to say, that was not the way the Lubavitchers felt, and I envied them their sureness, and the sheer weight it gave them. I had, of course, my family, my friends, my work, and the various pleasures, some profound, some fleeting, that came my way; but there was nothing beneath my feet. The Hasidim had a world without time, eternal life, and the extraordinary sense that everything they did counted. But traveling in the other direction, from Manhattan to Brooklyn, was even more disorienting for me. To the Konigsbergs and everyone else I encountered in Crown Heights, I was first and foremost a benighted secular Jew; whatever cultural breadth or knowledge of the world I could lay claim to counted for nothing. My worldliness was like a heavy suitcase full of clothes that turned out to be unsuitable for every occasion. This was brought home to me in quite a literal way one afternoon when, having spent a large part of the day at the zoo, I hurriedly caught the subway to Crown Heights (where I had an appointment with a Lubavitcher official) and realized only after I was halfway there that I was still wearing jeans. No Orthodox woman wears pants. According to law, it is forbidden to dress like a man. Heretofore I had always worn a dress or a skirt on my visits to the neighborhood. It seemed the polite and the expedient thing to do. That day, however, I had been in a tremendous rush and forgotten to change. I knew that a woman in Levi's would make the man I had my appointment with uncomfortable. I glanced at my watch. Too late to do anything about it. My appointment was in five minutes. He would just have to put up with it, I thought, as I stepped out of the subway into the bright afternoon light. But when I entered the building where the man's office was, a clutch of Hasidim who were standing in the entranceway stared at me with such consternation that I weakened and bolted. Cursing under my breath as I did it, I found a telephone, told the man that I was supposed to meet that I had been delayed, and changed our appointment to later that evening. Then I went home, changed clothes, and returned several hours later. It probably should be said that I am not the sort of person who wears jeans to a fancy restaurant or, conversely, fancy clothes to the movies. So why was I so angry about such a trivial matter, one that in the great scheme of things probably had as little importance as

Sheina's abandonment of tennis? Did my Levi's represent something more, perhaps? Had the cumulative effect of repeatedly leaving my own world behind finally caught up with me? It had. The question, of course, was not "Does God really care if I wear jeans?" but "Can anyone who finds crucial nourishment in the outside world still function within the framework of the Hasidic world?" I felt that there had to be people who had grappled with this question and might be willing to talk to me, and eventually I found some.

On a chilly Sunday morning several months after Yom Kippur, I arrived, somewhat late, at a large meeting room in the basement of an Upper East Side synagogue. I had come to hear Rabbi Zalman Schachter talk to a group of fifty people about "Exploring Jewish Spirituality." I was interested in Rabbi Schachter because he had once been a Lubavitcher but had left them in the late sixties and now ran a fellowship in Philadelphia called *B'nai Or* (Children of Light), a center for what some people referred to as "new-age Hasidism." Rabbi Schachter is considered by many to be the avatar of a burgeoning Jewish spiritual movement that bypasses the traditional synagogue, liturgy, and rabbinate and stresses instead heightened spirituality, an egalitarian liturgy, a more linguistically relevant service and a strong spirit of communality. Many of the movement's acolytes are former sojourners in the bazaars of Eastern mysticism; others are attracted to the antisecular, antirationalist spirit of the movement; and still others, disaffected by traditional Orthodox upbringings, are attracted to the vitality of the relaxed, largely leaderless Jewish study groups, reportedly numbering in the thousands, that the movement has spawned.

When I telephoned Rabbi Schachter in Philadelphia, he told me that he had arrived in the country only the day before for a brief visit. He was teaching in Germany for a year (he was on sabbatical from his regular teaching job in

the Department of Religion at Temple University) and
would be returning there in a few weeks. But he was scheduled to speak in New York the first week in January, he said,
and invited me to come hear him. His talk turned out to be
a seven-and-a-half-hour cram course in new-age Hasidism.
When I arrived, I found the rabbi and a guitarist assistant
standing in the center of two wide concentric circles of
people of diverse ages, who were walking in different di-
rections but facing each other. A portly, kindly looking
man, he was dressed that day in a loose black cotton shirt
over a white turtleneck, baggy black cotton pants, leather
sandals over socks, and a quite unyarmulke-like woven
black beanie. He had a medium-length gray beard but the
skin between his sideburns and beard was clean shaven,
a slight but significant departure from the full-bearded Hasidic style which tended to give his face a slightly oriental
appearance. One of the women in the outer circle told me
that the rabbi, whom she referred to as Zalman, had directed the two lines of people to "get in touch" with one
another by staring into one another's eyes as they moved
along. Rabbi Schachter has conducted seminars like this
one all around the country, but you could tell that the exercise was difficult for this particular crowd of spiritual pil-
grims. New Yorkers are, after all, trained from birth to avoid
eye contact with strangers at any cost, and it is hard to
change the habits of a lifetime in just one afternoon.

Under Rabbi Schachter's direction, the group tried
many other exercises, some mental, some physical. Traditional prayers were rephrased and reiterated en masse,
breathing exercises were combined with prayer, expressive
non-conventional body movements to accompany prayers
were encouraged, and the circles broke up into small
groups to discuss their reaction to what they were doing.
(My group's reactions: "Interesting." "Silly." "My wife's
probably enjoying this." "Is this est?") After lunch, the
rabbi answered questions and gave an oddly endearing

talk about "trying to find a language" for people with a religious impulse who were put off by most of the formal structure around religion, such as the language and tone of the *siddur* (the daily prayer book).

"Most people are simply overwhelmed by the *siddur,*" he said. "It just looks like there's too much to do. If I had my way, the portions of the *siddur* which have to do with doing things would be printed on one kind of paper, the portions which have to do with feeling on another, and so on. We must try to demonstrate that people don't have to spend all their time with irrelevancies, like trying to appease that grouchy old man up there . . . Rabbinical schools are teaching only with a rear-view mirror. They don't teach young men and women how to live in the world today. They should leave theology alone and teach about the living God as opposed to a God modeled after an Oriental potentate. We should learn how to keep our religion without separating ourselves from the rest of the world or each other. The denominations, for example, are as defunct as the dodo. The Orthodox are embattled with the Hasidim, the Conservative Jews with the Reform Jews, and there's no dialogue between any of them. I *talk* to my peers, some of whom are gentiles. I compare notes. I learn things. When was the last time the Klausenberger rebbe talked to the Bobover rebbe, or the Satmar rebbe talked to the Lubavitcher rebbe? How come they're not trying to help the world be at peace?"

At one point in his remarks, which were peppered with modern slang and four-letter words, Rabbi Schachter paid tribute to the Lubavitchers for the spiritual training they had given him. "For a young Jew interested in a contemplative life," he said, "they offered a lot." He recalled how he had hung on the previous rebbe's every word when he was a young man and how, when the old rebbe became paralyzed and could barely be heard in shul, he and his fellow students would lean forward and mouth every word he said. He did not want to disavow that part of his past, he said, but to illustrate the difference between his own orientation and theirs he made an analogy, suggested to him by the psychoanalyst and Catholic convert Karl Stern, between the Freudian developmental stages—oral, anal, phallic, latency, and genital—and those of many religious people, especially those who have returned to their faith. The oral stage is one of total acceptance, "introjecting mama." The acolyte "buys the whole package, hook, line and sinker. There are people who remain suckers their whole lives." Next comes the anal stage, during which obsession with the rules becomes paramount and all the restraints and strictures are in the foreground. Memorizing the rules takes up a lot of time, said Rabbi Schachter, and "some people in the spiritual supermarket never get out of that aisle." In the phallic stage, the obsession is with symbolism. Everything seems to stand for something else, and clues for secret messages and signs are discovered everywhere. Newly religious people very often get bogged down in this stage, he said, because they are like children with trading cards, entranced with all the secrets they can find in religious texts and comparing notes on them; the next stage is latency, in which *the group* takes on primary importance, and the overriding emotion is "I'll do anything for my gang." The last stage, parallel to the Freudian genital phase, arrives when someone feels truly intimate with God. Many conventionally religious people never achieved this, the Rabbi said, because they were stuck in an infantilized way in one of the earlier stages. Somehow, he said, organized theology had become a conspiracy to keep people from changing and looking within. Someone once asked Alan Watts, the popularizer of Eastern mysticism, why he had given up the Church. He replied that he had not given it up, he had simply graduated. In the same way, Rabbi Schachter said, he had graduated from the Lubavitchers.

Later that evening I found myself remembering how

awkwardly and self-consciously Rabbi Schachter's audience had carried out his instructions for making the process
of praying more "organic." It was impossible not to compare the scene with its equivalent in Crown Heights, where
the congregation, led by the Rebbe, had seemed to me
almost like one living body. Was that how they felt? It
was impossible to know. I tried to imagine the assorted
doctors, lawyers, students, and spiritual high rollers who
had been present that afternoon conjoined in a similar
way, and I could not.

Shlomo Ashkinazy is a thirty-six-year-old social worker
and *baal teshuvah* who lives in Manhattan but has spent
long hours studying in the Crown Heights community and
in Israel. A mutual acquaintance introduced us. He is small,
soft-spoken, has a neatly trimmed chestnut-colored beard,
milky blue eyes and exudes a spirit of indefatigable de-
termination. In the course of a long conversation we had in
his office on East Twenty-third Street one afternoon, he
said that he believed that the Torah-based model of society
in Crown Heights was about as ideal as any that could exist
on earth, despite the fact that there was no real place for
him in that world. Mr. Ashkinazy is the clinical director of
the Institute for the Protection of Lesbian and Gay Youth,
Inc., an educational and counseling agency, and is himself
a homosexual. He says that some of the rabbis he has
studied with in Crown Heights have told him that he is the
first homosexual that they have ever met. He does not
doubt that they are telling the truth. The official Orthodox
view of homosexuality is unequivocal: It is forbidden. In a
Crown Heights bookstore, I bought a book by Rabbi S.
Suchard published in 1981 and entitled *Make Your Marriage Work*, whose final page pretty well summarizes the
Orthodox position:

"Homosexuality is a vexing problem. What stand in
society do homosexuals have? Are they an accepted norm

or should they be ostracized from society? Especially in
America, 'gay' movements are gaining momentum. They
feel they have nothing to hide and must be accepted as a
norm in society. There are inherent questions about such
individuals. How safe are children with homosexuals? Can
they make deviants of otherwise normal people? Should
these people be allowed into a classroom?"

Rabbi Suchard acknowledges that there are "divergent
opinions" about these matters, and seems to hesitate on
the brink of doubt himself when he observes: "Some
say if a person has such tendencies, why should he be
branded as an outcast? He was born that way." He quickly
dismisses this view as being mere faulty human logic,
however. Citing scripture (Leviticus 8:22: "A man may
not live with another man, as he would with a woman. It
is an abomination"), he says confidently: "The Torah is
strictly against such an act, and this then is the norm. It
means that people who openly proclaim their homosexuality must be treated as deviants from society and the *hala-
chah*. They are not to be trusted with children and are not
a legitimate social group who are entitled to their own gay
rights. They are either sinners or sick people; if sinners,
they must be punished, and if sick, they must be given
medical or psychiatric treatment. Our dilemma as to what
is right and what is wrong is solved. All that remains is to
explain the correct point of view and deal with the problem
on that basis."

Although Mr. Ashkinazy has personally found tolerant
and even understanding mentors in Crown Heights, his
position is somewhat anomalous. He is a politically sophisticated, college-educated outsider who approached the
Lubavitchers as a man who wanted "to learn and to
grow." They consider him a man in transition. He tells those
who he feels can deal with it that he is gay and avoids the
issue with those he feels cannot deal with it. He accepts
the idea that all six hundred and thirteen commandments

are there to be followed, but takes the position with those who accuse him of picking and choosing which he will follow and which he will not that, as is the case with every other Jew, there are some precepts that he is simply not going to be able to fulfill.

For young homosexual men and women growing up in the community, the picture is quite different. Mr. Ashkinazy knows this, because he has counseled and befriended a number of them.

"Some of them have forced themselves to lead the lives expected of them," he told me. "They lead outwardly 'normal' married lives, have lots of children, and really try to push their homosexuality out of their lives. Sometimes they manage to subdue their feelings and control themselves for as long as fifteen or twenty years and then they become depressed and break down. I know one man who used to be extremely outgoing and reasonable, who has become neurotic and depressed since he's gotten married. No one wants to be around him. Others lead secret homosexual lives but try to keep up appearances. It's a tremendous strain."

"Some people believe that the separation of the sexes in so many areas of life and the extraordinary amount of time the men spend together in the Hasidic world must foster a kind of homoerotic atmosphere," I said.

"That hasn't been my observation. The separation of the sexes only seems to stir the imagination of most men and intensify their interest in women, and, curiously, while it is true that the men scrub each other's backs in the *mikvahs*, study together all the time, dance together constantly, and in the European manner are always kissing each other, this overt physicality, with some homosexual men, sublimates the need for a stronger kind.

"But, you know, for Lubavitchers the most important issue is 'Where can I grow most in religious terms, and where can I learn most,' and the answer usually is, Right

there in the community. The men I mentioned who have
opted to stay and try to play by the rules have just not
been able to imagine leading the religious life they want
to in the outside world. But I know more people who felt
that there was no way for them to remain. They couldn't
discuss their so-called problem with their families. They
couldn't discuss it with their friends. Just last week, as a
matter of fact, a young man from Crown Heights called me
for help. He was awfully depressed. Someone's treating
him for the depression with medicine, which is a good
idea for the moment, but it's not going to solve things for
him."

"How did he learn about this place?" I asked.

"From the *Village Voice*. We ran an ad in the paper."

I expressed surprise that the *Voice* would circulate in
Crown Heights. He laughed. "It gets read. They smuggle
copies of it into the dormitories. It's sort of the *Playboy*
of the New York Hasidic community. Mostly they just
make fun of it. It confirms the boys' ideas about how pre-
posterous the secular world is."

As he was seeing me out of his office, Mr. Ashkinazy
expressed the view that he believed things would eventually change for homosexuals in Hasidic communities.
He cited the altered view of polygamy as an example of
how a custom once thought to be unalterable outlived its
tenability.

"But of course I'm an optimist," he said. "I've been politically active in the gay movement for years and I've seen
changes that no one thought possible ten years ago.
Changes in laws, changes in attitudes. I don't think a religious Jew ought to be isolated. Just studying isn't enough.
A community is needed, and no one else comes close, in my
opinion, to creating the kind of community that the Lubavitchers have. But when I even suggest to men who have
suffered so much in that world that there's bound to be
more understanding eventually, most of them say, 'Impos-

sible!' That's why they leave. I wish that they didn't feel that they had to."

When Kalman Dubov was a young man, growing up in Boro Park in Brooklyn, he had a secret: He used to sneak off to the local public library to read novels. He never talked about the books he read because no one he knew would have read any of them or approved of his reading them. None of the books were scandalous; when he was quite young he read "The Hardy Boys." Later on, there was Dickens and Arthur Conan Doyle. But his sessions at the library were an important part of his life. Mr. Dubov was part of a small Lubavitcher community in Boro Park. He knew no one who had even been inside a secular library, and he would not have dared to tell anyone how much he enjoyed his extracurricular reading. Dubov, who is thirty-four now, eventually received his ordination but left the Lubavitcher community because he wanted to "live more like other men." He lives in Sacramento, California, where he is studying at the McGeorge School of Law.

"I can't say precisely when I decided to leave the Lubavitchers," he said to me in a telephone interview, "but I think that I was always a little uncomfortable with Hasidic life. I come from a family that has been Lubavitch for four generations and I'm the oldest of thirteen children, but I was always a bit of a loner. I kept my doubts entirely to myself, though every once in a while they would surface and get me in trouble. My parents wanted to marry me off when I was eighteen, but I refused. They were terribly disappointed. Then, one day in school when I ought to have been reading Talmud, I was caught reading a Sherlock Holmes story. The book I was supposed to have been reading was on top of the desk and I had the Conan Doyle half on my lap, half inside a sort of shelf in the desk. Actually, I'd been reading it all week in class. I just

couldn't put it down. Well, the teacher noticed that I'd
been staring at my lap for hours and he came over to see
what was going on and found the book. He was stunned.
He didn't know what to say. First he put it on top of his
desk. Then he put it in his desk drawer; then he took it out
again and kept looking at it. He kept shaking his head and
looking at me. He didn't punish me, he talked to my parents. Nothing really came of it, except that the teacher and
my parents gave me odd looks for a while. Then I went to
France. I was in Paris for two years studying with a very
holy, very tyrannical man. He knew absolutely nothing
about the real world. I hated it. After that I returned to
Newark, where the older boys' yeshiva was before it
moved to Morristown. Finally, I came to the last stage of
study before ordination, which then took place at 770 in
the main hall. It was an awful place to study—cavernous,
cold. Now the older boys have a better place, on Albany
Avenue. But it wasn't just the physical coldness of the place
that got me depressed. I felt that I wasn't accomplishing
anything, that I was doing everything by rote. I felt con-
gested, miserable. I didn't participate. I couldn't really
stand the method of study, which is meandering and un-
structured. I couldn't stand the fact that what I was being
taught was totally unrelated to the history of the rest of the
world. I felt trapped. Well, then I decided to do something
that by Lubavitcher standards was inconceivable. I started
taking judo and karate lessons. I was twenty-one by then
and I'd never really done anything with my body, I'd always done everything with my mind. I guess I just wanted
to do something physical. Anyway, I loved it and eventually I became friends with the manager of the place. He
was a nonreligious Jew, the first I'd ever really gotten to
know, who was taking his M.A. in history at City College. I
helped him with his studies and he helped me by introduc-
ing me to his friends and giving me small glimpses of what
the secular world was like. I liked it a lot. I liked his friends.

I liked his friends' girlfriends. I loved the lack of constraint
in their world. I wanted to be reading the books he was
reading."

"Is that when you left?"

"No. I wanted to, but I thought that I should get my
ordination first. I also realized that if I wanted to go on to
college I'd have to take the high-school equivalency test.
Many of the boys didn't bother with their high-school degrees. They knew that they didn't really need one and
nobody really presses you about it; religious studies are
what count. But I took it and did well and then I tried to
get into some non-Lubavitcher yeshivas that seemed to
offer a somewhat broader education than the Lubavitcher
ones, but they were suspicious of me, probably because I
was doing everything on my own, without the help or
stamp of approval from any parent or teacher, and they
wouldn't let me in. They told me to go back where I belonged. I didn't tell anybody that I was doing this, but
somehow my father must have found out, because he spoke
to the head of the Lubavitcher schools, a tough customer if
there ever was one, and told him that I should be prevented
from getting ordination."

"But you got it anyway?"

"Yes. I went to Israel for a year and my parents tried to
arrange another marriage there. But I didn't want it, and
they got mad again. Then I came home and just studied
hard and took the tests for my ordination. My father wasn't
really pleased with my ordination. There were no hand-
shakes or hugs. Nothing. It kind of hurt."

"What did you do then?"

"Well, I knew that I wanted to go to college but a cer-
tificate of ordination does not get you into college without
transcripts, and *there* was the rub. They don't want anyone except a select few that they think are totally reliable
going to college, so they had this policy of just not releas-
ing transcripts. Period. They just wouldn't give them up.

This nearly drove me crazy for two years, but I finally got them, don't ask me how. Then came the problem of where to go. I had once overheard someone mention that L.I.U. accepted rabbinical transcripts for their Master's program—lots of schools don't—so that's where I went. I went to the Department of Guidance and Counseling and explained my situation and I was accepted. I applied for a student loan and I got one. It was like a dream. That was in seventy-six and I was twenty-four and I just started attending classes. I loved it. I was terrified at first. It was all so strange. They asked me to write a paper. I'd never written a paper in my life."

"How did your family feel about your being there?"

(A long sigh.) "Well, I was still living at home because I couldn't afford to live anywhere else. I just didn't talk about it. But at the end of my first day my father said, 'Where were you today?' I said, 'I was at Long Island University. I'm studying for a Master's degree in education.' He said, 'You're going to continue doing this?' I said, 'Yes.' He said nothing but turned around and left the room. He hasn't spoken to me since."

"Did your mother feel the same way?"

"My mother thought I would fail. But I didn't. I got three A's and a B-plus that first semester. I was quite proud of myself. When she found out that I was doing so well, she was obviously disappointed. That summer she said to me, 'You can have your choice: either leave college or stop eating with your family and stop associating with your brothers and sisters.' When it became clear that I was not going to stop going to school, I was no longer allowed to join my family at the table and if my mother was leaving me alone in the house she actually put the bread, fruit, and canned goods in a carton and tried to hide it. I know it sounds hard to believe, but that's what she did."

"How did you eat?"

"By then, I'd gotten a fellowship, but I still didn't have

very much money. I ate poorly. I lived on slices of pizza and knishes from the kosher pizza parlors. I became hypo-glycemic. They told me that I needed a high-protein diet. I didn't know what to do. I solved my problem by becom-ing a volunteer at the Social Services Department of Brooklyn Hospital. If you worked there, you could eat in their cafeteria, which had cheap food that was pretty good. The food wasn't kosher, of course, and it didn't feel right eating non-kosher food, but I decided that it was either that or get sick, so I ate it."

Rabbi Dubov eventually received two degrees from Long Island University, one in education and another in sociology. He went on to become a chaplain in the Navy, and served in Rhode Island, the Philippines and Bethesda, Maryland. While he was in the Philippines he fell in love with a gentile girl. She converted, they married and they now have a two-year-old son. He no longer wears a beard, but he does keep a kosher home. For a while he was a Re-form rabbi in Longview, Texas, and then he served as the rabbi of a Conservative synagogue in Reno, Nevada. He left his last post, he says, because he did not feel comfortable with the values of many of his congregants. I asked him if he had thought about whether he would send his child to a religious or secular school. He said he thought that he would leave that decision up to the boy. His family has never become reconciled to any of the changes in his life. I asked if he ever missed Crown Heights.

"I miss the depth and fervor of the true Hasids. I miss the religious emotionality. I miss the dancing and singing. It was awesome to be among so many people all giving up their egos. But I feel that I have enough to do as a rabbi to create some warmth and normalcy. I am not going to worry about the Messiah."

CHAPTER THIRTEEN

A Wedding

NOT long after he announced his engagement, Shmuel married and moved around the corner with his new wife. A few months later, Bassy told me that she was getting married, too. She had known her fiancé's sister at camp, and his parents had known her family for years. His name was Aaron Hoffman. Aaron's uncle had telephoned her father to ask if she might be interested in his nephew, and she was. Very. Aaron was well-known in the community as a brilliant young scholar blessed with so prodigious a memory that, along with only a handful of other men, he was entrusted with the task of providing written translations of the Rebbe's talks. Before the advent of the tape recorder, the handwritten transcriptions and translations of the Lubavitcher leader's talks were the sole means of retaining them for posterity. Tape recorders and videotapes have diminished the role of the scribes, but they have not made the task of translating the talks less diffi-

cult, and on the Sabbath and the numerous holidays when
writing and tape-recording are forbidden, it is only the excellent memories of this small circle of men that make it
possible to preserve the talks. To be asked to translate
the Rebbe's words was considered an honor, and Aaron's
job, though unpaid, was regarded as a great plum. (After
Aaron married, when he moved out of his family's house
and incurred the obligations of a husband, a small salary
would be given to him.) As Bassy glowingly described her
future husband, I gathered that Aaron himself, the son of
a writer for a Jewish paper, was also considered a plum.
I asked Bassy if she would mind telling me a bit about her
courtship.

"No problem. After his uncle called, Aaron called. We
went to the beach even though it was a bit chilly and just
walked along the water and talked. We walked a lot together. We went to Manhattan. We walked around Rocke-
feller Center, and we went to the Hotel Pierre cocktail
lounge. After a couple of times together, we knew that
this was it. It just seemed right. He's very handsome. He
has dark, serious eyes . . . and, uh, he's twenty-six."

I wanted to ask Bassy if she had any idea of what life
with a man was going to be like. I knew she didn't. I knew
that she would tell me she did. It seemed silly to ask. I
confined myself to two narrow questions. Did Sheina or
anyone else prepare her in any special way for marriage?
Did anybody talk to her about sex? Bassy closed a barrette
that had sprung open in her long, chestnut-colored hair.

"A rabbi teaches the boys. A woman teaches the girls.
A bunch of girls who are getting married go to this woman
and, ah, she tells us what to expect. She is quite frank. But
what's the problem? I've been around men all my life. I
mean, I have brothers. My friends have brothers. It's not
exactly as if I'm meeting a man for the first time in my
life."

.   .   .

The day of the wedding has arrived. Even though it is winter, the wedding ceremony will take place outdoors, under a *chupah*, or wedding canopy, outside 770. The reception is being held at the Brooklyn Jewish Center, a few blocks away on Eastern Parkway. Shmuel's wedding reception had been held there, too, as had Mirriam's and Chanah's and most of the young Lubavitcher couples. At certain times of the year, Sheina had once told me, it was not unusual for her to find herself attending wedding receptions at the center two or three times a week.

The wedding was scheduled for six, but, as at most Lubavitcher events, no one seriously believed that it would take place on time; at 5:45 the guests were still ambling into the center, greeting friends, and nibbling hors d'oeuvres, confident that there was time to spare. For most of the evening, the men and women, including Bassy and Aaron, would sit in separate places: the women in a large mirrored ballroom festooned with pink, blue, and white balloons downstairs, the men in a smaller room (sans balloons) upstairs. But in this prelude to the evening they strolled around the ballroom together. Every stratum of the Lubavitcher community was represented, from the butcher to the rov; indeed most of Lubavitcher Crown Heights seemed to be present. The elaborate predinner smorgasbord, arrayed on a thirty-two-foot buffet table, included three or four kinds of cold fish, two fruit fantasies with lovebirds on top, five chicken liver platters, numerous savory hot dishes, and several cornucopias of raw vegetables. The chef, caterer, and overseer for the Center were all Lubavitchers. The orchestra was non-Lubavitcher, but only because the Eli Lipsker Orchestra, the ubiquitous Lubavitcher ensemble, had been engaged elsewhere that evening. Bassy, wearing a white satin dress with a many-layered scalloped hem, was seated on a throne-like white wicker chair, flanked by Bubbe, Sheina (who was wearing new rimless glasses and looked quite elegant in a pearl gray

dress), and her future mother-in-law, a slim sleek "blonde."
Bassy looked like a flower. A photographer assembled the
two families and snapped their pictures in various combina-
tions and poses. He worked with alacrity but several people
in both families looked as if they would rather have been
somewhere else. Moshe looked particularly uneasy. Sheina
whispered to me that he hated all the fuss and thought it
unnecessary. She disagreed. She thought that "it's nice to
look back on." There was a leather-covered Book of Psalms
on Bassy's lap. Both she and Aaron had been reading the
Psalms today, as is the custom, and she glanced in the book
from time to time like someone with a school assignment
she had to finish. A friend of Bassy's came up and led her to
the dance floor and the two girls, together with four or five
of their friends, two old ladies, and a handful of five- and
six-year-old girls formed a circle and began to dance. Soon,
other circles formed in the mirrored room and before long
nearly all the women were dancing. The room was aflutter
with Albert Nipons. A somewhat less stylish, more matter-
of-factly dressed group that did not join the dancers was in
evidence, most of whom turned out to be either colleagues
or the wives of colleagues of Aaron's father. The husbands in this largely European, non-Hasidic group lingered with their wives long after most of the other men
repaired to the men's reception room upstairs where another small band was playing. One of the women in the
newspaper group struck up a conversation with me. She
told me that though she was not Hasidic she was religious.
She was in a concentration camp during the war, she said,
and the Hasidic inmates bore up better than other people.
She had endured terrible hardships, like giving away her
daughter to a gentile for safekeeping for the duration of
the war and having to clean the camp latrines with tooth-
brushes every day; but even when she felt most despair-
ing, her faith kept her going. "Sometimes," she said, looking at the dancers, "all my life after the war seems like a

dream, and I'm afraid I'll wake up and find myself back
at the camp."

It was 6:30. No one seemed to have noticed that the
wedding ceremony was supposed to have taken place half
an hour ago. The orchestra was playing "The Impossible
Dream" from *Man of La Mancha*. Bubbe, looking frailer
than the last time I had seen her, was dancing a sedate
two-step with Sheina. She smiled at everyone but her eyes
bore the evidence of some kind of strain. Bassy's future
mother-in-law was doing a dance that looked like something from *Saturday Night Fever* with her older daughter,
and a few women, including one wearing a jaunty veiled
hat and a nineteen-fortyish style suit, were dancing by
themselves. When Bassy returned to her seat there was
sweat on her brow. Bubbe's wig was slightly askew and she
looked exhausted. The bandleader looked toward the door
and immediately began to lead the musicians in a beautiful,
melancholy melody, "The Alter Rebbe's Nigun," a song
written by the first Lubavitcher rebbe which is traditionally played during the prewedding ritual in which the
groom covers the bride's face with a veil. Aaron, his eyes
closed and wearing his white *kittel*, was slowly led into the
room by his father and Shmuel. The rest of the men followed behind in a slow-moving procession. When the cor-
tege reached Bassy, Aaron opened his eyes, looked at her
intently, then dropped a white cloth over her face (a custom associated with Isaac's meeting with Rebecca). Then
Moshe exclaimed, in Hebrew, "Oh, sister! May you be the
mother of thousands of myriads," a phrase from Genesis.
After Aaron covered Bassy's face, he closed his eyes again
and was led out of the room, through the Center's marble
entranceway, down the front steps, and across Eastern
Parkway to 770, where the gold-fringed, blue velvet
canopy, supported by four stout poles, awaited him.
Hasidim marry under the stars because the stars are associated with God's promise to Abraham to "Bless thee

. . . and multiply thy seed as the stars of the heaven . . ."
The groom's escorts carried candles, and in the dark night
the candlelight added a soft burnish to the already irre-
sistibly charming, old-fashioned scene in front of the synagogue. According to one mystical tradition, the men carry
candles as symbolic reminders of the lightning that appeared when Israel (the bride) accepted God (the bridegroom) at Mount Sinai.

Several hundred people had now assembled on the sidewalks near the wedding canopy. The deceased grand-
parents of the bride and groom, though unseen, were also
believed to be among the guests. It was a cold night, and
those who forgot to don their coats before they left the
Center were shivering. It was difficult to see much of what
was happening under the canopy, but most of the people
were able to catch a glimpse of the bride as she and her
father and stepmother and the groom's family circled the
bridegroom seven times. Many interpretations have been
given of this ritual, the most widely held being that it is
performed to protect the husband from the evil spirits
who seek to harm him and deny the couple a fruitful
marriage. Seven, as mentioned earlier, is considered a particularly holy number. Seven blessings are said during the
wedding ceremony and after the wedding feast, and for
seven nights after the wedding relatives and friends give
lavish dinner parties for the newlyweds. The couple is
escorted to these parties and is generally treated like
royalty at them. The custom serves a practical purpose as
well, that of distracting the couple from the ineluctable
halakic fact that after their wedding night together they
are not allowed to touch each other for eleven days. Not
more than four days before the wedding, the bride is expected to immerse herself in the ritual bath, provided, of
course, that she is not menstruating. To help young brides
understand the minutiae of the strict laws governing married sexual life, scores of books have been published. The

books take nothing for granted. In Moishe Sternbuch's *Laws of Jewish Family Life*, for example, it is suggested that a girl should be "sure" of the location of her private parts before she examines herself. If the bride has had the misfortune of miscalculating the time of her period and is menstruating at the time of her wedding, then (Rabbi Sternbuch again) "two guardians are needed. The custom is to have a young boy with the groom and a young girl with the bride. They should be children of about nine years old (the age by which a child talks freely in public). Some hold that they can be even younger, six years old (when a child is able to describe what he sees). Where there are no younger children, one can be lenient and take older ones. This is for the night, but during the daytime, although they are still forbidden to be completely alone together, one child—either a boy or a girl—is sufficient. Some stricter authorities hold that . . . they should sleep in separate rooms, he with the men, and she with the women . . . The husband should be careful not to speak words of endearment to his wife . . . because this could, Heaven forbid, lead to an erection and unnecessary emission of semen which is a very serious sin."

In sharp contrast to the various ancient customs observed during the ceremony, including the reading of the marriage contract in Aramaic, there were photographers' lights that bathed the wedding party in a harsh, bright light and a microphone that projected the celebrants' voices far from the *chupah*. The family was videotaping the event. As the ceremony went on, the younger children, who of course had witnessed this scene many times, began to giggle, run around, and even shout a bit. No one tried to stop them or took much notice of the noise, although a few of the children could not have been more than ten feet from the canopy. At the end of the ceremony, Aaron broke a cloth-wrapped glass (this custom, observed by almost all Jewish bridegrooms who have religious weddings, is supposed to be a reminder of the fall of the Temple—a kind of warning to the bride and groom that, as one religious author put it, "the wedding day will not continue indefinitely; and that the young couple ought to prepare itself for all of life's eventualities"). The ritual probably originated in the Middle Ages, when it was the custom for the groom to taste a glass of wine after the seven benedictions were recited, offer some to his bride, then smash the glass against the nearest northern wall. In Jewish folklore, evil spirits come from the north. The prophet Jeremiah, too, said that "evil appeareth" from the north. Noise, such as that made when a glass is broken, is supposed to fend the spirits off. It is hoped that the spirits who might be intent on destroying a bride and groom's happiness will be mollified, or at least distracted, by the destruction of a glass.

After the glass was broken, everyone shouted *"mazel tov!"* ("good luck"), the men embraced, and the wedding party trooped back to the reception hall. There the bride and groom spent a short period of time together in a private room—a carryover from the time when a groom brought his bride to his home immediately after the ceremony to consummate the marriage. When they came out of the room, Aaron crossed the red carpeted hallway to rejoin the men, Bassy crossed over the other way, to rejoin the women, and a different, more unbridled kind of dancing began in both rooms. It is considered a blessing to dance and sing the praises of a bride, and rabbis in ancient times sometimes danced and performed juggling acts to entertain brides. So great is the virtue accrued from dancing at weddings that, according to one story, even though Queen Jezebel was wicked and died ignominiously, dogs did not eat the soles of her feet because she had danced at weddings.

Bassy's friends had obviously only been warming up earlier; as the evening progressed the dances got faster and faster. Bassy's feet barely touched the floor. Her eyes shone, she developed a bright pink spot on each cheek and ringlets of hair rested damply on her brow. By midnight, her laughter and energy were like something boiling over in a pot.

In the men's reception room, the dancing, fueled by a better-stocked bar, was even wilder. I peeked in from the doorway and saw the butcher, a man widely known for his dancing talent, waving a handkerchief above his head and leading the men in a spirited *kazatski*, a Russian dance done on bended knees. In the blur of whirling black figures I saw many familiar faces. The men were having trouble keeping their hats on. Aaron's face was red. Moshe was clapping on the sidelines and singing. Mendel, who had recently become engaged to a Canadian girl, was watching Aaron with a reflective expression. Shmuel, who had now been married for a few months, was standing next to him. His hands were clasped behind his back and he, too, was looking at Aaron thoughtfully.

CHAPTER FOURTEEN

A Death, A Birth

I n the months following Bassy's wedding, her grandmother began having frequent dizzy spells, and she became weaker and weaker. By early spring she began to look almost translucent, and her movements became increasingly hesitant. One evening, at a Sabbath meal, she pressed her hand in mine; it felt like a dry leaf. She pretended that she was not actually sick, Miriam later told me, but eventually it was discovered that she had cancer of the colon and had to be hospitalized. By that time, Mendel's amiable new wife was expecting a baby, and Shmuel's wife and Bassy were pregnant, too. Bubbe called all three women close to her bedside one afternoon and blessed her future great-grandchildren. Not long afterward, she died. She was eighty-six.

Three weeks later, a wide-eyed baby, swaddled in a white jacket and soft white woolen cap, was being transported on a large embroidered pillow through a room

crowded with women. The baby was Bassy and Aaron's
as yet unnamed eight-day-old son. Ten months had passed
since their wedding day. The woman carrying the baby
was Bassy's oldest sister-in-law. Upstairs, waiting for the
baby in a small, sunny room, was the *mohel*, or ritual cir-
cumciser, surrounded by a large crowd of men. Besides
Aaron, there was Moshe, Shmuel, Mendel, Bassy's father-
in-law, several brothers-in-law, and a healthy sampling of
both families' male friends and relations.

An empty chair had been set aside for the Prophet
Elijah, who is believed to put in an appearance at all circumcision ceremonies. The *mohel*, who wore a white doctor's coat over his suit, was Aaron's great-uncle. The *bris*,
as the circumcision ceremony is called (*bris* is the Hebrew
word for covenant), is one of those community events that
people learn about through the grapevine, and anyone
who thinks that he or she should attend does. It was
taking place at Bassy's in-laws' place, a narrow but comfortable two-story building on one of the more gentrified
stretches of Crown Street, several blocks away from the
Konigsberg house. Nearby sections of the same street
looked like post-war Berlin.

This was actually the second social event inspired by
the baby's entrance into the world. The first was a party
given for him on the Friday night after his birth. According to the Talmud, the embryo in its mother's womb
is in a sanctified state because while it is there, it is taught
the entire Torah. Just before the child is born, the Talmud
says, an angel taps him on the lips, making him forget all
that he has learned *in utero*, so that he can choose between right and wrong as a fallible mortal. This "forgetting" also desanctifies him, of course, so a party is thrown
by his fellow fallible mortals to console him. Among the
foods served at the celebration are cooked legumes, which
are believed to be effective charms against demons, who
might want to harm the child. Talmudic literature takes

the presence of angels and demons for granted. Only a few scholars, including Maimonides, rejected the idea of such spirits.

The Bible does not account for the creation of demons, but according to Talmudic tradition they made their debut on the first Sabbath eve, when God was putting the finishing touches on the world. As the day was waning, according to one source, He turned his attention to those beings "who, though included in the plan of things as they were to be, might well be left for last. He had not progressed beyond the fashioning of their souls, however, when the hastening Sabbath overtook Him, and He was obliged to sanctify the first day of rest. So it is, that demons have no bodies, but are constituted wholly of spirit."

Perceptions of the physical appearance of demons have varied, but the basic outlines were drawn in Talmudic times. This is one Talmudist's description: "In accordance with their origin, [the demons] are between angels and men. They have wings like the former, and move about from one end of the earth to the other, and know what will come to pass; but, like the latter, they eat and drink, propagate their kind, and die." One medieval scholar believed that they sustained themselves on fire, water, air, and slime; another said that they could transform themselves into any shape they wished and might appear as cats, rabbits, or wolves. Demons were said to thrive in dirty places. Thus, as Joshua Trachtenberg points out in *Jewish Magic and Superstition*, "even on Yom Kippur, when no ablutions might be performed, the hands must be washed in the morning."

When we talked about this subject, Sheina told me that she believed in the presence of spirits but that she couldn't say what form they took. Moshe said that neither he nor anyone he knew believed in demons or angels with a tangible shape, but that he did believe in good and bad spirits, in a more abstract sense.

"Think of it this way," he said. "You know you get a different feeling standing on Forty-second Street and standing in Crown Heights. It's obvious that certain places are filled with an atmosphere of good, and others are not. It says in the Talmud that every time you do a *mitzvah* you create an angel; that doesn't mean that every time you fulfill one of God's commandments a little winged creature pops up, but that you are adding to the world's store of goodness. Maybe in previous times people actually saw these spirits in a physical shape. Certainly the more spiritual a person is, the more palpably he feels the presence of good and evil."

Few Jewish demons were known by special names, and those that were played no significant role in Jewish history and have largely been forgotten. A notable exception is the wild-eyed, disheveled Lilith, seducer of men and nemesis of pregnant women and babies, who some believe was an embodiment of the Jews' patriarchal fears centering on rebellious women. But, feared as she was, Lilith was a flyweight of demonic animus compared to the "evil eye" which, unlike Lilith, is still feared today. There are two kinds of evil eyes. One is a spiritual malignancy attributed to ordinary people who sow trouble wherever they go, and the other—"rooted in the pagan belief that the gods and spirits are envious and spiteful and essentially wish men ill," according to Trachtenberg—is attributed to evil spirits. To avoid arousing the enmity and jealousy of such spirits, Jews have since Talmudic times avoided complimenting one another too much, or boasting, or speaking in too fulsome a manner about anyone's good fortune. Medieval Jews had various linguistic devices to counteract this danger, such as saying the phrases "May the Lord protect thee" and "No evil eye" after any flattering remark was made. They would also try to fool malevolent spirits by purposely saying patently untrue, unflattering things.

For example, they would call a handsome son ugly. This tradition is very much alive today. The automatic response anyone in Crown Heights has to "How are you?" is *"Baruch Hashem,* fine." This is not merely an appreciative nod to the Creator for making the person fine but a protective invocation of God's name. Similarly, it is not unusual in casual conversation for people to append prophylactic phrases to their own words, as in "You look particularly beautiful today—no evil eye intended." The profound lack of interest on the part of Lubavitcher officialdom in taking any sort of census of the Rebbe's followers can also be attributed, at least in part, to fears relating to the evil eye. As Trachtenberg points out, "Any act or condition that in itself may excite the envy of the spirits is subject to the evil eye; taking a census or even estimating the size of a crowd, possession of wealth, performing an act which is normally a source of pride or joy—all evoke its pernicious effects."

I inadvertently bumped into peculiar reticences from time to time in Lubavitcher circles which perplexed me when they occurred but which I later attributed to this belief. Ask any official how many Lubavitchers are in a certain city, or how many belong to some Lubavitcher organization, or how many people attended a certain meeting, and the reply will usually be something like "Quite a few," or "Hard to say," or—usually said with an expression of benign tolerance—"Do numbers matter that much?"

One day, as I was walking down the street with Sheina, whose oldest daughter had just had a baby, and a young woman friend, I asked Sheina how many grandchildren she now had. As a semi-newcomer to the Hasidic world, Sheina still reacts to some things the way she would have in her old life; so she answered me with a placid smile, "Six." The young woman walking with us, who had been raised in a Lubavitcher family, looked stricken. She admonished Sheina gently, mumbled something that was inaudible but obviously prophylactic, and sighed deeply.

The angels, of course, are the protectors of men and work as assiduously for good as demons work for evil, except, of course, for the angel of death, the cruel messenger who along with his emissaries is depicted in the Bible as a smiter and destroyer. Luckily, the demons are subservient to the angels, and, since according to Jewish mystical belief every man, woman, beast, and flower has its angelic source, goodness has a fair chance of prevailing. A variety of opinions exist as to the origin and function of angels. The second, fourth, and fifth days of creation have all been advanced as the most likely days on which they made their first appearance. In earlier eras, it was generally assumed that angels walked upright, spoke Hebrew, could fly from one end of the world to the other, could prophesy, were human in shape (though, like demons, they could assume any form they wished to), and could make mistakes, although they were entirely free from the "evil inclination." Some early scholars distinguished between various categories of angels: angels of mercy and angels of judgment, angels with masculine qualities and angels with feminine ones, and so on.

The night before the *bris,* a *wachnacht* (vigil) had been held at the baby's house. A gaggle of schoolboys had gathered around his cradle and piped the *Shema* aloud, and afterward, Aaron and other male friends and relatives spent much of the night studying and praying. This custom, which is kabbalistic in origin, is practiced to guard the baby from any attempt by Satan to harm him in order to prevent him from fulfilling this crucial part of the covenant. Many now largely forgotten customs were associated with the birth of boys, but infants of both sexes are still protected today by the "Song of Ascent," an assemblage of selected Psalms, names of patriarchs and matriarchs, and scriptural and kabbalistic phrases written on a piece of paper and taped by Lubavitcher Hasidim to the front door and the doorway of an infant's room when it is brought home from the hospital. In medieval times, a circle was sometimes drawn around the lying-in bed, an inscription protecting the mother and child from Lilith was sometimes chalked upon the walls or door of the room, and mothers were not allowed to stir out of the house alone until after their sons were circumcised.

The *bris* was scheduled to take place at 9:00 in the morning but guests were still pouring through the front door at 9:40. There were no more coat hooks or hangers left, so everyone tossed his coat on a great mound in the hallway. Heavily laden platters of smoked fish, salads, bread, fruit, puddings, olives, and cake had been set out on several paper-cloth-covered tables, and at least twenty children were admiring a large red, white, and blue soldier-shaped cake, emblazoned with the legend, "We Want Moshiach Now." Chanah flew up from Virginia to be here, and she and Miriam (whose seventh child, a girl, was now a few months old) and Bassy's two younger sisters-in-law, both pregnant, fluttered protectively around the baby as he was borne up the stairs to the *mohel*. The baby gazed at the crowd with that serious, otherworldly expression peculiar to newborn babies and maintained an air of silent calm until the *mohel*'s scalpel pierced his flesh. Then he wailed (if the tiny mews of a newborn can be called a wail) pitifully. The thirty-odd men standing around the *mohel* looked stricken. As they watched the ceremony and listened to the prayers that were recited, their expressions shifted from pity, to resignation, to encouragement, to something akin to rueful amusement. In the course of the ceremony, the baby received the name Menachem Mendel. The Rebbe's name, of course, is Menachem Mendel, but since Jews are not allowed to name a child after any living person, the letter of the law was observed by saying

that the child was being named after the third Lubavitcher rebbe, the present Rebbe's namesake. Bassy's baby
is not the first Menachem Mendel in the family. Miriam's
fifth child and Chanah's third bear the same name. It is a
rare Lubavitcher family, in truth, that does not boast at
least one Menachem Mendel.

After the baby was rewrapped in his swaddling, the
mohel sang to him, rocked him on a pillow, and danced
him around the room. The dance was a rollicking bouncy
one, and considering what had just transpired, I expected
the baby to object. But the dancing seemed to please or
stun him, and, while the *mohel* whirled him around, he
maintained a princely silence.

Outside the room, the women waited for the baby to be
returned to them. Quite a few of them were on the staircase, talking quietly. Sheina was bustling back and forth
downstairs, helping some elderly ladies find places at the
table. Bassy, who had managed to find a wig that looked
exactly like her own long, thick chestnut tresses, and wore
a barrette in it in exactly the same place she had worn it in
her own hair, gazed unhappily toward the room where the
baby was. I asked Miriam, who was standing next to me,
if Bassy and the other women learned the Lamaze method
to help them in their labor. She told me that they learned
it but that the men did not attend the classes, as she understood they did in the secular world. They were not allowed to touch their wives during labor, either, though
they were allowed to be in the labor room with them to
pray. Just before the *mohel* handed the baby back to
Bassy, I caught a glimpse of Moshe hovering protectively
over his grandson. For a few seconds, their faces were
inches away from each other—two bald pates, two sets of
luminous hooded eyes, two expressions of dreamy wonder.
Then the baby was borne downstairs to a room full of so-
licitous women and wide-eyed little girls. The conversation
among the women during the circumcision ceremony had

been subdued, and when the small plaintive wail of the baby alerted them to the fact that the rite was taking place, the room became very quiet. If the men had looked implicated and rueful, the women looked appalled. Thank God, they all seemed to be silently saying, that we were not born men.

Succoth

FROM time to time, Sheina attended a "Women's Group."
Its members were mostly *baalot teshuvah* or women who
were still on the fringes of the Lubavitcher world, and it
was led by a well-liked Crown Heights teacher named
Frimet Kline. The very existence of a group of this kind
bespoke a certain amount of seepage from popular culture.
Before the sixties, there were no Lubavitcher "women's
groups," apart from the various service organizations.
There still were not many, so I was pleased when Sheina
invited me to attend a meeting. I had a fairly clear idea of
what subjects would not be discussed by the women, but
none whatever of what they would talk about.

The meeting took place on an early October evening in
the tiny Manhattan apartment of an attractive, vivacious
TV producer in her mid-thirties. As she led me into the
living room, she told me that she had become religious
only recently and had married a religious fellow who was

"completely unlike anyone else in my professional or private life." There were eight other women at the meeting: a few Europeans, an Israeli, and three or four Americans. The group was well-dressed, mostly middle-aged, and urbane looking. A glass-topped coffee table completely covered with bowls of nuts, figs, dates, potato chips, crackers, and cookies occupied everyone's attention for a while, then the group settled down and looked expectantly at a plump, pretty, watchful-looking woman who sat on a straight-back chair: Frimet Kline. Mrs. Kline said that they would be talking that evening about the upcoming holiday of Succoth, and I grasped at once what I should have realized beforehand; this was a *religious* study group. The modernity of it was that there were women present instead of men.

Some of the women in the room knew a lot about religious customs, others knew very little, so Mrs. Kline began by speaking in general terms about the holiday—noting that it was celebrated for seven days and commemorated the forty years in which the wandering Israelites lived in temporary dwellings; that *Succoth* meant "tabernacles" or "booths" and the chief obligation of the festival was to build a *succah,* a windowless rectangular structure of at least three sides covered with bamboo poles or woven boughs, and "dwell" in it; and that in cold climates "dwell" has come to mean "eat meals in."

One of the women interrupted Mrs. Kline to ask her why the holiday was celebrated for seven days.

"Well," said Mrs. Kline, who had a high-pitched voice, a full bosom, and extremely intelligent, dark, searching eyes, "on the simplest level, Leviticus says that it should be celebrated for that many days, the same place where it says to take the four 'species' [a citron, palm branch, myrtle branch, and willow branch] and 'rejoice' with them during the festival. But let's look at it another way. We went out of Egypt as a preparation, to get the

Torah, and during the period of the Exodus God helped the Israelites to endure their hardships by making them comfortable. While they were not yet spiritually united, he helped them to be united physically. The seven days of Succoth commemorate the seven clouds God created to protect the Israelites. As they crossed the desert there were four clouds around them to protect them from their enemies; there was one above them to shield them from the desert sun; there was one under their feet to protect them from the hot sands and refresh them; and there was one going ahead of them to show the way, to remove obstacles and kill scorpions. Actually, there was an eighth cloud which served as a chariot for the old and infirm, and as many of you know, there is a concluding day of celebration which is technically independent of Succoth but is meant to end the Succoth festival. In the diaspora, it has been stretched to two days to include Simchat Torah, the most joyous celebration of the year."

Our hostess, who was wearing a lavender panné velvet dressing gown, asked Mrs. Kline why it was that most people decorated their *succahs* with fruits, Indian corn, and even pictures and small tapestries whereas the *succahs* in Crown Heights were always bare of decoration.

Frimet Kline: "We never decorate our *succahs* because it's unnecessary to. It's a *mitzvah* to build a *succah* and eat in it. That's what God asked us to do. Anything else is gilding the lily."

Hostess: "But people like to decorate their *succahs*. It makes them happy to see them looking festive. I don't see the harm of it."

Frimet Kline: "Okay, okay, it makes them happy; good! But I'm saying that it's irrelevant to the *mitzvah*. Maybe people need to do it, but God doesn't need it, that's all I'm saying."

Hostess (sounding quite annoyed): "Well, I think if

people like doing it, they should. I mean who needs the whole idea of Succoth? What's it for? If people personalize it, I think that they're going to be more involved in it."

Frimet Kline (sounding exasperated, her voice at a high pitch): "No. I'm not saying that it's a crime, but the point is that personalizing customs gets you into trouble. To add a bunch of stupid grapes to a *succah* suggests that the *succah* is not enough." She looked at her hands for a second, then added, in a quiet voice, "We need the *succah*, just as we need all the other holidays, to connect us with our past. When we're connected with our past the present flows naturally from it. When you try to change the *succah* into something out of *House & Garden* you're losing some of the meaning of the thing. The *succah* has a semi-open reed or bamboo roof because it's supposed to be somewhat exposed to the elements. When you're outdoors in a *succah*, you're out of your comfortable house. The holiday comes at a time when the harvest is in. It seems like a time to take it easy. But God said He wanted us to be outside. Why? Because you're closer to the realm of nature where it's more physically obvious that God is in charge of things. It's the very primitiveness of the structure that counts. Do you see what I mean?"

Hostess (looking mollified): "I guess I do."

A short time later the group broke up. As everyone was putting their coats on, our hostess's husband walked in the door, and husband and wife exchanged cool hellos. He was plump, quite shy, and clearly uncomfortable with all the women around. He looked like someone who had wandered into the wrong apartment.

On another bright October day, I walked slowly down President Street toward the Konigsberg house, where I was going to spend an afternoon of Succoth with the family. The air was crisp and the sidewalks thick with fallen leaves. Almost every yard I passed had a *succah* in it, and almost every *succah* had a family in it. Small children, shouting to one another in Yiddish, ran up and down stoops and along the sidewalks, as they had the day I'd wandered along these streets for the first time. A powerful, homely scent wafted out of all the kitchens, and families and friends clustered in convivial groups on stucco porches innocent of furniture and lawns whose crabgrass provoked no animosity or even interest.

The Konigsbergs' *succah*, which was in their driveway, was built to last, even though it had to be taken apart every year. It had three walls made of wood paneling framed by two-by-fours, and a roof of evergreen boughs supported by more two-by-fours and sticks. Narrow, bright rays of light filtered through the roof and dappled the table, large enough to accommodate sixteen people, that was set beneath it. Sheina, wearing an apron over the raincoat she had on to keep warm, was carefully placing some wine bottles on the table and examining the labels. "Hi," she said, giving me a little hug. "You'd better keep your coat on. It's a bit chilly out here. The roof has to be open enough to let the rain fall through, which can be a problem if it rains on Succoth. That's what happened last year, and the men had to stay out in it. Not I. What a mess."

Friends and various family members milled around the table. Even when the meal began in earnest the milling continued. People would appear at the open side of the *succah* like unannounced visitors in a Chekhov play and somehow find a place to squeeze into. Moshe sat at the head of the table amusing half a dozen grandchildren. All the guests got a chance to hold the palm, willow, and myrtle branches in their right hand and the citron in their left hand, and to recite a benediction. Everybody ate chicken, and noodle pudding. But there was more singing than eating, and, for once, more singing than talking. One of the guests sang a plaintive Yiddish song, "Mein Stetle Belz," with his small daughter. The song was so moving that a few of the guests wept, and when the duo had finished all the guests cheered. The sound of loud rock music drifted over from a neighbor's house. Moshe shrugged and rolled his eyes; the neighbor's son had a rock band, he said, and they had been rehearsing all afternoon. After a while, the quiet melodic songs that filled the *succah* somehow blotted out the rock music—a genuine Hasidic miracle.

About four hours later, I left. The table had been cleared but all the chairs around it were occupied and the singing was still going strong. As I walked down the street, a rolling wave of song followed along from every backyard.

Near the subway station, on Eastern Parkway, I saw the Rebbe coming toward me on the sidewalk. Three small boys and five men trailed along behind him at a respectful distance as an escort. His hands were clasped behind his back, and he seemed absorbed in his own thoughts. But as we passed each other he looked up and we both smiled, in the way that strangers sometimes do. As soon as he was a safe distance away, an old woman popped out from behind a nearby tree and rushed up to me. She must have been at least seventy-five years old. She patted and pinched my cheeks and put her face close to mine to scrutinize me.

"So, little *maidele*, I don't know who you are, but I know you're lucky. I saw the Rebbe smile at you. Something wonderful will happen to you soon." (Pat, pat. Pinch.) "You'll see."

She invited me to join her in shul to say a Succoth blessing, but I declined, saying that I had already said it and was anxious to get home.

"Well, go along then," she said, giving me one last pat

and reluctantly letting me go. I felt like a good-luck penny. At the end of the block, just before I descended into the subway entrance, I turned around. She was still there, beaming at me.

ABOUT THE AUTHOR

Lis Harris is a staff writer for *The New Yorker*. She lives in New York City with her husband and two sons.